W9-BWM-208

REFERENCE WORKS FOR THEOLOGICAL RESEARCH

3RD EDITION – 1991

Robert J. Kepple and John R. Muether

WITHDRAWN

kenrick

seminary library

Charles L. Souvay Memorial

UNIVERSITY
PRESS OF
AMERICA

Lanham • New York • London

92808

Copyright © 1992 by
University Press of America®, Inc.
4720 Boston Way
Lanham, Maryland 20706

3 Henrietta Street
London WC2E 8LU England

Library of Congress Cataloging-in-Publication Data

Kepple, Robert J.
Reference works for theological research : an annotated selective
bibliographical guide / Robert J. Kepple, John R. Muether. — 3rd ed.
    p.   cm.
Includes index.
  1. Theology—Bibliography. 2. Religion—Bibliography.
I. Muether, John R. II. Title.
Z7751.K46   1992   [BR118] 016.2—dc20   91–42222 CIP

ISBN 0–8191–8564–7 (cloth : alk. paper)
ISBN 0–8191–8565–5 (pbk. : alk. paper)

 ^{TM} The paper used in this publication meets the minimum requirements of
American National Standard for Information Sciences—Permanence
of Paper for Printed Library Materials, ANSI Z39.48–1984.

ACKNOWLEDGEMENTS

Several people were helpful in the production of this third edition. Tim Erdel and Jim Pakala both called our attention to some important works we had overlooked, and they made several other helpful suggestions. Mark Stover provided a great deal of advice on the chapter on computer-assisted research.

William Brailsford and David Wilson proofread the manuscript through several stages of production. Peter Bartuska and F. Todd Williams provided valuable assistance in formatting camera ready copy.

Robert J. Kepple   John R. Muether
Vice President   Library Director
Library Technologies, Inc.   Reformed Theological Seminary
Abington, Pennsylvania   Maitland, Florida

TABLE OF CONTENTS

GENERAL INTRODUCTION

PURPOSE AND SCOPE

This work is designed to serve as a major resource both for the student and for the instructor in the study of the reference works useful in theological research. It is intended both as a textbook (where students can find the basic "facts" about theological reference works) and as a future resource (to which students may refer to refresh their memory as to the most useful works in a given area.

The first edition of this work, which appeared in 1978, was an unannotated list of about 450 tools. The second edition, published in 1981, was considerably expanded and restructured, and included descriptive annotations. This edition adds a chapter on computer-assisted research, makes some minor changes in format, and adds a significant number of additions and new editions of reference works. It now includes over 800 titles.

It should be stressed that, even at its current size, this bibliography is selective, and only a limited number of works are included. For additional reference works, particularly the very specialized, the user is urged to consult the various bibliographical guides and bibliographies for each subject area.

In order to avoid duplication with James McCabe's useful work, *A Critical Guide to Catholic Reference Works* (see A7), this guide has been highly restrictive in including works about the Roman Catholic church or produced under its auspices. However, Roman Catholic works important to the study of Christianity (e.g. *The Catholic Encyclopedia*) have been included. Those studying the Roman Catholic church or a topic closely related to it will also need to use McCabe's work.

STRUCTURE AND USE

The table of contents outlines, in some detail, the topical chapters and sections into which this work is divided.

The first 19 chapters form Part I, the General and General Religious/Theological Lists. These are works that cover knowledge in general or religion and theology in general. These are divided into chapters primarily on the basis of the bibliographic or reference function of the work.

The last 20 chapters form Part II, the Subject Area Lists. These are works limited by subject to covering, fully or in part, one of the subfields of theological study. These are divided into sections first by the subfield covered, then by type of tool within the subfield (e.g. chapters 20-25), by time period within the subfield (chapters 26-31), or by topical subfields (chapters 32-39) as appropriate.

In the annotations, material placed within quotation marks is from the subtitle or the preface of the work described.

PART I :

THE GENERAL AND GENERAL RELIGIOUS / THEOLOGICAL LISTS

INTRODUCTION

The following chapters cover the general reference tools frequently of use in theological study and the reference works covering theology or religion in general. Those reference works covering only one of the subfields of theology are listed in Part II.

Note that the listings of general reference works are very selective. Only those that are heavily used and widely available are listed. If one of the listed works is not available, your library may have others that serve the same purpose.

CHAPTER 1
BIBLIOGRAPHICAL GUIDES

Bibliographical guides are reference tools designed to refer the user to the reference works available on a particular topic and to the "standard" or "best" works on a given topic. Most include brief annotations describing each work, and many provide brief essays on the literature of the various fields and on the methodology of research in those fields.

** GENERAL COVERAGE

A1   *Guide to Reference Books.* Eugene P. Sheehy. 10th ed. Chicago: American Library Association, 1986.
The basic working tool of reference librarians. Gives extensive lists of reference tools arranged by subject and function. Most entries have brief annotations. A first place to go to discover what the basic reference tools are in a particular area. Religion is treated on pp. 340-391. Be certain to use the index.

A2   *Guide to Reference Material: vol. 2, Social & Historical Sciences, Philosophy & Religion.* A.J. Walford, ed. 4th ed. London: Library Association, 1982.
The British equivalent of Sheehy. While coverage complements Sheehy, Walford lists important issues of journals, articles, and other minor works which Sheehy does not. See also vol. 1 (Science and Technology) and vol. 3 (Generalia, Language and Literature, the Arts).

A3   *American Reference Books Annual.* Littleton, CO: Libraries Unlimited, 1970- . Annual.
Intended as a comprehensive review of new reference books published in the U.S. Contains long, critical, signed evaluations of about 1,500 new titles each year. Classified arrangement. Five-year cumulative author, title, and subject indexes are available. A good place to check out new reference materials.

A4   *The Humanities: A Selective Guide to Information Sources.* Ron Blazek and Elizabeth Smith Aversa. 3rd ed. Littleton, CO: Libraries Unlimited, 1988.
A basic and helpful survey. Chapters 1-2 cover general reference tools. Chapters 3-12 treat Philosophy, Religion, the Visual Arts, the Performing Arts, and Languages and Literature. History is not included. Each section includes a discussion of computer-aided research. In all, lists and annotates about 1,000 titles. Author/title and subject indexes.

A5   *The Social Sciences: A Cross-Disciplinary Guide to Selected Sources.*
       Nancy L. Herron, ed. Englewood, Col.: Libraries Unlimited, 1989.
An annotated bibliography of 790 predominantly English-language resources in
the social sciences.   A chapter covering general tools is followed by ones on
political science, economics and business, history, law, anthropology, sociology,
education, psychology, communications, geography, and statistics.   Includes
discussions of computer databases. Author, title, and subject indexes.

** RELIGIOUS / THEOLOGICAL

A6   *The Literature of Theology: A Guide for Students and Pastors.* John A.
       Bollier. Philadelphia: Westminster, 1979.
A very helpful introductory guide. Lists and annotates 543 works, almost all in
English.   Classified arrangement with short introductions to each part. Includes
lists of Bible versions and commentary series. Author and title index.

A7   *Critical Guide to Catholic Reference Books.* James Patrick McCabe. 3rd
       ed. Littleton, CO: Libraries Unlimited, 1989.
An extensive guide listing over 1,500 "of the most important reference books in
English and foreign languages whose contents or point of view relate in some way
to Catholicism." Emphasis on published works available to the U.S. researcher.
Based on a Ph.D. dissertation at the University of Michigan. Author, title, and
subject indexes. The place to go if studying the Catholic Church or a closely
related topic.

A8   *Theological and Religious Reference Materials.* G.E. Gorman and Lyn
       Gorman, with the assistance of Donald N. Matthews. 4 vols. Westport,
       CT: Greenwood Press, 1984-
Vols. 1-3 (General Resources and Biblical Studies; Systematic Theology and
Church History; Practical Theology) now published. Vol. 4 (Comparative and
Non-Christian Religions) is forthcoming. An international guide to theological
reference tools that aims at inclusion rather than selectivity. Its broad subject
arrangement can make for difficult use (e.g. under "Church History: Handbooks"
there are 451 entries). Rather than encouraging "browsing from the neophyte
theologian," this may frustrate the user trying to find the best books. Author, title,
and subject indexes.

A9   *Research Guide to Religious Studies.* John F. Wilson and Thomas P.
       Slavens. Chicago: American Library Association, 1982.
Part 1 is a helpful 104-page survey of religious studies that stresses the important
bibliography of each area of inquiry. Part 2, a 50-page annotated list of major

reference works used in religious studies, is somewhat dated and lists only English-language tools, and relatively few of those. Has author/title and subject indexes. May be useful for getting started in a new area of study.

A10   *ADRIS Newsletter: Newsletter of the Association for the Development of Religious Information Systems*. Bronx, NY: Dept. of Theology at Fordham University, 1971- . Quarterly.

This is an important source for current information on publications and activities in theology. Includes sections on: calendar of coming events; news, announcements, organizations, and directories; bibliography, information, research, and reference matters (including brief reviews of new works); information from and about serials and periodicals (including reviews and comments); and bulletin of recent books (with brief reviews).

** GUIDES TO THEOLOGICAL RESEARCH AND LIBRARY USE

In addition to functioning as bibliographical guides, the following offer guidance in conducting theological research.

A11   *Library Research Guide to Religion and Theology*. James R. Kennedy, Jr. 2nd rev. ed. Ann Arbor: Pierian, 1984.

A good "how to" introduction for those writing papers. Treats both research techniques and use of selected reference tools. Geared more to undergraduate work, but also helpful for the graduate student. The 2nd edition includes newer tools and a brief discussion of computerized bibliographic research. An appendix lists about 350 theological reference works.

A12   *How to Find Information in the Seminary Library*. John Allen Delivuk. St. Louis: Concordia Seminary Library, 1985.

A collection of 18 guides to the use of various theological reference tools. Arranged in four sections: the subject catalog, periodical indexes, essays and dissertations, and finding information on selected topics. The guides vary in length and quality; the detailed directions on the use of periodical indexes are especially helpful.

A13   *Introduction to Theological Research*. Cyril J. Barber. Chicago: Moody Press, 1982.

A mediocre introduction that stresses methods of theological research rather than the tools available. Heavy emphasis on using biblical studies tools to do exegetical study and relatively dated bibliography. No index.

A14   *A Guide to Library Research Methods.* Thomas Mann. New York: Oxford, 1987.

An instructive summary of the principles of library research, written by a general reference librarian at the Library of Congress. 13 chapters cover a wide range of approaches such as encyclopedias, card catalogs, published bibliographies, and computer searches. An appendix describes 21 "special cases," from archives to translations. There is a combined subject and title index.

CHAPTER 2
GENERAL ENCYCLOPEDIAS, HANDBOOKS AND DIRECTORIES

** ENCYCLOPEDIAS

These are works that contain articles on all branches of knowledge or that comprehensively treat a particular branch of knowledge. They are usually arranged A to Z by subject.

Note that some encyclopedias, particularly those limited to one subject area, are titled "dictionary" by the publisher, but they really function as encyclopedias.

** GENERAL COVERAGE -- ENGLISH LANGUAGE

B1   *Encyclopaedia Britannica.* 1st-14th editions. Chicago: Encyclopaedia Britannica, 1763-1973.
Generally considered the leading English-language encyclopedia. For the complete history of the 14 editions and their numerous printings, see Sheehy, pp. 134-135 (A1 above). The following editions are the more important:
      (a) 9th ed., 25 vols., 1875-1889.
          As with the 11th, an outstanding scholarly edition. Emphasis on long detailed articles. Weak index.
      (b) 11th ed., 29 vols., 1911.
          Contains a larger number of more specific articles. Good index.
      (c) 14th ed., 24 vols., 1929-1973.
          With this edition, the encyclopedia began the policy of continuous revision where each year various articles are updated as needed, or left unchanged if still current. Be certain to use the comprehensive index to find all the information on a topic.

B2   *The New Encyclopaedia Britannica.* 15th ed. 30 vols. Chicago: Encyclopaedia Britannica, 1974- .
A radical restructuring of the encyclopedia which includes: the *Propaedia* (outline of knowledge) [1 vol.]; the *Micropaedia* (ready reference and index) [10 vols.]; and the *Macropaedia* (knowledge in depth) [19 vols.]. The 102,214 short articles in the *Micropaedia* summarize a subject and refer the user to relevant articles and parts of articles in the *Macropaedia*. Although it is a poor substitute for the index of the 14th ed., always use the *Micropaedia* before the *Macropaedia*. The 4,207 "in-depth" articles in the *Macropaedia* are signed by authorities in the field and include selected bibliographies. A continuous revision policy applies to each year's edition.

B3   *Encyclopedia Americana.* 30 vols. New York: Americana, 1903- .
A good general encyclopedia comparable in quality to the *Britannica*. Continuous revision policy. Mostly short specific articles, some with bibliographies (which may not be up-to-date). The last volume is a detailed index which should always be consulted.

B4   *The New Columbia Encyclopedia.* 4th ed. New York: Columbia University Press, 1975.
Considered the best one-volume encyclopedia available. Over 50,000 concise articles, many with brief selective bibliographies. Outstanding accuracy. Excellent source for brief, non-specialized, quick-reference information.

Note: A number of non-English encyclopedias are generally recognized as even more extensive and authoritative than the Britannica. They are usually strongest on subjects related to their own and neighboring countries. For a description of important foreign encyclopedias, see Sheehy, pp. 138-145 (A1 above).

** SOCIAL SCIENCES

B5   *Encyclopaedia of the Social Sciences.* 15 vols. New York: Macmillan, 1930-1935.
The first comprehensive work in the area. Signed articles by specialists with bibliographies. Especially strong on biography of those active in the social sciences up to 1930.

B6   *International Encyclopedia of the Social Sciences.* Edited by David L. Sills. 17 vols. New York: Macmillan, 1968.
Based on and complements the above work. "Topical articles are devoted to concepts, principles, theories, and methods in the disciplines of anthropology, economics, geography, law, political science, psychiatry, psychology, sociology, and statistics." Lengthy, comparative, analytical articles -- use the index to locate desired information. Weak on biography. Includes bibliographies.

B7   *International Encyclopedia of the Social Sciences, vol. 18: Biographical Supplement.* New York: Macmillan, 1979.
Includes 215 additional biographies, emphasizing the "intellectual development and contributions to the social sciences" of those included. Those social scientists included have died since the preparation of the original volumes or are now over 70 years old. The bibliographies include materials by and about the biographees. No index, but table of contents of biographees.

** FACT / STATISTICAL HANDBOOKS AND DIRECTORIES

Fact or statistical handbooks are such reference works as yearbooks, almanacs, manuals, etc., which are generally published at regular intervals and provide a source of quick, up-to-date, brief information on various topics. Directories may be considered specialized fact/statistical handbooks concerned with listing various items, such as denominations, associations, addresses, etc. Most often, you will probably use these tools for specific pieces of information: a group's official name, membership, address, publications, etc.

B8   *World Almanac and Book of Facts.* New York: Newspaper Enterprise Association, 1868-   . Annual.
Still the best almanac available, it is "a compendium of facts and useful information," e.g. the dates of Easter, cost-of-living statistics, denominational information, etc. Includes extensive index at the front of each volume. If the *World Almanac* is not available, other almanacs will often fill its place (e.g. *Information Please Almanac, Reader's Digest Almanac*).

B9   *Europa Year Book.* 1st- ed. London: Europa Publications, 1959-   . Annual.
Now 2 vols. Has detailed up-to-date information on each country of the world including: historical survey, statistical survey, government, political parties, religion, press, etc. Contains a section on international organizations, as well as maps.

B10   *Statesman's Yearbook: Statistical and Historical Annual of the States of the World.* New York: St. Martins, 1864-   . Annual.
Publisher varies. Includes the same type of information as Europa Yearbook but in more compact form. Also includes selective bibliographies of statistical sources and reference books for each country. Detailed index.

B11   *Statistical Abstract of the United States, 1878-* . United States. Bureau of the Census. Washington, DC: U.S. Government Printing Office, 1879-   . Annual.
The standard source for social, political, and economic statistics about the U.S. Besides the current-year data, it often has statistics for the last 5 to 15 years, sometimes back to 1790.

B12   *The World of Learning.* 2 vols. London: Europa Publ., 1947-   . Annual.
        Lists, country by country, the academies, learned societies, research institutes, libraries and archives, museums, universities and colleges, and other schools of higher education. Gives addresses, officers, selective listings of faculty,

brief description and statistics, etc., as appropriate. Provides a wealth of information. At the back of vol. 2 is an index of institutions by name.

B13   *Encyclopedia of Associations.* 5 vols. Detroit: Gale, 1961-   . Annual.
        Contents: v. 1 -- National Organizations of the U.S.; v. 2 -- Geographic and Executive Indexes; v. 3 -- New Associations and Projects; v. 4 -- International Organizations; v. 5 -- Research Activities and Funding Programs. Lists over 18,000 active associations, including information on full name, address, officers, purposes, activities, membership, publications, etc. Extensive indexes provide access to each entry by name, important words in the name, and by specific subject.

CHAPTER 3
RELIGIOUS / THEOLOGICAL ENCYCLOPEDIAS

Included here are encyclopedias covering religion or theology in general. Encyclopedias covering one subfield of theology are found in the subject area lists.

** ALL RELIGIONS -- MAJOR WORKS

C1   *The Encyclopedia of Religion.* Mircea Eliade, chief ed. 16 vols. New York: Macmillan, 1986.
A major new work with 2,750 articles by 1,400 recognized scholars covering all aspects of religion, past and present. Emphasizes the history of religious traditions, cross-cultural religious ideas, and the role of religion in culture. Somewhat disappointing; negative reviews have criticized a lack of theoretical analysis and noted that some articles are out-of-date. Annotated bibliographies accompany articles. Vol. 16 is an extensive index.

C2   *Encyclopaedia of Religion and Ethics.* Ed. by James Hastings. 13 vols. New York: Scribners, 1908-28.
A comprehensive work on religion in the English language, limited only by its obvious age. Wide coverage of all aspects of religion and ethics. Signed articles with good bibliographies covering all religions, as well as people and places associated with them. Excellent indexing.

C3   *Die Religion in Geschichte und Gegenwart: Handwörterbuch für Theologie und Religionswissenschaft.* Hrsg. von Kurt Galling. 3d. vollig neubearb. Aufl. 7 vols. Tübingen: Mohr, 1957-65.
Known as "RGG," this is an authoritative work in the field. The 1st ed. (1909-13) and 2nd ed. (1927-32) are also still useful, containing excellent articles by specialists with good bibliographies, as does this edition. Many biographies, including living people. German Protestant viewpoint. Vol. 7, the index, includes biographical notes on the contributors.

** ALL RELIGIONS -- ONE VOLUME

C4   *Abingdon Dictionary of Living Religions.* Keith Crim, ed. Nashville: Abingdon, 1981.
A well-done encyclopedia covering the historical development, doctrines, movements, objects, practices, sects, and writings of contemporary world religions. Includes both major articles on important topics and definitions of over 1,600 key words and phrases. Many of the articles have brief bibliographies.

C5   *Eerdmans' Handbook to the World's Religions.* R. Pierce Beaver et al.,
       eds. Grand Rapids: Eerdmans, 1982.
A well-done guide to the religions of mankind, both past and present. Includes
a "Rapid Fact-finder" (a short dictionary of persons, places, institutions, and ideas
of religions), a good general index, select bibliographies, maps and charts, and
numerous illustrations (many colored).

C6   *The Facts on File Dictionary of Religions.* John R. Hinnells. New York:
       Facts on File, 1984.
Twenty-nine scholars have written 1,150 entries on world religions. Emphasis is
on "living religions" although there is some discussion of ancient religions.
Concentrates on the terms used by the various religions, rather than on scholarly
and technical terms. Notation system links entries to an extensive bibliography.
In addition to a general index, there is a helpful "synoptic index" that lists all
terms covered in the dictionary under each of 29 different religions.

** CHRISTIANITY -- PROTESTANT VIEWPOINT

C7   *New Schaff-Herzog Encyclopedia of Religious Knowledge.* 13 vols. New
       York: Funk and Wagnalls, 1908-12.
A revision and translation of the 3rd. ed. (1896) of the *Herzog-Hauck
Realencyklopädie.* Preceded by the *Schaff-Herzog Encyclopedia* (1884-91 in
various editions) which is based on the 1st and 2nd editions of the *Herzog-Hauck
Realencyklopädie.* Strong on historical, biographical, ecclesiastical, and
theological topics -- weakest on Bible. Includes some information on
non-Christian religions as well. Note that a bibliography is found in three places:
a general bibliographical survey in the preface; a bibliographical appendix at the
beginning of each volume; and appended to the individual articles. Has good
index.

C8   *New Twentieth-Century Encyclopedia of Religious Knowledge.* J. D.
       Douglas, gen. ed. 2nd ed. Grand Rapids: Baker, 1991.
A major revision of the 2 vol. *Twentieth-Century Encyclopedia of Religious
Knowledge* (Grand Rapids: Baker, 1955), with two-thirds new material. The 1955
edition was itself a supplement to *Schaff-Herzog* (above). Over 2,000 articles by
250 contributors, concentrating on church history and biography, denominations,
ecclesiastical terms, and social and political issues. Emphasizes "evangelical
Christianity as a worldwide phenomenon."

C9   *Cyclopaedia of Biblical, Theological, and Ecclesiastical Literature.* Edited
       by John M'Clintock and James Strong. 10 vols. + 2 vol. supplement.
       New York: Harper, 1867-87.
Obviously not up-to-date, but a good source for the prevailing theological

viewpoint of that time. Good bibliographies of 19th century and earlier materials accompany the long articles.

C10   *Realencyklopädie für protestantische Theologie und Kirche.* Johann Jakob Herzog, ed. 3. verb. und verm. Aufl., hrsg. von Albert Hauck. 24 vols. Leipzig: Hinrichs, 1896-1913.

A basic and extensive German Protestant encyclopedia. Long signed articles by specialists with bibliographies. Still of value. Vol. 22 is an index, vols. 23-24 form a supplement.

C11   *Evangelisches Kirchenlexikon: kirchlich-theologisches Handwörterbuch.* Hrsg. von Heinz Brunotte and Otto Weber. 4 vol. Göttingen: Vandenhoek & Ruprecht, 1955-61.

Publication of third edition began in 1985. The new edition will have four volumes plus an index volume. German Protestant viewpoint, with about 800 contributors. The signed articles include bibliographies and emphasize recent literature. Vol. 4 is an important subject index and also includes a name index, the "Biographischer Anhang," which has brief biographical information on 15,000 persons.

C12   *Theologische Realenzyklopädie.* Hrsg. von Gerhard Krause und Gerhard Müller. Berlin: de Gruyter, 1977- .

A new Protestant encyclopedia, now complete through Bd. 17 (-- Katechismuspredigt). Much more theological than historical, with long discussions of selected theological issues by specialists. The forthcoming cumulative index will facilitate use (each volume also has its own index). The first volume published, the "Abkürzungsverzeichnis," is a useful list of abbreviations used by many works in theology, not just in the *TRE.*

** CHRISTIANITY -- CATHOLIC VIEWPOINT

C13   *Catholic Encyclopedia.* 16 vols. New York: Appleton, 1907-1914.

Subtitle: "An International Work of Reference on the Constitution, Doctrine, Discipline, and History of the Catholic Church." The predecessor of the *New Catholic Encyclopedia,* this set complements it on history and biography, especially of the medieval period. Reflects the older, more traditional theology of the Catholic Church.

C14 *New Catholic Encyclopedia.* 15 vols. New York: McGraw-Hill, 1967.
C15 *New Catholic Encyclopedia, vol. 16: Supplement, 1967-74.* New York: McGraw-Hill, 1974.
C16 *New Catholic Encyclopedia, vol. 17: Supplement, Change in the Church.* New York: McGraw-Hill, 1978.
C17 *New Catholic Encyclopedia, vol. 18: Supplement, 1978-1988.* Palatine, Ill.: Jack Heraty, 1989.
Not just a revision of the above work, but an entirely new production. International in scope, emphasis on American and English-speaking areas. Contains about 17,000 signed articles, most with bibliographies, by more than 4,800 contributors. Vol. 15 is a well-done index of about 600 pages, and also lists the abbreviations and contributors. Be sure to use the index to locate specific topics. Vols. 1-15 cover up to the close of Vatican II. The supplements update the earlier articles and cover new topics.

C18 *Encyclopédie des sciences ecclésiastiques redigée par les savants Catholiques le plus eminents de France et de l'étranger.* Paris: Letouzey, 1907- .
The most extensive theological encyclopedia. Represents the best scholarship of French Catholicism. Consists of five major parts, most of which are listed below in the appropriate subject lists. The parts are:
(1) *Dictionnaire d'archéologie chrétienne et de liturgie.*
(2) *Dictionnaire d'histoire et de géographie ecclésiastiques.*
(3) *Dictionnaire de théologie catholique.*
(4) *Dictionnaire de la Bible.*
(5) *Dictionnaire de droit canonique.*

C19 *Lexikon für Theologie und Kirche.* 2. völlig neu bearb. Aufl. hrsg. von Josef Höfer und Karl Rahner. Begrundet von Michael Buchberger. 10 vols. & Register. Freiburg: Herder, 1957-67.
One of the best Catholic encyclopedias. Primarily short signed articles with selective bibliographies, but has some extensive essays. The index volume has an extensive specific subject index, a classified subject index, a geographical index, and a list of the contributors indicating the entries contributed.

C20 *Lexikon für Theologie und Kirche: Ergänzungband, Teil 1-3: Das Zweite Vatikanische Konzil.* 3 vols. Freiburg: Herder, 1966-1968.
The supplements include the texts of the Vatican II documents (in Latin and German) along with extensive commentary, a bibliography, and an index.

** CHRISTIANITY -- DENOMINATIONAL

C21   *Baptist Atlas.* Albert W. Wardin; cartography by Don Fields. Nashville:
        Broadman, 1980.
A combination atlas and history of the Baptists. Each of the five chapters has
excellent maps and useful statistical tables. Topics covered are: origins in
Netherlands and England; U.S.A. Baptists (3 chapters); and Baptist movements of
the world.

C22   *Encyclopedia of Southern Baptists.* 4 vols. + index. Nashville, TN:
        Broadman, 1958-1982.
Treats the history, practices, and worship of the Southern Baptists. Includes
signed articles with bibliographies on the organizations, institutions, colleges,
newspapers, theology, important people, etc. Vol. 3 (1971) is a supplement with
a separate A-Z sequence. Vol. 4 (1982), covering 1971 to 1980, includes some
updating of previous entries as well as new entries on: topics of special interest
in the 70s; biographies of 400 Southern Baptist leaders; and new activities,
organizations, agencies, etc. of the church.

C23   *The Brethren Encyclopedia.* 3 vols. Philadelphia: Brethren Encyclopedia
        Inc., 1983.
"Attempts to present reasonably full coverage of Brethren life, practice, and
heritage." Vols. 1 and 2 contain articles in alphabetical order, and vol. 3 contains
appendixes, bibliography, maps, and statistical data. Includes many biographies,
2,300 entries on individual Brethren congregations, illustrations, and "sidebar"
anecdotes. No index, but extensive cross-references. The bibliography in vol. 3
includes material by and about Brethren. It is more comprehensive than and
supersedes *A Brethren Bibliography, 1719-1963* (Elgin, IL: Brethren Press, 1964).

C24   *The Encyclopedia of the Lutheran Church.* Julius Bodensieck. Edited for
        the Lutheran World Federation. 3 vols. Minneapolis: Augsburg, 1965.
Broad coverage of the Lutheran church, international and ecumenical in scope.
Covers Lutheran doctrine, history, practice, beliefs, persons, etc. Contains about
3,000 articles contributed by 723 Lutherans from 34 countries. No index, few
(and weak) bibliographies.

C25   *Lutheran Cyclopedia.* Erwin L. Lueker. Rev. ed. St. Louis: Concordia,
        1975.
Substantially revised and expanded from the 1st ed. of 1954. Strongest on
Lutheranism, but does include material on other denominations. Has brief articles
on history, practice, teaching, significant individuals, etc., of the Lutheran church.
Includes bibliographies.

C26   *Mennonitisches Lexikon.* Christian Hege and Christian Neff. 4 vols. Frankfort a. Main: the Authors, 1913-1967.
Issued in parts over 55 years! Has signed articles with bibliographies. International perspective with European emphasis.

C27   *The Mennonite Encyclopedia: a Comprehensive Reference Work on the Anabaptist-Mennonite Movement.* 4 vols. Hillsboro, KS: Mennonite Publishing House, 1955-1959.
C28   *The Mennonite Encyclopedia, vol. 5: Supplement.* ed. by Cornelius J. Dyck and Dennis D. Martin. Scottdale, Penn.: Herald Press, 1990.
Covers the history, theology, practices, ethics, biography, etc., of the Mennonites from their beginning to the present. Signed articles with bibliographies. Builds upon, but does not duplicate, the *Mennonitisches Lexikon* (above). The supplement updates articles and adds new articles, stressing global influence of the Mennonite movement.

C29   *Encyclopedia of World Methodism. History of the United Methodist Church.* Nolan B. Harmon. 2 vols. Nashville: United Methodist Publishing House, 1974.
Sponsored by the World Methodist Council and the Commission of Archives and contains articles on Methodist history, doctrine, biography, sites, etc. Emphasis on the coverage of the United Methodist Church and American Methodism. Signed articles with bibliographies, general index.

C30   *Encyclopaedia of the Presbyterian Church in the United States of America.* Alfred Nevin. Philadelphia: Presbyterian Publishing, 1884.
Includes articles on significant individuals, presbyteries, congregations, history and growth of Presbyterianism in the U.S., and other institutions and topics. Good coverage of the 19th century and earlier.

** JEWISH

Only two major English-language Jewish encyclopedias are included here. Students of the Christian religion will find them useful for backgrounds and Jewish perspectives.

C31   *Encyclopaedia Judaica.* 16 vols. Jerusalem: Encyclopaedia Judaica, 1971-1972.
Often cited as the authority on Jewish topics. A comprehensive view of world Jewry and its history. Over 25,000 signed articles, most with bibliographies, include many biographies, including living figures. Use the extensive (about 200,000 entries) index (vol. 1) for best results. This index uses letter-by-letter, not word-by-word, alphabetizing.

C32   *Jewish Encyclopedia.* Ed. by Isadore Singer. 12 vols. New York: Funk
       & Wagnalls, 1901-6.
Subtitle: "A Descriptive Record of the History, Religion, Literature, and Customs
of the Jewish People from the Earliest Times to the Present Day." The older
standard work, still useful for its bibliographies of older material and historical
and biographical information, and still preferred by some scholars.

CHAPTER 4
RELIGIOUS / THEOLOGICAL HANDBOOKS AND DIRECTORIES

Use these tools for information about religious organizations and denominations such as addresses, membership, names of officers, and other statistical information. Some of these tools also contain historical and/or theological information about the sects and denominations.

** INTERNATIONAL AND FOREIGN

D1   *World Christian Encyclopedia.* David B. Barrett, ed. New York: Oxford University Press, 1982.
"A comparative study of churches and religions in the modern world, AD 1900-2000." A massive international and interdenominational work by over 500 scholars. The major part of this work gives data on 150 ecclesiastical traditions, 20,800 denominations and subdivisions, and 15,000 Christian organizations. Also includes a "selective world bibliography on Christianity," an "atlas of Christianity and evangelization in the modern world," a "who's who in the Christian world, 1970-80," and a "topical directory of world Christianity." Contains numerous maps, diagrams, and illustrations, and seven quick reference indexes. A major and very important reference work on modern Christianity worldwide. Since 1985 David Barrett has updated the book's mission statistics in his series, "Annual Statistical Table on Global Mission," in the January issue of *International Bulletin of Missionary Research.*

D2   *Handbook, Member Churches, World Council of Churches.* A.J. van der Bent, ed. Rev. ed. Geneva: World Council of Churches, 1985.
Contains statistical, historical, and descriptive information on the over 300 churches that are members of the World Council of Churches. Arranged geographically by continent, region, and country -- with indexes by country, names of member churches, and the English names of member churches. Also includes information on other national and regional councils and conferences of churches. Contains helpful information, but limited to WCC membership.

D3   *UK Christian Handbook.* Peter Brierley, ed. 1989/90 ed. Bromley, Kent: MARC Europe, 1988.
A list of 4,000 Christian organizations, classified into several categories including accomodations, book stores, churches, educational institutions, media, overseas missions, and social services. Provides brief information about each group. Extensively indexed by personal names, location, and organization.

D4   *Annuaire protestant . . . la France protestante et les Églises de langue française.* Paris: Centrale du livre protestant, 1862- . Annual.
Subtitle and publisher varies. Gives directory and institutional information on each entry for French protestant churches and other French-speaking churches.

** AMERICAN

D5   *The Encyclopedia of American Religions.* J. Gordon Melton. 3rd ed. Detroit: Gale, 1989.
Covers nearly 1,600 primary religious bodies in the United States. Classed arrangement, with each religious group placed within one of 22 "families" or listed under "unclassified" groups. Gives considerable detail and covers many minor groups. Indexed by religious organization, educational institution, personal names, publications, geographical location, and subject.

D6   *A Directory of Religious and Parareligious Bodies and Organizations in the United States.* James V. Geisendorfer. Lewiston, N.Y.: E. Mellen Press, 1989.
An alphabetical name-address listing of over 5,700 religious and parareligious groups in the U.S. Includes cross-references for alternative and former organizational names. Particularly helpful for its data on non-Christian (Hindu, Jewish, Sufi, Buddhist, Muslim, Sikh, etc.) groups.

D7   *Handbook of Denominations in the United States.* Frank S. Mead. New 9th ed. rev. by Samuel S. Hill. Nashville: Abingdon, 1990.
Intended to give a brief, impartial account of each body -- its history, doctrine, present status, etc. Also gives an evaluation of the group's doctrinal beliefs. Each denomination is listed under the religious tradition to which it belongs. Includes a glossary of terms, a list of addresses of denominational headquarters, a bibliography of material about each denomination, and a name and subject index.

D8   *Profiles in Belief: The Religious Bodies of the United States and Canada.* Arthur Carl Piepkorn. 7 vols. New York: Harper & Row, 1977- .
Four volumes published thus far -- vols. 3 and 4 in one physical volume (1979). No additional volumes published since then and the status of vols. 5-7 is unclear. Classed arrangement; strong on the historical background of each group and in describing the origin, significance, and meaning of the many sub-branches of each group. Includes indexes and bibliographical notes. Contents: v. 1 -- Roman Catholic, Old Catholic, Eastern Orthodox; v. 2 -- Protestant; v. 3 -- Holiness and Pentecostal; v. 4 -- Evangelical, Fundamentalist, and other Christian churches; v. 5 -- Metaphysical bodies; v. 6 -- Judaism; v. 7 -- Oriental, Humanist, and Unclassified.

D9   *The Directory of Religious Organizations in the United States.* 2nd ed.
       Falls Church, VA: McGrath Publishing Co., 1982.
Describes 1,628 general organizations active in the field of religion, excluding
religious bodies and religious orders. For each gives (as applicable): the full
name, the religious affiliation, address and telephone number, chief officer, staff
& membership size, a brief summary of the purpose and work of the organization,
and its specific activities (publications, radio/TV programs, meetings, etc.).
Entries are arranged alphabetically with no indexes. The 1st ed. (Consortium,
1977) listed 328 religious orders (dropped from the 2nd ed.) and 1,241 general
organizations, arranged topically with a name index.

D10   *Religion in America, 1975- .* Princeton: Princeton Religion Research
       Center, 1975- .
A series of studies (published more or less annually) which provides current
statistics and interpretive comments on the state of religion in America. Prepared
by a non-denominational group using the research facilities of the Gallup
Organization.

D11   *Religion in America: 50 Years, 1935-1985.* Princeton: Gallup Report,
       1985.
A summary of fifty years of Gallup survey data on American religion,
documenting trends in religious identification, practices, and belief.

D12   *Yearbook of American and Canadian Churches.* Nashville: Abingdon,
       1916- . Annual.
Exact title varies. The standard directory, sponsored by the National Council of
Churches. Does not include cults and small groups. Gives extensive information
on each group, including: various sub-bodies within the denomination, addresses,
brief description of its organizational set-up, names and addresses of officers,
membership statistics, etc. Indexed by name of organization and denomination.
Along with the directory this work also contains a statistical and historical section
on Christianity in the U.S. and Canada.

D13   *Churches and Church Membership in the United States, 1980.* Bernard
       Quinn et al. Atlanta: Glenmary Research Center, 1982.
"An enumeration by region, state and county based on data reported by 111
church bodies." The best single source for information on the membership of
major Christian and Jewish groups in the United States. Presents a wealth of
statistical data in four major parts: summary information and statistics on the 111
participating religious bodies; regional summaries for the nine census regions;
summaries for each state; and the same data for each of the 3,102 counties in the
U.S. Very valuable tool for study in this area.

D14   *National Evangelical Directory, 1989/90.* Wheaton, IL: National
Association of Evangelicals, 1989.

Published biennially, this is the seventh edition. Intended to be a "national listing of evangelical schools, missions, organizations, and associations." The 4,000 entries (which give name, address, and phone number) are logically divided into different lists by the type and purpose of organization. Also included is an alphabetical index of all organizations, etc. listed in the directory. Includes some hard-to-find lists of of evangelical organizations such as: Christian camps, retirement facilities, youth and campus organizations, film distributors, record companies, and Christian day school organizations.

D15   *Directory of Religious Broadcasters.* Ben Armstrong, ed. Morristown, NJ: National Religious Broadcasters, 1977- . Annual.

Title varies. An important source of information on the electronic church. Lists radio, TV, and cable stations that offer full or partial religious programming; producers of religious programming; and individual programs. Also contains sections on international broadcasting, equipment, consultants, etc. Includes indexes of radio call number, TV call number, television/film producer, and radio producer.

D16   *Catholic Almanac.* 65th- ed. Huntington, IN: Our Sunday Visitor, 1969- . Annual.

Previously titled the *National Catholic Almanac.* Gives information primarily for the U.S., but covers the entire Roman Catholic Church worldwide. Includes: special reports; the history, hierarchy, and government of the Catholic Church; biographical data on officials, saints, and popes; and summaries of the beliefs, practices, and activities of the Catholic Church. Use the extensive index at the front.

Note: Most denominations also publish directories of their churches, officers, etc. If you are working with a particular denomination, use their directory.

CHAPTER 5
DIRECTORIES OF UNIVERSITIES, COLLEGES, AND LIBRARIES

** UNIVERSITIES AND COLLEGES -- GENERAL

There are numerous directories of universities and colleges. Listed below are just two of the better known guides. If they are not available, most libraries will have some other directory of this type.

E1   *Peterson's Annual Guides to Graduate Study: Book 2, Graduate Programs in the Humanities and Social Sciences.* Princeton, NJ: Peterson Guides, 1966- . Annual.
New edition each year. The 24th edition (1989) was arranged in 34 major subject areas. Under each subject area are: brief definitions of the various specialized fields within the subject; a directory to which schools offer training in each field (with brief descriptions of the program); and a section containing two-page descriptions of some of the schools listed in the directory.

E2   *Lovejoy's College Guide.* Charles T. Straughn and Barbarasue Lovejoy Straughn, eds. 19th ed. New York: Monarch Press, 1989.
A directory, with brief information, of undergraduate schools. Arranged by state, subarranged by name of the school. Indexed by school and by "career curricula and special programs."

E3   *Guide to American Graduate Schools.* Harold R. Doughty. 5th ed., completely rev. New York: Penguin Books, 1986.
Lists over 1,200 accredited programs in all subject areas, with brief but fairly comprehensive information on each program. Arranged alphabetically by school with "location by state" and "fields of study" indexes. The latter index is somewhat difficult to use because the "fields of study" terms are too few and too broad.

** CHRISTIAN COLLEGES, BIBLE COLLEGES, SEMINARIES

E4   "Church-Related and Accredited Colleges and Universities in the United States." Section in each volume of *Yearbook of American and Canadian Churches* (see D12 above).
Includes all colleges in some way related to those groups listed in the Yearbook. Does not include Bible colleges.

E5 *Consider a Christian College.* Christian College Coalition. 2nd ed. Princeton, NJ: Peterson Guides, 1990.
Subtitle: "A guide to 78 private liberal arts colleges and univeristies combining academic excellence and enduring spiritual values." Includes one-page summaries of Christian liberal arts colleges, with descriptions of spiritual emphases, academics, student life, and annual costs. A helpful guide to the schools covered.

E6 *Directory, American Association of Bible Colleges.* Wheaton, IL: AABC, 1948- . Annual.
Lists all members and candidates for membership. Gives name, address, church affiliation, brief statistical information, and names of officials. The AABC is the major accrediting body for Bible colleges.

E7 *Directory of Departments and Programs of Religious Studies in North America.* Watson E. Mills, ed. 1989 ed. Macon, GA: Council on the Study of Religion, 1989.
Includes, for each of the more than 400 schools which paid to be included, a one-page description which includes a department profile, descriptions of the undergraduate and/or graduate programs offered in religion, and a list of faculty members. Appendix A lists "United States: names and addresses of four-year schools, and graduate schools not located in theological schools, with departments or programs of religious studies." Appendix B does the same for Canada. Appendix C lists "Names and addresses of theological schools in the United States and Canada." Includes a geographical directory and an index of "faculty members at participating schools."

E8 *Directory, Association of Theological Schools in the United States and Canada.* Vandalia, OH: ATS, 1975- . Annual.
Previous editions under old name, American Association of Theological Schools. Published as an issue of the Association's Bulletin. ATS is the major accrediting body for graduate seminaries in the U.S. and Canada. Lists accredited and associate members. Gives address and brief statistical information about each school. Appendices list schools by denominational affiliation and nation, and by geographical location.

E9 *Guide to Schools and Departments of Religion and Seminaries in the United States and Canada: Degree Programs in Religious Studies.* William Burgess, ed. New York: Macmillan, 1986.
Lists over 700 accredited programs of religion and theology in North America. Entries are listed alphabetically under each province or state. Each listing includes: address, tuition and fees, calendar, entrance requirements, degrees granted, and description of the background and mission of each school. Institutional and denominational affiliation indexes.

** LIBRARY DIRECTORIES

Library directories provide helpful information about the libraries included such as location, hours, personnel, address, size, collection strengths, and lending policies. Most are arranged or indexed by location, subject, and/or institutional name.

** FOREIGN LIBRARIES

E10   *World Guide to Libraries.* Helga Lengenfelder, ed. 9th ed. Munich: K.G. Sauer, 1989.
Lists over 37,000 libraries from 167 countries. Arranged by country, subarranged by nine types of library (including "ecclesiastical libraries") and then by city. Information includes address, phone number, and important holdings and special collections.

E11   *A World Directory of Theological Libraries.*   George M. Ruoss. Metuchen, NJ: Scarecrow Press, 1968.
Gives basic information on 1,779 theological libraries (Catholic, Jewish, Orthodox, and Protestant) in the world. Arranged by country, then by city. Effective date of contents: December 1966. Index of institutions and religious groups but no subject index.

E12   *Subject Collections in European Libraries.* Richard C. Lewanski. 2nd ed. New York: Bowker, 1978.
Lists around 10,000 special subject collections, primarily in northwest Europe. Arranged by subject using the Dewey classification: then, within each subject, alphabetically by country. Subject index. Gives for each collection its size, location, and special conditions of access.

E13   *Research Libraries and Collections in the United Kingdom: a Selective Inventory and Guide.* Stephen Andrew Roberts, et al. Hamden, CT: Linnet Books, 1978.
Contains four major sections, each arranged alphabetically: national, special, and public libraries; university libraries; polytechnical libraries; and Scottish central institutions. For each, it gives the library name, address, collection strength(s), use and access policies, etc. Three indexes: by subject, by name of collection, and by geographical location.

** AMERICAN LIBRARIES

E14   *American Library Directory.* 2 vols. New York: Bowker, 1923-   .
       Annual.
Frequency, subtitle, and compiler varies. The 42nd ed. (1989-90) lists over 30,000
U.S. and over 3,000 Canadian academic, public, special, and government
libraries. Arranged by state or province, then by city, then alphabetically by
name. Also includes over 400 networks, consortia, and cooperative efforts. The
information given includes: full name, address, telephone, personnel names,
special collections owned, statistics on size and service. Has name index. Very
helpful for locating most libraries in a given geographical area.

E15   *Subject Collections: a Guide to Special Book Collections and Subject Em-*
       phases. Lee Ash and William G. Miller, with the collaboration of Barbara
       J. McQuitty. 6th ed. 2 vols. New York: Bowker, 1985.
"As Reported by University, College, Public, and Special Libraries and Museums
in the United States and Canada." Entries are arranged under numerous specific
subject headings which are in alphabetical order. Under each subject, libraries
with strengths in that subject are listed, along with brief address and holdings
information.

Note: In addition to the directories listed above, many state, city, and regional
library groups issue directories of libraries within their scope. Check with your
reference librarian to find out what is available for your area.

CHAPTER 6
BIOGRAPHICAL SOURCES

There are numerous publications designed to provide biographical information on individuals of note -- a small sample of some of the more important and useful for your purposes are listed below. Remember that most encyclopedias include biographical articles. In addition, biographical encyclopedias for church history figures are given in the church history chapters, rather than here.

Many denominations also issue a biographical dictionary, a ministerial directory, "fasti," etc., of ministers and leading figures of the denomination, past and/or present. These types of works are *not* included in this list.

** INTERNATIONAL -- INDEXES

F1   *Biography and Geneology Master Index.* Miranda C. Herbert & Barbara McNeil, eds. 2nd ed. 8 vols. Detroit: Gale, 1980.
"A consolidated index to more than 3,200,000 biographical sketches in over 350 current and retrospective biographical dictionaries." A major resource for locating biographical information, emphasizing the United States. All of the works indexed are in the English language and almost all were published in the United States. The first edition was titled: *Biographical Dictionaries Master Index* (1975-76). See also the smaller Gale publication, *Historical Biographical Dictionaries Master Index.* Kept up-to-date by annual supplements and five-year cumulations (see below).

F2   *Biography and Geneology Master Index: 1981-1985 Cumulation.* Barbara McNeil, ed. 5 vols. Detroit: Gale, 1985.
"A consolidated index to more than 2,250,000 biographical sketches in over 215 current and retrospective biographical dictionaries." Supplements the above work.

F3   *Biography and Geneology Master Index: 1986-1990 Cumulation.* Barbara McNeil, ed. 3 vols. Detroit: Gale, 1990.
"A consolidated index to more than 1,895,000 biographical sketches in over 250 current and retrospective biographical dictionaries."

F4   *Dictionary of Universal Biography of All Ages and of All People.* Albert M. Hyamson. 2nd ed. New York: Dutton, 1951.
An index to 23 major biographical sources, e.g. the *Dictionary of National Biography.* Includes individuals who died before the late 1940s, but stronger on 19th century and earlier. Lists about 120,000 individuals alphabetically and directs the user to the appropriate biographical tool.

F5   *Internationale Personalbibliographie, 1800-1943.* Max Arnim. 2 Aufl.
      2 vols. Stuttgart: Hiersemann, 1952.
Primarily a list of bibliographies of materials by and about individuals, but
includes some basic biographical information (e.g. occupation/profession, dates)
and often leads to other biographical tools. International in scope, but emphasis
on Germany.

F6   *Internationale Personalbibliographie Bd. III-IV, 1944-1975.* Max Arnim.
      Fortgefuhrt von Franz Hodes. 2. uberarbeitete & bis zum Berichtsjahr
      1975 fortgefuhrte Aufl. von Bd. III (1944-1959). Mit Nachträgen zur
      zweiten Aufl. von Bd. I/II (1800-1943) Hrsg. Gerhard Bock. Stuttgart:
      Hiersemann, 1978-   .
Currently being published by fascicle. Extends coverage of the original set up
through 1975, and includes new references for individuals already included in
vols. 1 and 2. Vol. 4 of this work will provide an index to all four volumes.

F7   *Biography Index: a Cumulative Index to Biographical Material in Books
      and Magazines.* New York: Wilson, 1947- . Quarterly.
Annual and three-year cumulations. Indexes all types of biographical material
found in English-language periodicals (articles, tributes, obituaries, etc.). Arranged
by name of biographee, indexed by occupation or profession.

** INTERNATIONAL -- SOURCES

F8   *Webster's New Biographical Dictionary.* Springfield, MA: Merriam-
      Webster, 1988.
Concise information on over 30,000 deceased persons. Helpful in giving a
syllabic division and pronunciation for all names included. This edition includes
greater coverage of the non-English speaking world than its predecessor.

F9   *Who's Who in the World.* 1st ed.- . Chicago: Marquis, 1971- .
      Published about every three years. Includes 25,000 living biographees
from over 150 countries.

F10   *International Who's Who.* London: Europa, 1935- .
      Gives short (100-150 word) biographies of living world notables. Includes
an obituary list of those in the previous edition who have died. Particularly good
coverage of heads of state, the performing arts, and writers.

F11   *New York Times Obituary Index, 1858-1968.* New York: New York
      Times, 1970.
Lists more than 353,000 names which have appeared under the heading "Deaths"
in the *New York Times Index* from 1858-1968. Gives year, day, section, page, and

column where the notice is located in the *New York Times* (available on microfilm at many libraries).

F12   *New York Times Obituary Index, 1869-1978.* New York: New York Times, 1980.

Lists more than 36,000 names which have appeared under the heading "Deaths" in the *New York Times Index* from 1869-1978. Gives year, day, section, page, and column where the notice is located in the *New York Times*. Supplement to the above (also called *New York Times Obituary Index, II*).

** AMERICAN -- GENERAL

F13   *Who's Who in America.* Chicago: Marquis, 1899- . Annual.

Subtitle varies. Now published in two volumes. Brief biographical information on living prominent Americans. Includes addresses and lists of published works. Accuracy of information included varies -- it is supplied by the biographee.

F14   *Who Was Who in America: Historical Volume, 1607-1896.* Chicago: Marquis, 1963.

Includes "individuals who have made a contribution to or whose activity was in some manner related to the history of the U.S." Other features: lists of major historical events, vice-presidents and presidents, cabinet officers, supreme court justices, congressional leaders, state governors, etc.

F15   *Who Was Who in America: a Companion Biographical Reference Work to "Who's Who in America."* Chicago: Marquis, 1942- .

Now eight volumes, covering 1897-1985. Includes the biographical entry (with death date) of those who were dropped from Who's Who in America at death. A cumulative index for 1607-1985 was published as a separate volume.

F16   *Dictionary of American Biography.* Published under the Auspices of the American Council of Learned Societies. 20 vols. and Index. New York: Scribner, 1928-37.

The major scholarly American biographical tool. Includes long essays with bibliographies by specialists. Planned to include all noteworthy persons of all periods who lived in the area of the U.S. Indexed by: names of biographees, contributors, birthplaces, schools and colleges attended, occupations, and topical subjects.

F17   *Dictionary of American Biography: Supplement 1- .* New York: Scribner, 1944-

Now eight volumes, including individuals who died up to 1970. Supplements the above and is similar in scope and purpose. Each supplementary volume also includes a cumulative index to the individuals included in all supplements.

F18   *Dictionary of American Biography: Complete Index Guide -- Volumes I-X, Supplements 1-7.* New York: Scribner, 1981.
A one volume cumulative index to DAB and its first seven supplements.

** AMERICAN -- RELIGIOUS

Works covering 20th century only. See chapter 31, "American Church History," for other works covering American religious biography.

F19   *Who's Who in Religion.* 3rd ed. Chicago, Marquis, 1985.
        Includes over 7,000 living religious figures in the United States, 4,000 of whom are new entries. Gives brief biographical data on each individual as supplied by the biographee. Older editions (1st ed. 1975, 2nd ed. 1977) are still useful as they contain many more entries.

F20   *Biographical Directory of Negro Ministers.* Ethel L. Williams. 3rd ed. Boston: G. K. Hall, 1975.
1st ed., 1965; 2nd ed., 1970. Gives basic biographical data on living black ministers who are active and influential in local or national affairs. Geographical index.

F21   *Biographical Dictionary of American Cult and Sect Leaders.* J. Gordon Melton. New York: Garland, 1986.
Contains 300-500 word biographical sketches of 213 founders and major leaders of American cults and sects. Only individuals who died before 1983 are listed. Includes selected list of primary and secondary works for each entry. Appendixes group entries by religious tradition, birthplace, and religious background.

F22   *Dictionary of American Religious Biography.* Henry Warner Bowden. Westport, CT: Greenwood, 1977.
Brief articles on 425 individuals "from all denominations who played a significant role in our nation's past." Emphasizes the wide pluralism of American religion. Includes bibliographies of material by and about each individual.

F23   *Who's Who in the Clergy: Vol. 1, 1935-36.* Edited by J.C. Schwarz. New York: the author, 1936.
Lists about 7,000 clergy alive and prominent in 1936. Gives brief biographical data including birthdate, education, positions and posts, and publications. This work, and the volume below, will provide information on the more obscure religious authors of the period who are not included in other biographial sources.

F24   *Religious Leaders of America: Vol. 2, 1941-42.* Edited by J.C. Schwarz.
      New York: the author, 1941.
Later edition of the above work, similar in form and content.

** AMERICAN -- SCHOLARS

F25   *Directory of American Scholars: a Biographical Directory.* Ed. by the
      Jacques Cattell Press. 8th ed. 4 vols. New York: Bowker, 1982.
Includes around 39,000 scholars "currently active in teaching, research, and
writing." The 4 vols. are divided by subject -- vol. 4 includes Philosophy,
Religion, and Law. Each volume has geographic index. Vol. 4 has a cumulative
index of the persons found in all four volumes. Gives brief biographical
information, stressing academic background and accomplishments. Includes
current addresses.

F26   *National Faculty Directory.* 1st- ed. Detroit: Gale, 1970- . Annual.
      An alphabetical listing of about 650,000 faculty members at junior
colleges, colleges, and universities in the United States as well as at selected
schools in Canada. Gives name, address, and department, but no other
information.

F27   *Directory of Faculty in Departments and Programs of Religious Studies in
      North America.* Watson E. Mills, ed. 1988 ed. Macon, GA: Council on
      the Study of Religion, 1988.
A companion to the CSSR's *Directory of Departments* (E7), providing
biographical information on over 3,200 individuals. Includes name, address,
phone numbers, schools attended and degrees earned, writings, employment
history, areas of specialization, and other personal information.

** BRITISH

F28   *Who's Who: an Annual Biographical Dictionary, with which is
      Incorporated "Men and Women of the Time."* London: Black, 1849- .
Includes brief biographical sketches of living prominent British persons. Also has
a list of the members of the royal family. An obituary section lists those who
have died who were in the previous edition.

F29   *Who Was Who, a Companion to Who's Who.* London: Black, 1929- .
      Now six vols., covering 1897-1970. Includes the entries for those who
were removed from Who's Who at death. Each new supplement includes a
cumulative index for itself and the previous volumes.

F30   *Dictionary of National Biography.* Edited by Leslie Stephen and Sidney
        Lee. 22 vols. London: Smith, Elder, 1908-09.
A scholarly biographic source for Britons and those of significance to the history
of Britain who died before 1900, including numerous clergymen. Long articles
by specialists with bibliographies.

F31   *Dictionary of National Biography: Index and Epitome.* Edited by Sidney
        Lee. 2 vols. London: Smith, Elder, 1903-13.
Adds new entries to the above. The index contains very brief biographical data
on each man and gives the location in the DNB of the full article.

F32   *Dictionary of National Biography 2nd- Supplements.* Oxford: University
        Press, 1912-   .
Now nine volumes, covering 1901-1980. Same scope and purpose as the main
work. Each new volume includes a cumulative index to the individuals in itself
and in the previous supplements.

CHAPTER 7
BIBLIOGRAPHIES OF BIBLIOGRAPHIES

A bibliography of bibliographies is a work limited to listing bibliographies. It may be universal or limited by subject, date, language, or other considerations.

These tools may be used to determine if a bibliography has ever been produced which covers an area of interest. If one is listed, the user must then go to that bibliography to find the listing of works on that topic.

** GUIDES

G1   *Bibliographies, Subject and National: a Guide to Their Contents, Arrangement, and Use.* Robert L. Collison. 3rd ed. London: Lockwood, 1968.
A good basic guide to major bibliographies in a given field or country. Lists 400-500 works with annotations. Includes entries for major works containing bibliographies (e.g. encyclopedias). Part 1 lists subject bibliographies by major subjects; Part 2 lists universal and national bibliographies. Includes an interesting introduction about bibliographies and their compilation.

G2   *Religious Bibliographies in Serial Literature: a Guide.* Michael J. Walsh, ed. Westport, CT: Greenwood Press, 1981.
Lists 178 bibliographical tools which are published regularly and which contain bibliographies of use in religious studies. Many of the items listed are bibliographies published within periodicals or are more general bibliographies of use in studying religion. Arranged alphabetically by title with subject and title indexes. Includes lengthy annotations as to each item's characteristics and usefulness.

** GENERAL

G3   *A World Bibliography of Bibliographies and Bibliographical Catalogues, Calendars, Abstracts, Digests, Indexes   and the Like.* Theodore Besterman. 4th ed. 5 vols. Lausanne: Societas Bibliographica, 1965-66.
The major listing by the all-time great bibliographer. Includes about 117,000 separately published bibliographies. This edition covers through 1963. Arranged by specific subject headings in alphabetical order (about 16,000 headings and subheadings). Gives the number of items in each bibliography. An author index is in vol. 5. Some sections of this work have also been reprinted separately.

G4   *A World Bibliography of Bibliographies, 1964-1974.* Alice F. Toomey.
2 vols. Totowa, NJ: Rowman & Littlefield, 1977.
Subtitle: "A list of works represented by Library of Congress printed catalog
cards: a decennial supplement to Theodore Besterman, *A World Bibliography of
Bibliographies.*" The subtitle describes its purpose and extent, which is much
more limited than Besterman. Consists of reproductions of about 18,000 LC
printed cards arranged under 6,000 specific subject headings. Note the headings
of "Dissertations, Academic," and "Festschriften." Somewhat disappointing
considering its predecessor, but helpful.

G5   *Bibliographic Index: A Cumulative Bibliography of Bibliographies,
1937- .* New York: Wilson, 1938- . 3x a year.
Annual cumulations. Intends to list any published bibliography (whether separate
or part of a larger work) with 50 or more entries. Surveys about 2,200 periodicals
as well as books and other materials. Arranged by specific subject headings.
Fairly comprehensive, strongest in the Western European languages.

** RELIGIOUS / THEOLOGICAL

G6   *A Bibliography of Bibliographies in Religion.* John G. Barrow. Ann
Arbor: Edwards, 1955.
Lists about 4,000 separately published bibliographies; see pp. iii-iv for types of
works not included. Covers up to about 1952, fairly complete to 1950. Dated but
not superseded. Classified arrangement, (but no section for Systematic Theology)
-- use the detailed table of contents for specific subjects. Title and author index.
Includes fairly good critical annotations and some information on the location of
copies.

G7   *Personal-Bibliographien aus Theologie und Religionswissenschaft mit ihren
Grenzgebieten: eine Bibliographie.* Hermann Erbacher. Neustadt:
Degener, 1976.
An index to where bibliographies of works by or about 1,843 persons of
significance in the study of religion and theology can be found. Arranged by
names of the individuals included. Lists nearly 2,500 items found in books,
periodical articles, etc.

G8   *A List of Bibliographies of Theological and Biblical Literature Published
in Great Britain and America, 1595-1931: with Critical, Biographical, and
Bibliographical Notes.* Wilbur M. Smith. Coatesville, PA: the author,
1931.
Note limits of coverage: "theology" in strict "systematic theology" sense; does not
include church history or practical theology. Lists only separately published
materials. Includes brief annotations and biographical information on the author

of each bibliography. Well done, but hard to use since entries are arranged by date. Author index.

G9   *Bibliography of Jewish Bibliographies.* Shlomo Shunami. 2nd enl. ed.
      with corrections. Jerusalem: Magnes, 1969.
Introductory matter in English and Hebrew. Includes 4,700 entries for bibliographies on Jewish literature, ancient Israel, the Bible and books about it. A supplement was published in 1975.

CHAPTER 8
RELIGIOUS / THEOLOGICAL BIBLIOGRAPHIES

Two primary uses for these bibliographies are a subject approach to theological literature, and verification and location of the more obscure, esoteric, or rare works in the field of religion.

Note that bibliographies covering only one subfield of religious or theological studies are *not* included here (they are in the subject area lists), and none of the bibliographies listed here are comprehensive; each employs some set of criteria to limit its contents.

** RELIGIONS

Only three of the better and more recent of the bibliographies covering religion in general are listed below.

H1   *Religious Books, 1876-1982.* 4 vols. Ann Arbor: Bowker, 1983.
        Lists over 130,000 titles covering all aspects of religion which were published or distributed in the U.S. The full bibliographical entries are arranged under 27,000 Library of Congress subject headings. The fourth volume contains author and title indexes with abbreviated entries that give the location of the item in the main listing. A highly important bibliography of American religious books.

H2   *A Reader's Guide to the Great Religions.* Charles J. Adams. 2nd ed.
        New York: Free Press, 1977.
lst ed., 1965. A collection of authoritative bibliographical essays on the world's major religions as well as ancient and primitive religions by 13 outstanding scholars. Each essay is a brief, thorough, and well-written introduction to the basic and important works for study of the respective religion. Includes author and subject indexes.

H3   *The Religious Life of Man: Guide to Basic Literature.* Leszak M.
        Karpinski. Metuchen, NJ: Scarecrow, 1978.
A well-written survey primarily for undergraduates and the public, but also helpful for advanced students. Classified arrangement with index of authors, titles, and subjects. Entries have brief annotations. Includes, for each major subsection in the bibliography, a list of major periodicals.

** LIBRARY CATALOGS

H4   *Alphabetical Arrangement of the Main Entries from the Shelf List of the Union Theological Seminary in New York City.* 10 vols. Boston: G.K. Hall, 1960.

A listing of the more than 191,000 titles held in 1961 by one of the largest seminary libraries in the world. Only one listing per title, usually the author (main entry), arranged in alphabetical order. Very helpful for verifying older and obscure theological titles.

H5   *The Shelf List of the Union Theological Seminary in New York City in Classification Order.* 10 vols. Boston: G.K. Hall, 1960.

Includes the same books as the above set, but now arranged by call number. This allows the listing to be used as a classified subject listing. You must determine the Union Seminary call number where the subject you are interested in will be found -- see next entry.

H6   *Classification of the Library of Union Theological Seminary.* Julia Pettee. rev. and enl. ed. New York: the Seminary, 1967.

A listing of the classification system used at Union Theological Seminary which will enable you to effectively use the above set. Use the index of this work to find the call number(s) of the topic of interest. Then, use that call number to find the correct location in the above set listing books on that topic.

H7   *Dictionary Catalog of the Klau Library, Cincinnati.* Hebrew Union College -- Jewish Institute of Religion. 32 vols. Boston: G.K. Hall, 1964.

Includes author, title, and subject entries (in one alphabetical listing) for c. 200,000 volumes of Judaica and related materials. Vols. 1-27 are of Roman alphabet materials, vols. 28-32 of Hebrew-language materials.

H8   *Union Catalog of the Graduate Theological Union Library.* 15 vols. Berkeley, CA: the Library, 1972.

An author-entry only catalog covering up to 1972. Includes the holdings of the San Francisco/Berkeley area Graduate Theological Union libraries. Helpful as an extensive general theological bibliography up to 1972.

** LIBRARY CATALOGS -- MICROFICHE

H9   *The Library of Congress Shelflist: Religion, BL-BX.* microfiche ed. Ann Arbor: University Microfilms, 1979.

These 156 microfiche are part of a larger project which filmed the entire LC shelflist. Reproduces, in call number order, the catalog cards for over 332,000 titles classified by the Library of Congress under "religion." Using the LC classification guides, you can determine the call numbers for specific subjects and use this as a subject listing.

H10   *Chicago Union Catalog of Religion and Theology.* Chicago: Chicago
       Cluster of Theological Schools, 1981.
A microfiche union catalog of the holdings of the member libraries of the Chicago Cluster of Theological Schools as well as the religion titles in the University of Chicago and Newberry libraries. The list is arranged by title and is complete through mid-1978.

H11   *CORECAT: Cooperative Religion Catalog, 1/1/1979-   .* Princeton, NJ:
       Committee for Theological Library Development, 1979-   . Semiannual.
A union catalog which lists all works cataloged by the theological libraries at Andover-Harvard, Princeton Seminary, Union Seminary in New York, and Yale Divinity School since 1978. Each new set of microfiche cumulates and completely supersedes the previous. Includes entries for authors, titles, series, subjects, etc., in one alphabet. Publication suspended in 1985.

** LISTS OF SELECTED WORKS -- GENERAL

H12   *Aids to a Theological Library.* John Trotti, ed. Missoula, MT: Scholars
       Press for the American Theological Library Association, 1977.
Written as a guide for theological libraries, intends to stress the bibliographical, reference and book-buying resources that a theological library should have. Classed arrangement, but no table of contents or index. Earlier editions included a listing of scholarly periodicals in religion.

H13   *Guide to Catholic Literature: v. 1-8, 1888-1967.* Edited by Walter
       Romig. Detroit: Romig, 1940-1968.
Includes entries by author, title, and specific subject, but the full entry is found only under the author's name. Includes books by and about Catholics in all languages. In total, contains about 250,000 entries with notes. In 1968, merged with the *Catholic Periodical Index* to form the *Catholic Periodical and Literature Index.*

H14   *A Theological Book List.* Compiled by Raymond P. Morris. London: the
       Fund, 1960.
"Produced by the Theological Education Fund of the International Missionary Council for Theological Seminaries and Colleges in Africa, Asia, Latin America and the Southwest Pacific." Includes 5,472 works, primarily in English, considered to be basic for developing theological libraries in the Third World. Detailed classed arrangement, author index, brief annotations.

H15   *A Theological Book List, [1963].* London: the Fund, 1963.
H16   *A Theological Book List, 1968.* London: the Fund, 1968.
H17   *A Theological Book List, 1971.* London: the Fund, 1971.
    The above three works supplement the original work (H14). Compilers and subtitles vary from volume to volume. Each includes separate sections for works in English, French, German, Spanish, and Portuguese.

H18   *The Reader's Guide to the Best Evangelical Books.* Mark L. Branson. San Francisco: Harper & Row, 1982.
A classified bibliography of "the best evangelical literature" in over 50 "key categories of Christian life and thought." Each category has a brief bibliographical essay surveying the literature and an annotated list of books on the subject. Limited to English-language and post-1950 titles. Also scattered throughout are lists of the favorite books (personal and professional) of various evangelical leaders. Has author index but no subject index. Also presents a brief overview of "What is Evangelicalism." A useful starting point for surveying evangelical literature.

H19   *A Reader's Guide to Religious Literature.* Beatrice Batson. Chicago: Moody, 1968.
An introduction to the "classics" of Christian literature from the Middle Ages and later, including the influence of Christian thought on outstanding literary works. Concentrates on the 17th to 19th centuries. Each chapter surveys the historical and cultural developments of a period, briefly mentions its literary masterpieces, and then analyzes several important religious literary works of the period. Includes bibliography and index.

** LISTS OF SELECTED WORKS -- FOR PASTORS

A large number of these lists have been produced. Listed here are a few of the more recent and more widely circulated lists.

H20   *An Annotated Bibliography on the Bible and the Church.* Douglas Moo, ed. 2nd ed. Deerfield, IL: Trinity Evangelical Divinity School, 1986.
"Compiled for the Alumni Association of Trinity Evangelical Divinity School" by the faculty of that seminary. A substantial (112-page) bibliography listing books "most helpful to the local pastor," chosen from an evangelical theological perspective. Classified arrangement with an author index. While this is a useful list, the quality and extent of annotation, the bibliographical citation form, and the (implicit) criteria for inclusion vary greatly from section to section. A more detailed table of contents is needed.

H21   *Building a Pastor's Library.* Martha Aycock Sugg and John Trotti.
      Richmond, VA: Union Theological Seminary, 1991.
A revision of *Essential Books for a Pastor's Library* (5th ed., 1976). Intended to
list subject areas which should be represented in a pastor's library and to suggest,
in each category, one or more important books. Classified arrangement with brief
annotations. No indexes.

H22   *Essential Books for Christian Ministry: Basic Readings for Pastors,*
      Church Staff Leaders, and Laymen. Fort Worth, TX: Southwestern Baptist
      Theological Seminary, 1972.
Lists about 1,000 titles, selected by the seminary faculty, in order to "assist
students, alumni, and Christian lay workers in selecting the most helpful books for
their libraries" (preface). Classified arrangement with brief annotations but no
indexes. Includes 18 pages on church music and 15 pages on religious education.

H23   *The Minister's Library.* Cyril J. Barber. Grand Rapids: Baker, 1974.
      A classed bibliography with brief annotations intended for pastors.
Selections and annotations have a decidedly evangelical and dispensational
orientation. Childs (AB2) notes the misleading character of Barber's advice:
"Barber seems mainly concerned with the orthodoxy of the author and he has little
judgment of quality." Includes some information for the pastor on how to
organize his library. Author, title, and subject indexes.

H24   *The Minister's Library, Volume 2, 1972-1980.* Cyril J. Barber. Grand
      Rapids: Baker, 1983.
Cumulates four separately published supplements to the above into a single subject
arrangement with new cumulative indexes. Similar in format and scope to the
original volume.

** 19TH CENTURY

The nineteenth and early twentieth centuries were fruitful periods for extensive
bibliographies of theological works. Only a few of the more important works are
listed.

On the theological bibliography of the eighteenth century see Edgar Krentz's
"Theological Bibliography in the Eighteenth Century," pp. 47-66 in *Essays on
Theological Librarianship* (ed. by Peter de Klerk and Earle Hilgert, Philadelphia:
American Theological Library Association, 1980).

H25   *An Introduction to Theology: Its Principles, Its Branches, Its Results, and Its Literature.* Alfred Cave. 2nd ed. Edinburgh: T & T Clark, 1896.
1st ed., 1886. An introduction to the study of theology which includes large bibliographies of recommended books for each section. Includes English, German, and French works. Author and subject indexes. Strongest on biblical studies.

H26   *Cyclopedia Bibliographica.* James Darling. 2 vols. London: Darling, 1854-59.
Subtitle: "A Library Manual of Theological and General Literature, and Guide to Books for Authors, Preachers, Students, and Literary Men: Analytical, Bibliographical, and Biographical." Vol. 1 is a list of authors (with biographical information) and their writings. Vol. 2 is a classified bibliography of material on the Bible, the major portion of which is a listing, in Bible-passage order, of materials on particular passages (including sermons). A projected 3rd volume; "General Subjects in Theology," was never published.

H27   *Bibliography of British Theological Literature, 1850-1940.* Dikran Y. Hadidian. Pittsburgh: Clifford E. Barbour Library, Pittsburgh Theological Seminary, 1985.
A selective list of British theological imprints. Excludes most pamphlets. Dates were selected to continue Darling's bibliography (above) through to the end of the British empire. An introductory essay provides a bibliographical study of the direction of British theology during this period.

H28   *Theological Encyclopaedia and Methodology: on the Basis of Hagenbach.* Karl R. Hagenbach. Trans. & enl. by George R. Crooks & John F. Hurst. New York: Phillips & Hunt, 1884.
A comprehensive work on theology which also includes many extensive bibliographies that list about 5,000 books. Includes index. Based on the original German work, enlarged by the addition of English and American titles.

H29   *Literature of Theology: a Classified Bibliography of Theology and General Religious Literature.* John F. Hurst. New York: Hunt & Eaton, 1896.
Based on his 1882 work: *Bibliotheca Theologica.* An extensive classified bibliography of "the best and most desirable books in theology and general religious literature published in Great Britain, the United States, and the Dominion of Canada." Detailed classified arrangement, see nine-page table of contents. Includes author and subject index.

H30 *Theological Index: References to the Principle Works in Every Department of Religious Literature.* Howard Malcom. Boston: Gould & Lincoln, 1868.
Includes about 70,000 titles under 2,000 specific subject headings. Unfortunately, the entries are given in a very abridged form (author's last name, short title, and [sometimes] date) which makes identification difficult.

H31 *Theologischer Jahresbericht, 1881-1913.* 33 vols. Leipzig: Heinsius, 1882-1916.
Published annually in period indicated. Publisher varies. Arranged by a detailed classification system with author index. Each section of these listings has a bibliography of relevant materials, followed by a bibliographical essay discussing and evaluating each item.

** SPECIAL TOPICS

H32 *The Howard University Bibliography of African and Afro-American Religious Studies: with Locations in American Libraries.* Ethel L. Williams. Wilmington, DE: Scholarly Resources, 1977.
An updated version of the author's bibliography, *Afro-American Religious Studies* (Scarecrow, 1972). Lists over 13,000 items from 230 libraries and archives (gives location information). Includes all types of primary and secondary materials with brief descriptions of some items. Use the detailed table of contents to find the material classed under five major headings with numerous subdivisions. Author index.

H33 *South African Theological Bibliography: Suid-Afrikaanse Teologiese Bibliografie.* C. F. A. Borchardt and W. S. Vorster, eds. Pretoria: University of South Africa, 1980- .
A bibliography which aims "to index all Festschrifts and periodical literature published in South Africa covering the theological field." Also includes relevant dissertations submitted at South African universities. Classified arrangement with a detailed table of contents and an author index. Intended as an ongoing bibliography -- vol. 2 was published in 1983.

H34 *Bibliography of New Religious Movements in Primal Societies.* Harold W. Turner. Boston: G. K. Hall, 1977- .
4 vols. published so far (v. 1 -- Black Africa; v. 2 -- North America; v. 3 -- Oceania; v. 4 -- Europe and Asia). A comprehensive list (with brief annotations) of mostly English-language materials (books, articles, and dissertations) on religious movements "which arise in the interaction of a primal society with another society where there is a great disparity of power or sophistication."

Movements derived from or connected with Christianity receive extensive coverage. Each volume is arranged geographically and indexed by author and, except for v. 1, by movement/individuals.

H35   *Breaking Through: A Bibliography of Women and Religion.* Clare B. Fischer. Berkeley, CA: Graduate Theological Union Library, 1980.

A bibliography of materials on women in religion, on the role of women in the study of religion, and on feminist perspectives in the study of religion. Classified arrangement, no annotations, no indexes. Primarily lists books, but has a final short section listing periodical articles.

H36   "Bibliography [on Christianity and Literature]." In *Christianity and Literature,* 1970?-1988. Quarterly.

Each issue of the journal included abstracts of books, periodical articles, etc., in a classed arrangement. Discontinued in 1988, at which point there were a total of 9,042 abstracts.

** CONTINUING

H37   *Critical Review of Books in Religion.* Atlanta: Scholars Press, 1988- . Annual.

A 400-500 page annual sponsored by the American Academy of Religion and the Society of Biblical Literature. Each volume begins with lengthy review essays of major works, followed by 2-3 page signed reviews of books classified in about 20 categories. Includes a list of new editions and translations. Author and reviewer indexes.

H38   *Theology Digest.* St. Louis: St. Louis University, 1953- . Quarterly.

Contains both "condensations of recent significant articles selected from over 400 of the world's theological journals" (translated into English if in a foreign language) and a "book survey." The book survey lists, with descriptive annotations, a large number of new theological books.

H39   *Theologische Literaturzeitung: Monatsschrift für das gesamte Gebiet der Theologie und Religionswissenschaft.* Leipzig: Hinrichs, 1876- . Monthly.

A periodical which includes bibliographical essays on important topics and numerous reviews and short descriptions of numerous new books. Cumulative annual indexes. For the years 1921-1942 the publisher issued annual cumulations entitled *Bibliographisches Beiblatt der Theologischen Literaturzeitung.*

H40   *Theologische Rundschau.* Tübingen: Mohr, 1897- . Quarterly.
      Includes long bibliographical essays on the literature of various important
theological topics. Also includes additional brief book reviews. Contains many
valuable bibliographies and critical reviews of research by authorities in each field.

H41   *ATLA Religion Index Special Bibliographies.* Chicago: ATLA, 1982- .
A series of bibliographies on special topics. Entries are extracted from the ATLA
religion database and arranged under specific subject heads. "Produced from
magnetic tape by a laser-beam Xerox process on 8 1/2" by 11" paper" in an
all-upper-case typeface. Some topics covered: Culture and Religion, Missions,
Politics and Religion, Women and Religion, etc.

CHAPTER 9
U.S.A. BIBLIOGRAPHY

National and trade bibliographies are listings of the books published in a given country compiled by official ("national") agencies or by commercial ("trade") firms. Ideally, they provide a comprehensive listing of the works published in that country.

The United States has no official national library and no official national bibliography. The Library of Congress and its extensive National Union Catalog come closest to filling those roles. Remember, however, that the holdings of the Library of Congress, as well as the other members of the National Union Catalog group, include extensive amounts of non-U.S.-published materials. Thus the National Union Catalog functions both as a "selective universal" bibliography as well as a "national" bibliography.

** LIBRARY OF CONGRESS AND NATIONAL UNION CATALOGS

The sets of volumes listed here are inter-related and are based on two sets of catalog cards produced by and located at the Library of Congress (LC): (1) the LC printed catalog cards which LC sells to other libraries, and (2) the catalog cards of the National Union Catalog (NUC), which represents the books in 700 U.S. libraries (including LC) and indicates which of those libraries holds each title.

All the LC/NUC volumes listed below are arranged by the "main entry" (usually author) and *no* title or subject access is possible. Few cross-references are provided.

The LC/NUC catalogs are most useful for verification of bibliographical information when you have an incomplete or incorrect citation; when you are compiling a bibliography of works *by* (not *about*) an individual; and when you are locating libraries where copies of a wanted book are located so that it may be requested on interlibrary loan.

** PRE-56 SETS

J1   *National Union Catalog, Pre-1956 Imprints: a Cumulative Author List Representing Library of Congress Printed Cards and Titles Reported by Other American Libraries.* 685 vols. London: Mansell, 1968-1980.
Known as "Mansell" or "Pre-56." A bibliography of all books published before 1956 reported to the National Union Catalog. Very extensive (over 10 million books are included) and useful, essential for in-depth bibliographical research.

Under voluminous authors a logical classified arrangement (usually by original title, subarranged by language) is used. An outline of the arrangement used is given at the beginning of the entries for such authors.

Vols. 53-56 include all works entered under "Bible." See AA17 below for further information on these volumes.

Each entry also lists libraries reported as holding each title. The quality and accuracy of the entries varies considerably depending on the contributing library. Some duplicate or conflicting entries for the same works will be found. This work supersedes all of the earlier LC and NUC catalogs up to and including the 1953-1957 NUC cumulative (the 1956 and 1957 titles in the NUC were added to the 1958-1962 cumulation of the NUC).

J2   *National Union Catalog, Pre-56 Imprints: Supplement.* 69 vols. London: Mansell, 1980-1981.

A supplement listing titles and added locations reported to the National Union Catalog since the beginning of the Pre-56 project.

** POST-56 SETS

J3   *National Union Catalog: 1958-1962.* 54 vols. New York: Rowman & Littlefield, 1963.
J4   *National Union Catalog: 1963-1967.* 67 vols. Ann Arbor: Edwards, 1969.
J5   *National Union Catalog: 1968-1972.* 119 vols. Ann Arbor: Edwards, 1973.
J6   *National Union Catalog: 1973-1977.* 135 vols. Totowa, NJ: Rowman & Littlefield, 1978.

Subtitle: *"A Cumulative Author List Representing Library of Congress Printed Cards and Titles Reported by Other American Libraries."* The above works are five-year cumulations of the monthly NUC. Author-entry only, alphabetically arranged.

J7   *National Union Catalog: a Cumulative Author List.* Washington, DC: Library of Congress, Cataloging Distribution Service Division, 1959-   . Monthly.

Quarterly and annual cumulations. The information found in the above cumulations first appears in this monthly NUC listing. U.S. published books are usually listed 6 to 18 months after publication. Author-entry only.

Note: Some of the above sets have been reprinted by a number of commercial publishers, some in single-sequence cumulations. Often available in printed copy or on microfiche. Your library may have those instead of the above. In addition, some publishers have issued title or other indexes to the LC/NUC catalogs in various formats. Use them if they are available to you.

** TRADE LISTINGS -- IN-PRINT

Up-to-date listings of materials which are currently or will be shortly available for purchase.

J8   *Books in Print.* New York: Bowker, 1948- . Annual.
        Lists currently available books from 33,000 U.S. publishers and foreign publishers with an American distributor. Some types of publications are excluded and some publishers are not represented (esp. small and reprint publishers). Two separate A-Z sections: Authors and Titles. An additional volume lists publisher addresses. Use carefully: the alphabetizing of the publisher-supplied bibliographical entries results in some strange sequences.

J9   *Subject Guide to Books in Print.* New York: Bowker, 1957- . Annual.
        Similar in scope and form to the above, but lists books by subject, A-Z under Library of Congress subject headings.

J10   *Forthcoming Books; now including New Books in Print.* New York: Bowker, 1966- . Bimonthly.
Includes two types of books: those too new to be listed in the latest Books in Print and new books due to appear in the next five months (according to the publisher). Separate author and title lists. For forthcoming books, gives author, title, publisher, and projected date and price. A separate "Subject Guide" is also available.

J11   *Publishers' Trade List Annual.* New York: Bowker, 1873- . Annual.
        A uniformly sized and bound compilation of publisher catalogs, arranged alphabetically by publisher. Completeness, indexing, and accuracy of information varies since actual printing copy is supplied by the publishers -- who pay to be included. Thus, not all publishers are found herein. The yellow pages at the beginning of volume one include an alphabetical index of included publishers and brief catalogs, printed by Bowker, for the publishers not supplying catalogs for the main section.

J12   *American Book Publishing Record.* New York: Bowker, 1960- . Monthly.
Annual and 5-year cumulations. Also know as "BPR." A list of books actually published, arranged by dewey classification number. Author and title index. Useful for retrospective bibliography back to 1960, as a source of LC cataloging copy, and for current awareness of books newly published in the U.S.

J13   *Religious & Inspirational Books & Serials in Print.* New York: Bowker,
        1985- . Biennial.
Formerly titled *Religious Books and Serials in Print.* Includes over 61,000 entries
from about 3,000 publishers, retrieved from the BIP database. Lists BIP type of
information for each work. Author, title, and subject indexes. A useful "Sacred
Works Index" (including 69 headings for versions of the Bible) was eliminated in
the 1987 edition. High level of duplication with BIP.

** REPRINT

J14   *Guide to Reprints.* Kent, CT: Guide to Reprints, Inc., 1967- . Annual.
        An author listing much like *Books in Print.* Includes reprints of both
books and periodicals from nearly 500 reprint publishers, some of which are not
in *Books in Print* (including foreign publishers). A separately published *Subject
Guide to Reprints* has been discontinued.

J15   *Out-of-Print Books Author Guide, 1989-90.* Ann Arbor: University
        Microfilms, 1989.
Formerly titled *Books on Demand.* Issued in various forms with various
supplements, now published annually. A microfiche listing of "over 119,000 out-
of-print books available as reprints," in paperback or hardback on a 30-day
"demand" basis. Use cautiously, as some titles listed are still in print and are far
less expensive than the reprint price.

** MICROFORM

An ongoing project of the American Theological Library Association Preservation
Board has filmed thousands of theological materials, especially titles originally
published from 1860 to 1930. Lists of materials available for purchase from the
board are issued at irregular intervals.

J16   *Microform Research Collections: a Guide.* Edited by Suzanne Cates
        Dodson. 2nd ed. Westport, CT: Meckler, 1984.
A list of 374 microform collections arranged by title. For each collection
information is provided on the publisher, format, price, published reviews,
arrangement and bibliographical control, indexes to the collection, and scope and
content. Index provides access to authors, editors, compilers, titles, and subjects.
Helpful source of hard-to-find information.

J17   *Guide to Microforms in Print, Author/Title: Incorporating International
        Microforms In Print.* Westport, CT: Microform Review, 1977- . Annual.
Author and title entries arranged in one A-Z sequence. Includes bibliographical
information on each title and special coding which describes the type of

microform that is available. Includes University Microform materials, but is *not* a complete listing of them. Lists books, periodicals, newspapers, and other types of materials on microform. A "Subject Guide" companion volume is also available.

J18   *Micropublishers' Trade List Annual.* Westport, CT: Microform Review, 1979- . Annual.
An extensive collection of the catalogs of microform publishers from throughout the world. Issued on microfiche, with printed index to the catalogs and instructions for use. Necessary for any extensive microform buying.

J19   *National Register of Microform Masters, 1965-1975.* 6 vols. Washington, DC: Library of Congress, 1976.
"The Register reports master microfilms of foreign and domestic books, pamphlets, serials, and foreign doctoral dissertations." Includes a brief bibliographical entry, LC card number (when available), location of the master, and the form and character of the microform. Supplements, issued yearly, were discontinued in 1983.

J20   *Bibliographic Guide to Microform Publications.* Boston: G.K. Hall, 1987- . Annual.
A list of non-serial microforms cataloged by the New York Public Library and the Library of Congress, both original microforms published by these libraries and commercially available microforms purchased by them. Includes monographs, government publications, pamphlets, dissertations, technical reports, and manuscript collections. Provides bibliographical information and description of the form and character of the microform.

** RETROSPECTIVE

J21   *American Book Publishing Record Cumulative, 1876-1949: An American National Bibliography.* 14 vols. Ann Arbor: Bowker, 1980.
Intends to list "every book published and/or distributed in the United States during that 74-year span." Includes 600,000 entries arranged by subject via the Dewey Decimal System. Author, title, and subject indexes. Extensive and helpful.

J22   *American Book Publishing Record Cumulative, 1950-1977: An American National Bibliography.* 15 vols. Ann Arbor: Bowker, 1978.
Similar to the above. A massive bibliography of 920,000 titles arranged by Dewey Decimal number. Separate author, title, and subject indexes.

J23   *American Book Publishing Record, 1876-1981: Author/Title/Subject Indexes on Microfiche.* New York: Bowker, 1982.
Consists of 649 microfiches in three binders (author, title, and subject) which list 1.7 million titles published in the U.S. between 1876 and 1981. Does not include the full cataloging information found in the paper ABPR volumes, but does give sufficient bibliographic information for most purposes. Very useful for quick comprehensive searches, particularly valuable for the subject access offered.

J24   *Cumulative Book Index: A World List of Books in the English Language, 1928/32- .* New York: Wilson, 1933- . Monthly.
Quarterly, annual, and multi-year cumulations. An extensive and accurate worldwide listing of English-language books. Has author, title, and subject entries in one alphabetical list. The author entry for each book is the most complete.

J25   *The American Bibliography.* Charles Evans. 14 vols. Chicago: the Author, 1903-59.
"Chronological dictionary of all books, pamphlets and periodical publications printed in the United States of America from the genesis of printing in 1639 down to and including the year 1820." The subtitle describes the scope of this work. Works are arranged in chronological order. Each volume has author, subject and printer/publisher indexes. Vol. 14 is a cumulative author index. Gives full bibliographical information and locations of copies in American libraries.

CHAPTER 10
FOREIGN NATIONAL AND TRADE BIBLIOGRAPHY

See the introductory note to Chapter 9.

** GREAT BRITAIN -- NATIONAL LIBRARY

K1   *General Catalogue of Printed Books*. British Museum. Department of
      Printed Books. Photolithographic ed. to 1955. 263 vols. London: Trustees
      of the British Museum, 1959-66.

One of the most comprehensive listings of English-language books, this work
includes over four million entries for virtually all the printed books in the Library
of the British Museum. Also strong on French materials and other
foreign-language materials. Periodicals are listed in three separate volumes under
the word "Periodicals." Entries are primarily by author, with some title entries.
Entries under an author also include cross-references to works about the author.
Under an author, a logical classified arrangement of titles and editions is used.
Under the names of sacred books (primarily the Bible), are listed both texts of that
book and books about that sacred book (e.g. commentaries). There are three
volumes for the Bible with an index.

K2   *General Catalogue of Printed Books: Ten Year Supplement, 1956-1965*.
      British Museum. Department of Printed Books. 50 vols. London: Trustees
      of the British Museum, 1968.

K3   *General Catalogue of Printed Books: Five Year Supplement, 1966-1970*.
      British Museum. Department of Printed Books. 26 vols. London: Trustees
      of the British Museum, 1971-72.

Supplements to the above. Periodicals are now listed under title, not "Periodicals."

K4   *General Catalogue of Printed Books: Five-Year Supplement*. British
      Museum. Department of Printed Books. 13 vols. London: British Museum
      Publications, 1978-1979.

Includes 400,000 works under 600,000 entries. Printed in a new 3-column format.
Will be the last supplement published -- superseded by the cumulative volumes
of the *British National Bibliography* (see K6).

Note: A cumulation of all the above sets is in the process of being published by
C. Bingley and by Saur under the title: *The British Library General Catalogue of
Printed Books to 1975*. To be about 360 volumes.

** GREAT BRITAIN -- CURRENT TRADE

K5   *British Books in Print: the Reference Catalogue of Current Literature.*
       London: Whitaker, 1965- . Annual.
An annual listing of books currently in print and on sale in the United Kingdom.
A single alphabetical listing of author, title, and subject entries. Includes listing
of publishers and addresses.

K6   *The British National Bibliography.*   London: Council of the British
       National Bibliography, 1950- . Weekly.
Monthly, annual, and 5-year cumulations. An excellent listing of any work
published in Great Britain or by any publisher having an office there. Arranged
by detailed Dewey Decimal-like classification system, with author, title, and
extensive subject indexing. Excellent source for post-1949 bibliography of
English-language titles.

** GREAT BRITAIN -- RETROSPECTIVE

K7   *Short-Title Catalogue of Books Printed in England, Scotland, and Ireland,
       and of English Books Printed Abroad, 1475-1640.* Alfred W. Pollard and
       G.R. Redgrave. 2nd ed., rev. & enl., begun by W. A. Jackson and F. S.
       Ferguson, completed by Katharine F. Pantzer. 2 vols. London:
       Bibliographical Society, 1976-86.
Known as the "STC." Arranged alphabetically by author. Includes a
bibliographical description of each book and lists locations of copies (all locations
of rarer titles). The subtitle describes the scope of the books included.

K8   *Short-Title Catalogue of Books Printed in England, Scotland, Ireland,
       Wales, and British America, and of English Books Printed in Other
       Countries, 1641-1700.* Donald G. Wing. 2nd ed., rev. & enl. 3 vols.
       New York: Modern Language Association, 1972-1988.
Continues the STC for the time period indicated. Similar contents to the STC,
giving locations for about 200 libraries. Be sure to read the description of its
scope, entry form, and entry-selection policies in the introduction.

Note: For 1950- , the annual and cumulative volumes of *The British National
Bibliography* (K6) may also serve as a retrospective bibliography.

** GERMANY

K9   *Verzeichnis lieferbarer Bücher, 1971/72-* . Frankfurt am Main: Verlag der
      Buchhändler- Vereinigung, 1971- . Annual.
A German "Books in Print" of currently available titles. Now has five volumes,
forming a single alphabet of authors, titles, and subject key-words. Also lists
addresses of German publishers. A companion "Subject Guide" is also available.

K10   *Gesamtverzeichnis des deutschsprachigen Schrifttums (GV): 1911-1965.*
      Hrsg. von Reinhard Oberschelp; bearb. unter der Leitung von Willi
      Gorzny, mit einem Geleitwort von Wilhelm Totok. 150 vols. München:
      Verlag Dokumentation, 1976-1981.
A cumulation and single listing of the main entries from some 15
German-language bibliographical tools. Entries are from the *Deutsches
Bücherverzeichnis, Deutsche Bibliographie, Deutsche Nationalbibliographie* and
various dissertation lists. Does not entirely supersede these works, especially their
subject access.

K11   *Gesamtverzeichnis des deutschsprachigen Schrifttums (GV): 1700-1910.*
      Bearb. unter d. Leitung von Peter Geils und Willi Gorzny; bibliograph. und
      red. Beratung, Hans Popst & Rainer Schöller. 160 vols. München: Saur,
      1979-1987.
Similar to the above, but for the earlier period indicated.

** FRANCE

K12   *Catalogue général des livres imprimés: Auteurs.* Bibliothèque Nationale.
      Paris: Impr. Nationale, 1897- .
An alphabetical author list: does not include periodicals, government or corporate
authors, or entries for anonymous or classical works. Under voluminous authors,
a detailed title index shows volumes, title changes, editions, etc. Includes most
of the collection up through 1959, although the earlier volumes had earlier cut-off
dates. Some post-1959 supplements have been published and others are being
prepared.

K13   *Les Livres de l'année--Biblio, 1971-* . Paris: Cercle de la Librairie, 1972-
      . Annual.
An annual listing of all French-language books published in that year. Includes
author, title, and subject entries in a single alphabet.

K14   *Les Livres disponibles.* Paris: Cercle de la Librairie, 1977- .
        Also titled *French Books in Print.* Issued now in three parts: author, title, classified subject. Lists French-language books, regardless of place of publication. Includes a listing of publishers and distributors with addresses.

** OTHER

K15   *Guide to Current National Bibliographies in the Third World.* G. E.
        Gorman and J. J. Mills. 2nd rev. ed. London; New York: H. Zell, 1987. A bibliography of national bibliographies for six geographical regions and 60 third world countries. Extensive annotations (usually over two pages) include each work's history, scope, and contents. Title index. Important guide for third world bibliography.

For additional national and trade bibliographies of foreign countries, see the applicable section in Sheehy (A1).

CHAPTER 11
PERIODICAL INDEXES: GENERAL COVERAGE

Both indexes proper and abstracting tools are included in this list.

The main function of periodical indexes is to provide *subject* access to the individual articles published in magazines and journals. Many indexes also include access by the author of the article, and a few by title as well. Some indexes, particularly the more specialized subject ones, also index book reviews, books, dissertations, or articles in multi-author works. Abstracting tools, besides providing the subject (and usually author) access of the periodical index, also provide a short descriptive and/or critical summary of each item included.

Periodical indexes are arranged in a number of different ways. The most common is a single alphabetical listing of author and specific subject entries. Some are arranged in two sections: one for subjects and another for authors. Others have a classified arrangement with author or specific subject indexes. Be sure you understand the arrangement of each index which you use.

** GUIDES

L1   *Indexed Periodicals: a Guide to 170 Years of Coverage in 33 Indexing Services*. Joseph V. Marconi. Ann Arbor: Pierian, 1976.
A guide which tells the user where, in the 33 periodical indexes covered, over 11,000 periodicals have been indexed. Covers up to about 1973. Indexes included are the more popular ones, e.g. most of those published by Wilson. Religious periodical indexes analyzed are: *Index to Religious Periodical Literature*, *Index to Jewish Periodicals*, *Catholic Periodical Index*, and *Catholic Periodical and Literature Index*. Helpful for finding out where a particular periodical you are interested in has been indexed in the past.

** GENERAL -- AMERICAN

L2   *Poole's Index to Periodical Literature, 1802-1881.* rev. ed. 2 vols. Boston: Houghton, 1891.
L3   *Poole's Index to Periodical Literature: Supplements, 1882-1906.* 5 vols. Boston: Houghton, 1887-1908.
Provides only subject, not author, access. A general-coverage index, but much theological material is included. Indexes about 590,000 articles found in about 300 periodicals in the 19th century. The bibliographical citation gives only the volume number and the first page of the article. Despite problems, this is the major source of indexing of 19th-century English-language periodicals.

L4   *Cumulative Author Index for Poole's Index to Periodical Literature, 1802-1906.* C. Edward Wall. Ann Arbor: Pierian, 1971.

A "quick and dirty" computer-compiled author index to *Poole's Index.* Author names are cited as they appear in the original index -- no attempt has been made to make all the entries for the same person exactly the same. Under each author's name, the user is given a volume, page, and column in *Poole's Index* where an article by that author is listed. Better than no author access, but still difficult to use.

L5   *Nineteenth Century Readers' Guide to Periodical Literature, 1890-1899; with Supplementary Indexing 1900-1922.* 2 vols. New York: Wilson, 1944.

Originally intended to cover all of the 19th century, but only this volume was ever published. Same format and layout as *Readers' Guide* (see below). "Supplementary" in that it supplements the coverage of the first 22 years of *Readers' Guide* by indexing some additional titles.

L6   *The Readers' Guide to Periodical Literature, 1900- .* New York: Wilson, 1905- . Semi-monthly.

Annual and multi-year cumulations. A general index to popular periodical titles. Includes author and subject entries in a single alphabet. Stays very current in its coverage and is easy to use. Particularly useful for its indexing of news magazines. Available at most public libraries.

L7   *International Index: a Guide to Periodical Literature in the Social Sciences and Humanities.* 18 vols. New York: Wilson, 1907-1965.

A good general-coverage periodical index but of more scholarly magazines. Includes religion, philosophy, and psychology. Good indexing; easy to use. Superseded by the following title.

L8   *Social Sciences and Humanities Index.* 7 vols. New York: Wilson, 1966-1974.

Continues L7 above, but restricted to the humanities and social sciences. Indexes over 200 scholarly periodicals. Similar in layout, format, and ease-of-use to *Readers' Guide.* Continued by *Humanities Index* (L16) and *Social Sciences Index* (L19).

L9   *Bulletin.* Public Affairs Information Service. New York: the Service, 1915- . Weekly.

Ten-week and annual cumulations. Known as "PAIS." Selectively indexes about 1,000 English-language journals, government publications, books, pamphlets, and reports for material about political and social conditions.

L10   *New York Times Index.* New York: the Times, 1913- . Weekly.
  Quarterly and annual cumulations. A carefully done subject index to the news stories in the *New York Times.* A brief abstract of the article is also included. Very helpful in locating brief summaries of past news stories and for finding the location of the full text in the *New York Times.*

** GENERAL -- FOREIGN

L11   *Subject Index to Periodicals, 1915-1961.* 44 vols. London: Library
   Association, 1919-1962.
Primarily British, covering the humanities, technology, and education. Later volumes index over 300 British titles. Primary section is arranged by subject. Author index.

L12   *Bulletin signalétique.* Paris: Centre National de la Recherche Scientifique,
   1948- .
Actually an entire series of periodical indexing tools that includes abstracts of the articles (in French). International, attempts to be exhaustive. Each part has a classified arrangement, with specific subject and author indexes. Early coverage, up to about 1960, is somewhat sketchy. For religion and theology, see M13 below.

L13   *Internationale Bibliographie der Zeitschriftenliteratur aus allen Gebieten
   des Wissens, 1963/64- .* Osnabrück: Dietrich, 1965- . Semiannual.
Known as "IBZ." Arranged by specific subject entry, with author indexing. Uses German subject headings, with references to them from the French and English equivalents. Worldwide coverage of a large number of periodicals, transactions, yearbooks, etc. Continues the following two works.

L14   *Bibliographie der deutschen Zeitschriftenliteratur, mit Einschluss von
   Sammelwerken, 1896-1964.* 128 vols. Leipzig: Dietrich, 1897-1964.
An index of German-language periodicals, transactions, yearbooks, etc. Subject arrangement with author index. Original coverage of 275 periodicals grew to about 4,500 titles before it merged with L15 to form L13.

L15   *Bibliographie der fremdsprachigen Zeitschriftenliteratur; 1911-1915,
   1925/26-1962/64.* 73 vols. Leipzig: Dietrich, 1911-1964.
Complement to the above work for non-German-language periodicals, etc. The first series (1911-1915) has subject access only; the later series also includes an author index. Good coverage of American, English, French, and Italian periodicals. At the end, indexed about 1,400 titles.

** HUMANITIES

L16   *Humanities Index.* New York: Wilson, 1974- . Quarterly.

Annual cumulations. Continues, in part, *Social Sciences and Humanities Index* (L8). Includes history. Typical Wilson format, with a single alphabet of author and subject entries. Includes separate book review section. Indexes about 290 titles.

L17   *British Humanities Index, 1962-* . London: Library Association, 1963- . Quarterly.

Annual cumulations. Intends to cover "all material relating to the arts and humanities." In two parts, subject and author, each with full entries. Indexes around 380 British journals. Continues, in part, *Subject Index to Periodicals* (L11).

L18   *Arts and Humanities Citation Index.* Philadelphia: Institute for Scientific Information, 1978- . 3x a year.

Annual cumulations. Rather than indexing by subject, a citation index "indexes" the material by the works which are cited in the footnotes of the article being indexed. Thus, using this index, you can discover what articles have cited a given work or article and what works are cited by a given indexed article. Also provides for modified author and subject access. Includes some religious and theological journals. See U8 for an online version of this index.

** SOCIAL SCIENCES

L19   *Social Sciences Index.* New York: Wilson, 1974- . Quarterly.

Annual cumulations. Continues in part the *Social Sciences and Humanities Index* (L8). Regular Wilson layout with a single alphabet of author and subject entries. Includes separate book review section. Indexes about 350 titles.

L20   *Social Sciences Citation Index.* Philadelphia: Institute for Scientific Information, 1974- . 3x a year.

Annual and five-year cumulations. Rather than indexing by subject, a citation index indexes the material by the works which are cited in the footnotes of the article being indexed. Thus, using this index, you can discover what articles have cited a given work or article and what works are cited by a given indexed article. Also provides for modified author and subject access. See U9 for an online version of this index.

CHAPTER 12
PERIODICAL INDEXES: RELIGIOUS / THEOLOGICAL COVERAGE

Included here are periodical indexes that cover religion or theology in general. Periodical indexes covering one subfield of theological studies are found in the subject area lists.

** GUIDES

M1   *Religious Periodicals of the United States: Academic and Scholarly Journals.* Charles H. Lippy, ed. New York: Greenwood Press, 1986.
Surveys more than 100 American religious periodicals (past and present), including Protestant, Catholic, Jewish, and humanist, with lengthy signed articles describing for each periodical its editorial viewpoint, publication history, title changes, indexing, etc. Alphabetical arrangement, with appendices that provide a "chronological capsule" (listing journals according to their founding dates), and a grouping by religious orientation. Editor and title index.

M2   *Bibliographic Control in Selected Abstracting and Indexing Services for Religion: a Comparative Analysis.* Glenn R. Wittig. Ph.D. Dissertation, University of Michigan, 1984.
A study of the bibliographic control of the literature in 12 religious subject areas offered by nine indexes and abstracts. Literature coverage was examined by a detailed bibliometric analysis rather than by simple title count. An important work not only for its evaluation of religious indexing tools, but also for its description of the bibliographic structure of religious literature itself.

M3   *A Scholar's Guide to Academic Journals in Religion.* James Dawsey. Metuchen, NJ: Scarecrow Press, 1988.
An introduction to the religious journals market, organizing 530 journals into 33 categories. Information includes: editor, address, subject matter of articles, audience, submission requirements, and the selection process. A list of style manuals is included in an appendix. Important source of information for the aspiring author. Title index.

M4   *Religious Journals and Serials: An Analytical Guide.* Eugene C. Fieg. New York: Greenwood, 1988.
A guide to over 300 religious journals, "aimed primarily at helping the librarian to select journals for the library and at the scholar who wishes to read or subscribe to journals that fit his or her particular interests." Topical arrangement, with basic publication information. Most entries have lengthy annotations that describe each

journal's contents and compare it with other journals.   Indexes by place of publication, title, publisher, and subject.

M5   *A Study and Evaluation of Religious Periodical Indexing.* Robert J. Kepple. (ERIC document #ED 150 984). Arlington, VA: ERIC Document Reproduction Service, 1978.

Consists of two parts: part I is a detailed examination of 26 tools which provide indexing of religious periodical literature. Citation, frequency of publication, and a descriptive narrative on the state and usefulness of each tool is given. In part II, the coverage and completeness of past indexing is examined and the overlap of coverage among current indexes is evaluated.

M6   *A Guide to Indexed Periodicals in Religion.* John Regazzi and Theodore C. Hines. Metuchen, NJ: Scarecrow, 1975.

An alphabetical listing of some 2,700 periodicals indexed in 17 abstracting and indexing services. The title of each periodical is given and the indexing tools which cover it are indicated. Also included is a key-word index to aid in locating the periodical titles. As noted in several reviews, this work includes some inaccurate data.

** MORE IMPORTANT

M7   *Index to Religious Periodical Literature, 1949-1976.* 12 vols. Chicago: American Theological Library Association, 1953-1977.

M8   *Religion Index One: Periodicals.* Chicago: American Theological Library Association, 1977- .

Now issued semiannually with annual cumulations. "RIO," continuing "IRPL," is the major American religious periodical index. Now indexes over 400 journals mainly in English and from North America, although some other titles are included. Covers a wide range of journals from all areas of theology. Through 1976, this index had two A-Z sections: author and subject entries for the articles; and a listing of book reviews arranged by author of the book reviewed. From 1977-1985, had three A-Z sections: subject entries, author entries (with abstracts when available), and book reviews. Beginning with vol. 18 (1986) the abstracts and book review index were eliminated (but see R4) and a Biblical citation index was added. See chapter U5 and U15 for descriptions of computerized access to this database.

M9   *Religion Index One: Periodicals. Vol. 1-4, 1949-1959.* Chicago: American Theological Library Association, 1985.

A revision and expansion of v. 1-4 of IRPL (M7). Journal coverage is extended from 63 to 100 titles. Book reviews are omitted (but see R5).

M10   *Catholic Periodical Index.* 13 vols. Haverford, PA: Catholic Library
        Association, 1930-1966.
M11   *Catholic Periodical and Literature Index.* Haverford, PA: Catholic Library
        Association, 1967- . Bimonthly.
Two-year cumulations. The *Catholic Periodical and Literature Index* continues
both the *Catholic Periodical Index* and the *Guide to Catholic Literature* (see H13
above). Now indexes about 150 periodicals either by or of interest to Catholics.
Its periodical coverage deliberately minimizes overlap with *Religion Index One.*
Since 1967, it has also included books of interest to or by Catholics. For books
and periodical articles, the author and subject entries are arranged in a single A-Z
list. In the bimonthly issues, book reviews are listed under the heading "Book
Reviews." In the cumulations, they are gathered in a separate listing at the back
of the volume. Includes indexing of papal, conciliar, diocesan, and other official
church documents, whether in original language or in translation. Overall, a useful
index covering the literature and periodicals of the Catholic Church.

M12   "Elenchus Bibliographicus" in *Ephemerides Theologicae Lovanienses.*
        Louvain: Universitas Catholica Lovaniensis, 1924- . Annual.
"ETL." Currently published as a separately paged section of the journal, this is the
most extensive bibliography of theology and canon law published today. While it
covers all areas of theology, dogmatic theology is stressed. Lists monographs,
festschriften, conference proceedings, and dissertations, as well as indexing over
500 theological journals. The journals are in many languages, scholarly in nature,
and include a large number of Roman Catholic works. Entries are arranged by a
fairly detailed classified subject system -- see the table of contents at the back of
the volume. Author index. Very useful for current work but hard to search
retrospectively due to its numerous separate numbers. Particularly valuable for its
coverage of topics in systematic theology.

M13   *Bulletin signalétique 527: Histoire et sciences des religions.* Paris: Centre
        de Documentation du C.N.R.S., 1979- . Quarterly.
Published since 1947, title varies. Since 1970, a major international work,
indexing and abstracting relevant material in over 1,500 journals and proceedings
(both secular and religious). Book reviews are included, listed under the author
of the book. In its earlier numbers, coverage was much less extensive. BS527
covers all areas of religious studies including history of religion, comparative
religion, Christian doctrine, church history, biblical studies, and the study of
non-Christian religions. Organized in four parts: a classified listing of articles
with abstracts (in French); a detailed listing of the periodicals abstracted; a set of
detailed subject indexes; and an author index. Indexes are cumulated annually.
Valuable for its current and extensive coverage.

** MOST CURRENT

M14   *Zeitschriften Inhaltsdienst Theologie. Indices Theologici.* Tübingen: Universitätsbibliothek, 1975- . 12x a year.

Annual indexes. Provides very current coverage of theological journals by reproducing the tables of contents of over 400 journals received at the Tubingen University theological library. Also includes festschriften and collected-essay works. Arrangement is in 12 sections by major theological subject areas, subarranged by title of the journal. Includes author and biblical reference indexes. A convenient way to scan quickly a large number of recent journals.

** OTHER

M15   *Religious and Theological Abstracts.* Myerstown, PA: Religious and Theological Abstracts, Inc., 1958- . Quarterly.

Annual author and Scripture reference indexes. Includes brief (5-15 line) abstracts in English, arranged in classified subject order. Now indexes over 200 journals, primarily Protestant and English-language, although some French, German, and Dutch titles are included. Valuable for its abstracts, but it indexes many of the same titles as *Religion Index One.* For a CD-ROM version of this index see U16.

M16   *Christian Periodical Index.* Buffalo: Association of Christian Librarians, 1956- . Quarterly.

Annual and multi-year cumulations. Indexes about 80 popular and scholarly publications, primarily evangelical and fundamentalist. Includes entries for authors and specific subjects in a single alphabetic sequence. Book reviews are listed in a separate section at the back. Fairly current, provides needed coverage of popular evangelical literature.

M17   *Index to Jewish Periodicals.* Cleveland: College of Jewish Studies Press, 1963- . Semiannual.

Now indexes 44 English-language American and British Jewish periodicals. Lists author and subject entries in a single A-Z sequence. Book reviews are listed, by author of the book reviewed, within the main sequence. Valuable as a source of popular and scholarly Jewish opinion on a variety of topics.

M18   *Guide to Social Science and Religion in Periodical Literature.* National Periodical Library, 1970- . Quarterly.

Annual and three-year cumulations. Formerly titled *Guide to Religious and Semi-Religious Periodicals* (1965-1969) and *Guide to Religious Periodicals* (1964-1965). Indexes about 100 semi-scholarly and popular English-language periodicals in the fields of the social sciences and religion. Concentrates on material relating religion to the social sciences and to modern society. Only gives subject entries, and those are few and broad. Most of the periodicals indexed here are indexed elsewhere. While its less-than-perfect subject headings, subject-only indexing, and time lag detract from its value, it still is occasionally of some use for locating popular-level materials on the relationships between religion and the social sciences and with modern society.

M19   *An Alphabetical Subject Index and Index Encyclopedia to Periodical Articles on Religion, 1890-1899.* Ernest C. Richardson. 2 vols. New York: Scribners, 1907-1911.
Vol. 1 lists 58,000 articles from over 600 journals under specific subject headings. Vol. 2, which lists the same articles alphabetically by author, is titled *Periodical Articles on Religion.* Includes materials in French, German, Italian, and English. Each subject heading also gives references to encyclopedia articles on the topic and (for subjects) a brief definition of the term or (for people) brief biographical information. Gives extensive and well-indexed coverage for the 1890-1899 decade, attempting to list all religious articles published during that period.

** MAJOR DENOMINATIONAL

M20   *Southern Baptist Periodical Index.* Nashville: Historical Commission, Southern Baptist Convention, 1965- . Annual.
No cumulations. An author and specific subject index to Southern Baptist periodicals. Particularly helpful for its indexing of the popular and Christian education periodicals of that group.

M21   *United Methodist Periodical Index.* Nashville: United Methodist Publishing House, 1960-1980. Quarterly.
Annual and five-year cumulations. An author and subject index to about 60 Methodist periodicals, including a good deal of Christian education material. Vols. 1-5 were titled: *Methodist Periodical Index.*

M22   *Methodist Reviews Index, 1818-1985: A Retrospective Index of Periodical Articles and Book Reviews.* Elmer J. O'Brien, ed. Nashville: United Methodist Church, 1989-1990.
An index to five scholarly Methodist journals, covering 167 years. Vol. 1 provides author and subject access to journal articles; vol. 2 provides author, subject, reviewer, and Scripture indexes to book reviews. Entries are also accessible online through the ATLA Religion Index database (see U5 and U15).

CHAPTER 13
SERIAL PUBLICATION TOOLS

Periodicals, irregular and annual repeat publications, and monograph series are all included under the term "serial." This list includes several types of reference tools which will help you deal with these types of publications.

** UNION LISTS -- NATIONAL

Once you have located a periodical article of interest to you, it is still necessary to locate a copy of that periodical issue. If your library does not have it, a union list will help you find a library that does.

A union list is an alphabetical list of the serials (including periodicals) that are owned by the various libraries that contributed information to the union list. The list also specifies which issues of a serial the library does have, if it does not have them all.

N1   *Union List of Serials in Libraries of the United States and Canada.* 3rd
      ed. 5 vols. New York: Wilson, 1965.
Known as "ULS." Includes 156,000 periodical and serial titles which began publication before 1950 and are held by one or more of 956 libraries. Gives history of periodical name changes, numbering irregularities, etc. Libraries holding a given serial are indicated with a listing of the extent of their holdings. The abbreviations for holding libraries are not in complete alphabetical order; you must scan the entire list. In addition, discovering the form of name under which a periodical is entered may require several attempts.

N2   *New Serial Titles, a Union List of Serials Commencing Publication after*
      December 31, 1949: 1950-70 Cumulative. 4 vols. Washington, DC:
      Library of Congress, 1973.
N3   *New Serial Titles: 1971-75 Cumulation.* Washington, DC: Library of
      Congress, 1976.
N4   *New Serial Titles: 1976-80 Cumulation.* Washington, DC: Library of
      Congress, 1981.
N5   *New Serial Titles: 1981-85 Cumulation.* Washington, DC: Library of
      Congress, 1986.
Updates the above work for serials beginning or ending within the indicated time periods.

N6   *New Serial Titles.*   Washington, DC: Library of Congress, 1953- .
Monthly.
Annual cumulations.   An ongoing service which provides up-to-date
information on new serials and other serial changes.

** UNION LISTS -- REGIONAL THEOLOGICAL

Hundreds of various local and regional union lists exist. Your librarian will know
those most helpful in your location. Listed below are some of the more important
union lists involving theological libraries.

N7   *BTI Union List of Serials.* 13th ed. Boston: Boston Theological Institute,
1987.
Distributed on microfiche with printed instructions. Includes entries by corporate
author and by title -- full bibliographic information appears under the title entry.
Primarily lists periodicals, although some other types of serials are included. Lists
the periodical holdings of Andover Newton Theological School, Boston
College--Dept. of Theology, Boston University School of Theology, Episcopal
Divinity School/Weston School of Theology, Gordon-Conwell Seminary, Harvard
Divinity School, Holy Cross Greek Orthodox School of Theology, and St. John's
Seminary.

N8   *CATLA Union List of Serials.* Chicago: Chicago Area Theological Library
      Association, 1974.
N9   *CATLA Union List of Serials. Supplement.*   Chicago: Chicago Area
      Theological Library Association, 1980.
Lists the periodicals held by 23 theological libraries in the Chicago area, including
Seabury-Western,   The   University   of   Chicago   Divinity   School,   the
Jesuit-Kraus-McCormick Library, and others. Arranged by title with holdings
indicated.

N10   *Union List of Periodicals of the Southeastern Pennsylvania Theological
       Library Association.* Donald N. Matthews and Sara Mummert, eds. 3rd
       ed. Gettysburg, PA: SEPTLA, 1986.
A union list of the periodical holdings of 13 theological seminary libraries
primarily in southeastern Pennsylvania, including Westminster Theological
Seminary, Lutheran Theological Seminary (Philadelphia), Eastern Baptist
Seminary, and others. Entries are arranged by cover title of the periodical, with
cross-references linking the entries of the periodicals with title changes. Gives full
holding information for each library.

N11   *TEAM-A Serials: a Union List of the Serials Holdings.* Louisville, KY:
          Southern Baptist Theological Seminary, 1972.
TEAM-A (Theological Education Association of Mid-America) includes the
Southern Baptist, Asbury, Louisville Presbyterian, St. Meinrad, and Lexington
seminaries.

N12   *Union List of Periodicals of the Members of the Washington Theological
          Consortium and Contributing Institutions.* Donald N. Matthews, ed. 4th
          ed. Gettysburg, PA: Washington Theological Consortium, 1985.
A union list of periodical holdings of 17 theological libraries including Catholic
University of America, Howard University School of Religion, Union Theological
Seminary in Virginia, Wesley Theological Seminary, and the Washington
Theological Union Library.

** DIRECTORIES OF CURRENT TITLES

Several publishers issue listings of currently published serials. These tools give
such information as publisher, cost, and circulation; and are arranged by major
subject areas.   They are useful for finding subscription information, for
information on newer serials not yet in union lists, and for a broad subject
approach to serials. The three listed below are among the more comprehensive.
There are other similar tools by other publishers, and you may find that your
library has those as well.

N13   *Religious Periodicals Directory.* Graham Cornish, ed. Santa Barbara, CA:
          ABC-Clio Press, 1986.
Lists religious and theological journals which are current or which ceased
publication after 1960. Emphasis on scholarly publications and those which are
the only source of information on a particular group; excludes parish, mission, and
popular/edificatory magazines. For each, gives basic bibliographical information,
languages used, coverage by indexing services, brief description of its scope, and
an evaluation of the journal.

N14   *Oxbridge Directory of Religious Periodicals.*   New York: Oxbridge
          Communications, 1979- . Annual.
Lists over 3,000 U.S. and Canadian titles -- magazines, newspapers, directories,
educational materials, annual reports, etc. Entries include publisher, address and
phone, editor, year established, circulation, etc. Arranged by title with key-word
title index.

N15   *Ulrich's International Periodical Directory.* 1st-   ed. New York: Bowker, 1967- . Annual.

Beginning with 27th edition (1988-89), *Ulrich's* incorporated *Irregular Serials and Annuals*, formerly a separate publication. A classified guide to current periodicals, intending to give comprehensive coverage to all serials currently in print. Now in three vols., lists over 100,000 titles under 550 broad subject headings. Gives bibliographical and subscription information including price, circulation, and tools in which a title is indexed. Includes title, ISSN, and publishing organization indexes.

Note: For American religious serials in particular, see the list of religious serials in *Religious & Inspirational Books and Serials in Print* (J13).

** BOOKS IN SERIES -- BIBLIOGRAPHIES / INDEXES

Another problem with serials is determining the individual titles and authors of books which are part of a monograph series. The tools listed below are designed to provide author and title information on volumes in a series when only the series name (and possibly the number assigned to the book in the series) is known. Also helpful for their listing of titles included in each series.

N16   *Books in Series, 1876-1949.* 3 vols. New York: Bowker, 1982.

An extensive listing and index of about 70,000 titles, in over 9,000 monographic series, published and distributed in the U.S. between 1876 and 1949. Vol. 1 is arranged by the name of the series. Under each series, full bibliographical data is given for each title in that series. Vol. 1 also includes a "Series Heading Index" and a "Subject Index to Series." Vol. 2 lists each individual work by author; vol. 3 lists each individual work by title.

N17   *Books in Series, 1950-1984.* 6 vols. New York: Bowker, 1985.

"Original, reprinted, in-print, and out-of-print books, published or distributed in the United States in popular, scholarly, and professional series." Includes over 200,000 titles (in over 21,000 series) of all books in series published in the U.S. from 1950 to 1984. The main section is arranged in alphabetical order by the name of the series, with a listing of all included volumes under each series. Has author, title, and subject-of-series indexes. The "series heading index" serves as a table of contents.

N18   *Titles in Series: a Handbook for Librarians and Students.* Eleanora A. Baer. 3rd ed. 4 vols. New York: Scarecrow Press, 1978.

Lists series in order by title or responsible body. Under each series, the individual authors and titles of works in the series are listed. Indexed by authors, titles of individual volumes, titles of series, and alternative names and titles for series.

CHAPTER 14
DISSERTATIONS AND THESES

Unpublished dissertations and theses are often valuable sources for research in any field. Fortunately, a number of tools are available which list dissertations and theses, index them by author and subject, and/or give abstracts.

In general, doctoral dissertations receive much better coverage than masters theses. However, this list does include some bibliographies of masters theses as well.

** BIBLIOGRAPHICAL GUIDES

P1   *Guide to Theses and Dissertations: an Annotated Bibliography of Bibliographies.* Michael M. Reynolds. Rev. and enlarged ed. Phoenix, AZ: Oryx Press, 1985.
A "retrospective international listing of theses and dissertations bibliographies which have been published as separated entities, produced through 1983 and most of 1984." Arranged by subject with special sections for universal and national bibliographies of theses. See especially pages 233-238 which lists 75 bibliographies in theology and religion. Includes indexes of institutions, names and journal titles, and specific subjects. Has brief annotations.

P2   *Guide to the Availability of Theses.* D. H. Borchart and J. D. Thawley. Munich: Saur, 1981.
"Compiled for the Section of University Libraries and other General Research Libraries" of the International Federation of Library Associations. Gives information on the availability, through inter-library loan, photocopying, or microfilming, of theses from 698 institutions in 85 countries. Arranged by country, subarranged by name of institution, with an index of institution names.

P3   *Guide to the Availability of Theses: II, Non-University Institutions.* C. G. Allen and K. Deubert. Munich: Saur, 1984.
Supplements the above by listing, in similar arrangement, 199 institutions (in 24 countries) that are not formally designated as universities. Includes 43 institutions that grant theses in religion. Institution index and subject index.

P4   *Guide on the Availability of Theses.* Marc Chauveinc. Groningen: University Library, 1978.
Gives information on obtaining copies of theses from 60 institutions in 60 countries. Includes information on interlibrary loan, in-library use, availablity of copies, etc. The information was gathered by questionnaire and the quality of the information varies.

** BIBLIOGRAPHIES AND INDEXES -- AMERICAN DISSERTATIONS

P5   *Comprehensive Dissertation Index, 1861-1972.* 37 vols. Ann Arbor: University Microfilms, 1973.

Known as "CDI." Includes virtually all doctoral dissertations done in the U.S. up to 1973. Includes, but is not limited to, the entries in *Dissertation Abstracts* (see P9 below). Vols. 33-37 are a listing of the dissertations arranged by author. Vols. 1-32 are divided into six major subject sections including history (v. 28) and philosophy and religion (v. 32). Subject indexing is done by listing the dissertation under each of the important words that occur in its full title.   Thus, to use effectively you must think of the major words and their synonyms which dissertations of interest probably had in their title. Not perfect, but still very good subject access.

P6   *Comprehensive Dissertation Index: Ten-year Cumulation, 1973-1982.* 38 vols. Ann Arbor: University Microfilms, 1984.

A supplement to the above.   Same format, but also includes indexing by "key phrases" (i.e. multiple-word keys) as well as by key words.   Philosophy and religion are indexed in vol. 32.

P7   *Comprehensive Dissertation Index, [Annual Supplement], 1973- .* Ann Arbor: University Microfilms, 1974- . Annual.

Published yearly to update the above two works. Similar content and format.

P8   *American Doctoral Dissertations, 1955/56- .* Ann Arbor: University Microfilms, 1957- . Annual.

Earlier volumes (through 1962/63) had varying titles. Lists dissertations (without abstract) by subject area, then by school, then alphabetically by author and title. Includes author index.   Valuable for its relatively quick publication and for its breakdown of new dissertations by subject area and by granting institution.

P9   *Dissertation Abstracts International.* Ann Arbor: University Microfilms, 1938- . Monthly.

Often referred to as "DAI."   Title varies, v. 1-11: *Microfilm Abstracts*; v. 12-29: *Dissertation Abstracts.*   Now divided into three subseries: A = Humanities and Social Sciences; B = Sciences and Engineering; and C = European Abstracts. Dissertations are listed by broad subject areas with monthly key-word and author indexes that are cumulated annually.   Primarily valuable because it includes abstracts of each dissertation, generally written by the author.   To find dissertations, it is easier to use *Comprehensive Dissertations Index* (see above) and then read the abstracts here (CDI includes the DAI abstract location). Most of the dissertations listed can be ordered from University Microfilms.

** BIBLIOGRAPHIES AND INDEXES -- AMERICAN THESES

P10 *Masters Abstracts: A Catalog of Selected Masters Theses on Microfilm.*
Ann Arbor: University Microfilms, 1962- . Quarterly.
Subtitle and format vary slightly. Format is the same as in Dissertation Abstracts.
Indexes and abstracts selected masters theses from selected schools. Includes
relatively few of the masters theses done annually. Most issues have cumulative
author indexing for that year's preceding issues.

P11 *Cumulative Subject and Author Index to Volumes I-XV of Masters
Abstracts.* Ann Arbor: University Microfilms, 1978.
A complete author and subject index to the 10,500 theses listed in *Masters
Abstracts* up through 1977. Gives complete bibliographical and ordering
information, but not the abstract.

** BIBLIOGRAPHIES AND INDEXES -- FOREIGN DISSERTATIONS

P12 *Retrospective Index to Theses of Great Britain and Ireland, 1716-1950.
Vol. 1: Social Sciences and Humanities.* Santa Barbara, CA: Clio Press,
1975.
A listing of masters and doctoral level theses. Indexes are in two parts: specific
subject (not just key-word) and author. Both parts give full bibliographical
information including author, title, year, degree, and school -- no abstracts.
Includes some availability information.

P13 *Index to Theses Accepted for Higher Degrees in the Universities of Great
Britain and Ireland, 1950/51- .* London: ASLIB, 1953- . Annual.
Title varies. Theses and dissertations are listed in a classified subject
arrangement; then alphabetically by institution within each subject. Subject and
author indexes are provided. Includes information on availability.

P14 *Dissertation Abstracts International C: European Abstracts. Ann Arbor:
University Microfilms, 1976- .* Quarterly.
"Abstracts of Dissertations Submitted for Doctoral and Post-Doctoral Degrees at
European Institutions." Foreign-language dissertations include an English
translation of the title and an English abstract. Selective in the schools that are
included (seems to stress English-language dissertations). Many of the
dissertations are available from University Microfilms. Author and key-word
subject indexes. Includes a survey of "European Higher Education Practices."

** BIBLIOGRAPHIES AND INDEXES -- RELIGIOUS DISSERTATIONS

P15   *Doctoral Dissertations in the Field of Religion, 1940-1952.* Council on
        Graduate Studies in Religion. New York: Columbia University Press, 1954.
"Their titles, location, field, and short precis of contents." Published as a
supplement to the *Review of Religion*, v. 18. Only includes dissertations from
universities or seminaries offering a Ph.D. in religion. Lists 425 items with brief
abstracts arranged alphabetically by author. Of primary value where CDI or DAI
are not available. Includes an "index" listing entries under 14 subject headings.

P16   *Dissertation Title Index.* Iowa City, IA: Council on Graduate Studies in
        Religion, 1952-1977. Annual.
Continues the above. Annual listing of the titles of new dissertations in the area
of religion. Continued by the following item.

P17   *Religious Studies Review.* Waterloo, Ontario, Canada: Council on the
        Study of Religion, 1975- . Quarterly.
Regularly includes a list of "Recent Dissertations in Religion" and less frequently
a list of "Dissertations in Progress." Dissertations are primarily from schools in
the Council, but items from other schools are included if supplied. Arranged
under broad subject headings. Gives author, title, degree, school, and date, but
includes no abstract.

P18   *Theological Research Exchange Network Index.* Portland, OR: TREN,
        1990.
A list of masters theses (Th.M., M.Div, and M.A.) D.Min. projects, and some
doctoral dissertations available on microfiche for purchase from TREN. Lists
3,552 titles from over 50 participating schools, mostly evangelical theological
seminaries in the U.S. Subject and author indexes.

P19   *A Bibliography of Post-Graduate Master's Theses in Religion.* Niels H.
        Sonne. Chicago: American Theological Library Association, 1951.
Lists about 2,700 Th.M. and S.T.M. theses divided into 37 subject areas. Author
index. Dated but the only tool of this type. Does not include Catholic or Jewish
seminary theses.

P20   *Research in Ministry, 1981-* . Chicago: American Theological Library
        Association. Annual.
"An index to Doctor of Ministry project reports and theses submitted by reporting
ATS schools." Arranged in two sections -- a list by specific subject and a list by
author. Each entry gives the title, the degree, the school, and the year of the
project and the author list also includes an abstract and the name of the advisor.
A 1981-83 cumulation was issued in 1984.

CHAPTER 15
MULTI-AUTHOR WORKS

A number of books are published each year which consist of essays by different authors. These works are known as multi-author works (MAW). The most common of these in academic circles is the festschrift, "a volume of writings by different authors presented as a tribute or memorial especially to a scholar." Other types of MAWs include volumes of papers from conferences and volumes of essays on the same topic.

A number of special reference tools exist which index (usually by subject and author) the individual essays within these MAWs. Those of general interest and those relating to religious or theological studies are included in this list.

** GENERAL COVERAGE

Q1 *The "A.L.A." Index: an Index to General Literature.* American Library Association. 2nd ed. Boston: Houghton Mifflin, 1901.
The standard general-coverage MAW index, covering up to 1900. Includes only English-language titles. A supplement, published in 1914, indexes some additional works from 1901-1910, but these are largely incorporated in Q2 below.

Q2 *Essay and General Literature Index, 1900- .* New York: Wilson, 1934- . Semiannual.
Annual and five-year cumulations. Continues the coverage of the above work. Detailed indexing of MAWs by author, subject, and some titles. Covers English-language materials, primarily in the humanities. Indexes, in total, over 10,000 MAWs.

Q3 *Bibliography of Articles on the Humanities: British and American Festschriften Through 1980.* Charles Szabo, Christopher Kleinhenz, and James Brewer. 2 vols. Millwood, NY: Kraus, 1991?
Forthcoming. A long-delayed work that will cover over 10,000 festschriften published in North America, the United Kingdom, New Zealand, and Australia. Part I will list the festschriften, arranged by the person or thing commemorated, with full bibliographical information, including contents. Part II will be a comprehensive author, title, and subject index to all the articles in these festschriften. Should be a valuable tool covering a significant amount of material on religion.

** RELIGIOUS / THEOLOGICAL COVERAGE

Q4   *Religion Index Two: Festschriften, 1960-1969.* Edited by Betty O'Brien
       and Elmer O'Brien. Chicago: American Theological Library Association,
       1980.

An author and subject index to the individual essays in 783 religious festschriften
for the time period indicated. Same format and style as Q6 below. Includes over
13,000 author/editor entries and over 33,000 subject entries.

Q5   *Religion Index Two: Multi-Author Works, 1970-1975.* G. Fay Dickerson
       and Ernest Rubinstein, eds. 2 vols. Chicago: American Theological
       Library Association, 1982.

Designed to fill the gap between the O'Brien index and the first of the annual
Religion Index Two volumes, this work indexes 30,154 articles in 2,612 multi-
author works. Vol. 1 contains the author and editor indexing, vol. 2 has the
72,945 subject entries for the articles.

Q6   *Religion Index Two: Multi-Author Works, 1976- .* Chicago: American
       Theological Library Association, 1978- . Annual.

Two major sections: a name index for the editors (of the whole MAW) and
authors (of the individual essays); and a subject index that analyzes both the
whole MAW and the individual essay by subject. The entry under editor in the
first section has the full bibliographical information about the MAW and lists its
contents. Uses the same subject headings, format, and typeface as *Religion Index
One* (see M8 above). For computerized access to RIT, see U5 and U15.

Q7   *Religion Index Two: Multi-Author Works, 1976-1980.* 2 vol. Chicago:
       American Theological Library Association, 1989.

Five-year cumulation of RIT.

Q8   *Index to Festschriften in Jewish Studies.* Charles Berling. Cambridge:
       Harvard College Library, 1971.

Includes two listings, by author and by specific subject. The "List of Festschriften
Indexed" gives full bibliographical entries for the 243 volumes of festschriften
dealing with Jewish studies that are included.

Q9   *Bibliographie der Fest- und Gedenkschriften für Persönlichkeiten aus evangelischer Theologie und Kirche.* Hermann Erbacher. Neustadt: Verlag Degener, 1971- .

Two volumes thus far: vol. 1 covers 1881-1969; vol. 2 covers 1969-1975. Each volume has two sections. The first is a listing of the festschriften included (arranged by the name of the honoree), with indexing by key title words and by series or journal (if any) of which the festschrift is a part. The second is a classified subject listing of the individual articles, prefaced by a detailed outline of the subject classification scheme. Also has author, personal name, geographical name, subject, and biblical reference indexes.

CHAPTER 16
BOOK REVIEW INDEXES

A number of reference works which direct the user to reviews of a particular book are available. Most are arranged by author of the book reviewed, and several also provide subject access. Both the book's subject and its publication date are important when looking for a review. Choose a book review index with subject coverage the same as or broader than the subject of the book. Since most book reviews appear six months to three years after a book is published, look for reviews in journals published during that time period. When using the book review indexes, remember also that there is an additional time lag between when the journal issue appears and when the index which covers the journal issue appears.

** GENERAL COVERAGE

R1   *Book Review Digest.* New York: Wilson, 1905- . Monthly.
         Annual and multi-year cumulations. Indexes and briefly summarizes the reviews in about 75 English and American, general-coverage (four religious in nature) periodicals. Reviews are arranged by author of the book reviewed. Includes subject and author indexes. Very selective and generally not very helpful in theological studies.

R2   *Book Review Index.* Detroit: Gale, 1965- . Bimonthly.
         Annual cumulations. Indexes all reviews in 300 periodicals, about ten of which are religious in nature. Reviews are listed by author of the book reviewed; reviewer is not named in the index. Title index in 1976 and later issues.

R3   *Book Review Index 1965-1984: a Master Cumulation.* 10 vols. Detroit: Gale, 1985.
Subtitle: "A cumulated index to more than 1,650,000 reviews of approximately 740,000 titles." Cumulation of the first 20 years of *Book Review Index* (R2).

** RELIGIOUS / THEOLOGICAL

R4   *Index to Book Reviews in Religion.* Chicago: American Theological Library Association, 1986- . Quarterly.
Annual cumulations. Subtitled: "An author, title, reviewer, series, and annual classified index to reviews of books published in and of interest to the field of religion." Supersedes the "Book Review Index" of *Religion Index One* (M8). Good quick indexing of nearly 500 journals, with sections providing access by author and editor, title, series, and reviewer.

R5   *Index to Book Reviews in Religion, 1949-1974*. 3 vol. Evanston, Ill: American Theological Library Association, 1990-1991.

A cumulation and expansion of indexes to reviews from the journals that originally appeared in *Index to Religious Periodical Literature* (M7). Expanded coverage includes 120 journals not originally indexed by IRPL. Format similar to the above; access by author and editor, book title, and subject.

R6   *Theological Studies: Index, Volumes 1-40, 1940-1979*. Washington, DC: Theological Studies, 1982.

Includes indexes for authors, titles (arranged by subject) and books reviewed. Since *Theological Studies* has an extensive book review section, this will be a valuable guide to many reviews of theological books.

R7   *An Index of Reviews of New Testament Books Between 1900-1950*. Watson E. Mills. Danville: VA: Association of Baptist Professors of Religion, 1977.

Indexes the numerous reviews in 52 major journals of books on the New Testament published between 1900 and 1950. Arranged by author of the book reviewed. A helpful supplement to the listing of book reviews in *New Testament Abstracts*.

** OTHER SOURCES OF BOOK REVIEW CITATIONS

Many periodical indexes include sections listing book reviews, or include indexing of book reviews within the main index. Two of the religious periodical indexes that include book review indexing are listed below. See the main annotation for full information on each.

M10   *Catholic Periodical Index, 1930-1966*.
M11   *Catholic Periodical and Literature Index, 1967- .*

Book reviews are found under the heading "book reviews" in the bimonthly issues but in a separate section at the back of the cumulated volumes.

M16   *Christian Periodical Index, 1956- .*

Book reviews are found in a separate section at the back of each issue.

Note: Many of the specialized periodical indexes listed in Part II, "The Subject Area Lists," also index relevant book reviews.

CHAPTER 17
MANUSCRIPT MATERIALS AND GOVERNMENT PUBLICATIONS

** ARCHIVAL MATERIALS

Often, the primary materials for historical research will be the papers, original records, etc., of the individual or institution under study. The tools below help the researcher locate available materials and learn the conditions for using those materials.

S1   *National Union Catalog of Manuscript Collections, 1959/61-* .
      Washington, DC: Library of Congress, 1962- . Annual.
The major guide and index to mss. collections in the U.S. Gives a detailed description (contributed by the holding institution) of over 30,000 collections in over 900 repositories in the U.S. Information given includes number of items, scope and extent, access restrictions, location, microfilm copy availability, etc. Includes annual index (cumulated every five years) of those collections by topical subject, personal, family, corporate, and geographical names.

S2   *Directory of Archives and Manuscript Repositories.*   U.S. National
      Historical Publications and Records Commission. 2nd ed. Phoenix: Oryx
      Press, 1988.
Includes information on 4,225 archives and mss. repositories. Arranged geographically, extensive name and subject indexes. Includes information on hours, use provisions, and holdings; descriptions of special collections; and bibliographical citations to other material where the collections are described more fully.

S3   *Women Religious History Sources: A Guide to Repositories in the United
      States.* Evangeline Thomas, ed. New York: Bowker, 1983.
A guide to the archival and manuscript repositories of Catholic, Episcopal, and Orthodox sisterhoods, and Lutheran, Mennonite, and Methodist deaconesses. Arranged by state, with 569 such repositories listed and their contents described. Includes a biographical register, a bibliography of other sources, and an index.

** GOVERNMENT PUBLICATIONS

A government publication is any document published at government expense. Each year, the government publishes millions of pages of material, including a great deal of basic statistical information. For those working in religion and theology, particularly the sociological aspects, government documents may be a valuable source of information.

The methods of classification, the means of identification, and the reference tools for using government documents are quite specialized. Below are listed only two works which will provide an introduction to these documents and their use.

S4   *New Guide to Popular Government Publications for Libraries and Home Reference.* Walter L. Newsome. Littleton, CO: Libraries Unlimited, 1978.
A guide to over 2,500 government publications "that are of current or long-term popular interest." Entries are arranged by subject. Helpful in listing some of the better popular-level material, but does not serve as an introduction to the whole range of public documents as does the next work.

S5   *Introduction to United States Public Documents.* Joe Morehead. 3rd ed. Littleton, CO: Libraries Unlimited, 1983.
A good introduction to the use and bibliographical control of government publications. Covers the production, distribution, and control of government documents. Also explains the various bibliographical tools useful in accessing and using these publications.

CHAPTER 18
WRITING AND PUBLISHING TOOLS

In this section are listed some of the basic tools which should be used in writing in the field of theology. The list is highly selective and emphasizes basic tools of which any writer in theology should be aware.

** DICTIONARIES -- ENGLISH

T1   *Webster's Third New International Dictionary of the English Language, Unabridged.* Springfield, MA: Merriam, 1961.
Today's standard unabridged dictionary, used as an editorial standard by many publishers. Includes about 400,000 words; proper nouns are excluded. Note that meanings are given in chronological order, not in order of importance or frequency. Basic philosophy is to be "descriptive," i.e. how the language is used, not "prescriptive," i.e. how the language should be used. The 2nd ed. followed the prescriptive model and is still preferred by some users.

T2   *Webster's Ninth New Collegiate Dictionary.* Springfield, MA: Merriam-Webster, 1983.
An abridged desk dictionary based on Webster's 3rd (see T1 above), following the same principles and arrangement for use. Has over 160,000 entries, including 11,000 new words and meanings. Appendices include: abbreviations, foreign words and phrases, biographical names, geographical names, colleges and universities, signs and symbols, and a (revised and expanded) handbook of style. The one to own and to use in writing.

T3   *The American Heritage Dictionary.* William Morris, ed. 2nd college ed. Boston: Houghton Mifflin, 1982.
The "first complete revision" of *The American Heritage Dictionary of the English Language* (1969), incorporating 15,000 new words and adding separate biographical and geographical sections. An abridged desk dictionary but larger than most others, this work now includes over 160,000 words. The most prevalent, contemporary meaning of a word is given first, and (where applicable) usage is labeled "slang," "non-standard," or "regional." An acceptable alternative to Webster's.

T4   *The Oxford English Dictionary.* J. A. Simpson and E. S. C. Weiner. 2nd
       ed. 20 vols. New York: Oxford University Press, 1989.
Unlike standard dictionaries, the OED presents a historical record of the English
language. Describes the history of each word in use since 1150, with meaning,
pronunciation, and date of its first documented use. Altogether, defines over
500,000 words. The second edition incorporates the four supplements to the first
edition, along with additions and revisions, and attempts to reflect world-wide use
of the English language rather than the more British emphasis of the first edition.
Also available electronically on CD-ROM.

** DICTIONARIES -- OTHER

T5   *Dictionary of Foreign Phrases and Abbreviations.* Kevin Guinagh, comp.
       3rd ed. New York: Wilson, 1983.
Gives the pronunciation and a brief definition of 5,500 foreign-language phrases
used in English. Arranged in a single alphabetical sequence which does not
ignore initial articles. At the back is a list of the phrases by the language from
which they come (Latin and French predominate). A very helpful tool.

T6   *Dictionary of Modern Theological German.* Helmut W. Ziefle. Grand
       Rapids: Baker, 1982.
A compact, inexpensive, and very useful listing, with brief definitions, of about
10,000 German words which form a basic theological vocabulary for reading the
German Bible and German theological works. Appendices list irregular and
semi-irregular verbs and the German names for the books of the Bible.

** SYNONYMS AND ANTONYMS

T7   *Roget's International Thesaurus.* 4th ed. Revised by Robert L. Chapman.
       New York: Thomas Y. Crowell, 1977.
A major listing of synonyms and antonyms with a long publishing history. Entries
are put into categories by concept, grouping similar words together. Use the
alphabetical index of individual words to locate the needed section.

T8   *Webster's Collegiate Thesaurus.* Springfield, MA: G & C Merriam, 1976.
"A wholly new book resulting from long study and planning and differing from
existent thesauruses in a number of significant respects." Very helpful and easier
to use than Roget's. Entries are arranged in regular A-Z order. Each entry gives
synonyms and antonyms, related terms, contrasting terms, and cross-references.

** GRAMMAR AND USAGE

T9   *A Handbook for Scholars.* Mary-Claire van Leunen. New York: Knopf, 1978.

Billed as "the first complete modern guide to the mechanics of scholarly writing," this is a very useful book. Covers matters of form and style, the problem of when and where to quote and to footnote, and peculiarities of scholarly style. Includes a helpful appendix on the writing of academic resumes. Includes index.

T10   *The Harbrace College Handbook.* J. Hodges and M. Whitten. 10th ed. New York: Harbrace, 1986.

One of the many useful guides to English grammar, punctuation, etc. All writers should have at least one such work and consult it regularly.

T11   *Writer's Guide and Index to English.* Wilma R. Ebbitt and David R. Ebbitt. 7th ed. Glenview, IL: Scott, Foresman, & Co., 1982.

An established source of information about current written English. Part 1, the Writer's Guide, discusses such topics as writing, developing ideas, persuading and proving, elements of style, the research paper, etc. Part 2, the Index to English, lists in alphabetical order particular words and phrases which often trouble the writer and indicates correct use.

T12   *The Elements of Style.* William Strunk Jr. and E. B. White. 3rd ed. New York: Macmillan, 1979.

A small paperback which has become a classic on writing style. Covers elementary rules of usage, elementary principles of composition, matters of form, words and expressions commonly misused, and comments on style. Must reading.

T13   *A Dictionary of Modern English Usage.* H. W. Fowler. 2nd ed., rev. & ed. by Ernest Gowers. New York: Oxford Univ. Press, 1983.

A widely-used standard work on the English language and its usage. Now available in this revision which updates the original work and also takes some account of American usage.

** STYLE / FORM

T14   *The Chicago Manual of Style.* 13th ed. Chicago: University of Chicago Press, 1982.

Previously titled *A Manual of Style.* For theology, this is the style manual most widely used by book and journal publishers. Has a wealth of detailed information on many matters of style and publishing. An indispensable tool for writers. While Turabian (T15) summarizes parts of this work, it is still necessary for other features, e.g. the chapter on "Foreign Languages in Type" (which includes information on capitalization) and the chapter on "Indexes" and their preparation. The 13th edition is heavily revised and expanded, emphasizing "the impact of the new technology on the entire editing and publishing process" and which endorses the name-date and reference list style of footnoting. Has detailed index.

T15   *A Manual for Writers of Term Papers, Theses, and Dissertations.* Kate L. Turabian. 5th ed., rev. and expanded by Bonnie Birtwistle Honigsblum. Chicago: Univ. of Chicago Press, 1987.
Summarizes and adapts the *Chicago Manual of Style* for the person producing a typewritten thesis, dissertation, paper, etc. Stresses information on typewritten style and footnote and bibliography forms. Latest edition incorporates the "parenthetical reference" citation method, and has a section on computerized word processing. Many schools use this as their standard. Good index.

T16   "Instructions for Contributors." *Journal of Biblical Literature* 107 (1988): 579-596.
Gives instructions for handling special matters of style in biblical studies papers. Intended to supplement the *Chicago Manual of Style.* A number of other theological journals now follow these guidelines. In particular, it gives an extended list of permissible abbreviations for the biblical books, pseudepigraphical books, early patristic works, Dead Sea Scroll texts, Targumic materials, Mishnaic and related literature, other Rabbinic works, and the Nag Hammadi texts; and "abbreviations of commonly used periodicals, reference works, and serials."

T17   *Handbook for Academic Authors.* Beth Luey. Rev. ed. Cambridge: Cambridge University Press, 1990.
Covers to all aspects of academic publishing, including chapters on the mechanics of authorship, finding and working with publishers, multi-author works, textbooks, the finances of publishing, and revising dissertations for publication. The revised edition includes a chapter on electronic publishing. Annotated bibliography and index. A valuable tool for both experienced and aspiring authors.

** ABBREVIATIONS

T18   *An Illustrated Guide to Abbreviations: for Use in Religious Studies.* John T. Taylor. Enid, OK: Seminary Press, 1976.
Includes both an explanation of the use of abbreviations in religious studies and an extensive listing of abbreviations. Topics covered include abbreviations of journals and periodicals, reference materials, and classical and early Christian literature. Each section includes an extensive list of standard abbreviations. A helpful work, particularly for classical and early Christian literature. Note that these abbreviations do not always agree with the standard JBL list (see T16).

T19   *Internationales Abkürzungsverzeichnis für Theologie und Grenzgebiete:*
       Zeitschriften, Serien, Lexika, Quellenwerke, mit bibliographischen
       Angaben. Siegfried Schwertner. New York: de Gruyter, 1974.
An "International Glossary of Abbreviations for Theology and Related Subjects:
Periodicals, Series, Encyclopedias, Sources, with Bibliographical Notes. A
contribution towards the standardization of title abbreviations, offering suggested
standard abbreviations for about 7,500 titles." Includes two major sections: one
arranged alphabetically by the abbreviations and one arranged alphabetically by
the names being abbreviated.

Note: Another useful guide to theological abbreviations is the supplementary
volume, "Abkürzungsverzeichnis," in TRE (C12).

CHAPTER 19
COMPUTER - ASSISTED RESEARCH IN THEOLOGY

** GUIDES

U1   *Bits, Bytes, and Biblical Studies.* John J. Hughes. Grand Rapids: Zonder-
      van, 1987.
"A resource guide for the use of computers in biblical and classical studies."
Reviews software programs (word-processing, spelling, indexing, database
management, etc.), computer-assisted learning programs, online retrieval services,
projects that are producing machine-readable versions of the Bible and other
classical texts, etc. Extensive bibliography and glossary; indexed by proper name
and topics. Kept up-to-date by the following:

U2   *Bits & Bytes Review.* John J. Hughes, ed. Whitefish, Montana: Bits &
      Bytes Computer Resources, 1986- . 9x per year.
Subtitle: "Reviews and news of computer products and resources for the
humanities." Among the best of the many computer newsletters being published.
Each 20-page issue contains lengthy hardware and software product reviews, a
news section listing product updates and new releases, upcoming conferences,
workshops, etc., and a bibliography of recent publications.

U3   "Offline." Robert A. Kraft. *Religious Studies News.* Atlanta: Scholars
      Press, 1985- . 5x per year.
Was subtitled "Computer assisted research for religious studies" when it appeared
in RSN's predecessor, *Council on the Study of Religion Bulletin.* A useful
clearinghouse of information on new products, users groups, conferences, etc.

U4   *Online Searching in Religion Indexes.* Julie M. Hurd. Evanston, Ill.:
      American Theological Library Association, 1989.
An introduction to the organization and structure of online databases, and a guide
to searching the ATLA's *Religion Indexes* (U5), with specific examples of search
strategies, for both BRS and DIALOG users. A helpful handbook for online
searchers.

** ONLINE BIBLIOGRAPHIC DATABASES

There are many advantages to searching online bibliographic databases. A
properly executed computer search can save hours of research time. In addition,
online databases allow more sophisticated searching (e.g. by keyword or
"Boolean" combinations), and they are usually updated more frequently than their
offline counterparts.

However, the limitations of online searching should not be overlooked. Presently, the most thorough access to online data is not found in the humanities (much less in theology) but rather in the natural sciences, medicine, and law. Further, there is a substantial gap in retrospective indexing, which is only slowly being filled. Also, the costs of online searching are visible and direct, and many libraries pass these on to their patrons.

Among the dozens of existing databases, the following (generally available through both BRS and DIALOG) are particularly helpful for theological research.

U5   *Religion Indexes.*   Evanston, Ill.: American Theological Library Association.
Includes, in one database, all of the indexes produced by the ATLA, including *Religion Index One, Religion Index Two, Index to Book Reviews in Religion*, and *Research in Ministry.*

U6   *Dissertation Abstracts Online.*   Ann Arbor, MI: University Microfilms International.
Lists over 1,000,000 doctoral dissertations accepted at American universities since 1861. Includes some Canadian dissertations, and since 1988, British and European dissertations as well. (See P9 for corresponding print edition.)

U7   *Books in Print.* New York: R.R. Bowker Company.
       Provides author, title, and subject access and basic bibliographic data for over 1,000,000 American books that are in print. Also includes information on forthcoming books and books out-of-print. (See J8 - J10 for corresponding print editions.)

U8   *Arts and Humanities Search.*   Philadelphia: Institute for Scientific Information.
Online version of *Arts and Humanities Citation Index* (L18). Indexes over 1,300 arts and humanities journals as well as relevant articles from 5,000 science journals. Subject coverage includes archaeology, history, language, linguistics, literature, music, philosophy, and religion. Covers 1980 to present.

U9   *Social SciSearch.* Philadelphia: Institute for Scientific Information.
       Online version of *Social Sciences Citation Index* (L20). Indexes over 1,400 international journals in the social sciences, as well as relevant articles from over 3,300 journals in natural sciences and medicine. Covers 1972 to present.

U10   *Philosopher's Index.* Bowling Green, OH: Philosophical Documentation
          Center.
Indexes and abstracts over 270 journals in philosophy and related fields, from
1940 to present. (See CC7 - CC9 for corresponding print editions.)

U11   *PsycINFO.* Arlington, VA: American Pychological Association.
          Indexes over 1,300 journals, monographs, and dissertations in psychology
and related fields, from 1976 to present.

U12   *Sociological Abstracts.* San Diego: Sociological Abstracts.
          Indexes over 1,600 jounrals in sociology and related fields, from 1963 to
present. (See DA6 for corresponding print edition.)

U13   *Magazine Index.* Belmont, CA: Information Access Company.
          Subject access to articles in over 400 general interest magazines, from
1959 to present. Also includes full text articles from about 100 magazines from
1980 to present.

U14   *National Newspaper Index.* Belmont, CA: Information Access Co.
          Indexes articles from five American newspapers: *The Christian Science
Monitor, The Los Angeles Times, The New York Times, The Wall Street Journal,*
and *The Washington Post.* Covers from 1979 to present.

** BIBLIOGRAPHIC RETRIEVAL FROM CD-ROM

Many online databases are also available on compact disc (CD-ROM). Your local
library may use these as an alternative to online searching, and it may make them
available for public access. Often CD-ROM searches are cheaper than online
searches. Two important religious CD-ROMs are:

U15   *Religion Indexes on Wilsondisc.* Evanston, Ill.: American Theological
          Library Association.
Includes, on one disc, all of the indexes produced by the ATLA, including
Religion Index One, Religion Index Two, Index to Book Reviews in Religion, and
Research in Ministry.

U16   *R & T A on CD-ROM.* Myerstown, PA: Religious and Theological
          Abstracts.
A CD-ROM version of *Religious and Theological Abstracts* (see M15).

** OTHER CD-ROM TOOLS

U17   *CD-ROMs in Print: An International Guide.* Meckler, 1991. Annual.
Intended as "a comprehensive listing of commercially available CD-ROMs." Lists over 1,400 titles, describing contents, publishers, distributors, hardware and software configurations, and price.   Includes publisher, distributor, software provider, and subject indexes.

U18   *The Bible Library.* Edmond, OK: Ellis Enterprises.
        Contains several different versions of the Bible (in effect, multiple Bible concordances), including KJV, RSV, NIV, and LB. Includes ten other theological reference works including the *Evangelical Dictionary of Theology.*

U19   *CD Word Library.*   Dallas: CD Word Library and Dallas Theological
         Seminary.
Contains four English versions of the Bible (NIV, RSV, KJV, and NASB), along with the Septuagint and Greek NT.   Other reference texts include three Greek-English lexicons, *Harper's Bible Dictionary*, the *New Bible Dictionary*, and three Bible commentaries.

U20   *The FABS Reference Bible System.* Defuniak Springs, FL: Foundation for
         Advanced Biblical Research.
Includes several groups of biblical reference tools: the KJV, NIV, and RSV, the Greek NT, the Septuagint, the Hebrew Scriptures, a Hebrew-English lexicon, a Greek-English lexicon.   Other reference works include *Abingdon's Dictionary of the Bible and Religion*, the complete works of Josephus, and harmonies of the Gospels and Old Testament history. A "Multi-Lingual Bible," also included, provides the Latin Vulgate, and German, French, and Spanish translations of the Bible.

U21   *The Master Search Bible.* Fort Washington, PA: Tri-Star Publishing.
        Contains three Bible translations (KJV, NASB, and NIV), as well as several reference works, including the *Wycliffe Bible Encyclopedia*, the *Wycliffe Bible Commentary*, the *Expository Dictionary of Bible Words*, the *New International Dictionary of Biblical Archaeology*, and the *NIV Study Bible*.

PART II : THE SUBJECT AREA LISTS

INTRODUCTION

The following chapters cover the reference tools that are concerned only with a specific subfield of theological studies and the basic reference tools from related "secular" disciplines that may be helpful in that subfield.

Note that each of these subject areas will also require the use of reference works of "general" or general "religious/theological" coverage to fill the gaps where specialized tools are not available.

These lists are limited in scope and highly selective. The reader is urged to consult the bibliographical guides listed for each subject area in which descriptions of additional relevant works will be found.

The study in a number of specialized areas of theology may also require knowledge of the research methods and literature of a related "secular" discipline. While a few of the basic reference works in such fields are listed below at appropriate spots, it is imperative that the reader obtain one of the bibliographical guides available for that field and use it.

CHAPTER 20
BIBLICAL STUDIES, GENERAL: BIBLIOGRAPHIES / INDEXES

Most of the works listed here include both periodical articles and books. Usually, they give access to the material by subject and author.

** BIBLIOGRAPHICAL GUIDES

AA1 *An Introductory Bibliography for the Study of Scripture.* Joseph A.
      Fitzmyer. 3rd ed. Rome: Pontifical Biblical Institute Press, 1981.
Revision and expansion of the second edition (1981); now includes over 700 entries. Aims to cover "all the important aspects of serious biblical study," especially for those beginning study in the original languages. Coverage includes periodicals, series, grammars and lexicons, commentaries, texts, theology, backgrounds, archeology, early rabbinics, hermeneutics, etc. Author index. A valuable guide.

AA2 *Basic Tools for Bibical Exegesis: a Student's Manual.* Stanley B. Marrow.
      Rome: Pontifical Biblical Institute Press, 1976.
Well organized with an excellent selection of 215 scholarly tools, most with descriptive annotations. Includes an author/title index and a list of important biblical studies journals (p. 83). Covers the Apocrypha, pseudepigrapha, background studies, texts and versions, dictionaries, grammars, lexicons, and concordances. Does not include commentary listings. An excellent tool, always worth consulting.

AA3 *Multipurpose Tools for Bible Study.* Frederick W. Danker. 3rd ed. St.
      Louis: Concordia, 1970.
A basic work which discusses the bibliography, history, and use of the various biblical reference tools by a Lutheran biblical scholar. Covers texts, concordances, grammars, lexicons, dictionaries, versions, and commentaries. Particularly helpful for its examples of how various tools can be effectively used.

** BIBLIOGRAPHICAL GUIDES TO COMMENTARIES

Individual commentaries and sets of commentaries will not be enumerated in this guide. Rather, the user is referred to the bibliographies of commentaries given below.

AA4   *A Guide to Selecting and Using Bible Commentaries*. Douglas Stuart. Dallas: Word Publishing, 1990.

The bulk of this book lists over 1,100 modern, non-specialized English language commentaries, with short annotations that describe the work's size, detail, level (popular, serious, or technical), and theological perspective. Additional chapters evaluate single-volume commentaries and major commentary sets. In the last chapter, the best commentaries are treated to longer annotations. No index.

AA5   *Repertorium Biblicum Medii Aevi*. Friedrich Stegmuller. 7 vols. Madrid: Consejo Superior de Investigaciones Científicas, Instituto Francisco Suárez, 1950-1961.

A thorough treatment of early and medieval biblical commentaries. Vol. 1 covers apocryphal writings and lists prologues to the Bible. Vols. 2-7 list patristic and medieval biblical commentaries, giving the incipit, explicit, editions, manuscripts, and bibliographies.

AA6   *Commenting and Commentaries: a Reference Guide to Book Buying for Pastors, Students, and Christian Workers*. Charles H. Spurgeon. Grand Rapids: Baker, 1981.

First published in 1876.   An old classic that contains two lectures on commentaries and their use and an annotated bibliography (over 100 pages) of 1437 commentaries, arranged in canonical order.   Particularly valuable as an historical bibliography of pre-1900 commentaries.   Conservative theological viewpoint but good critical judgment.

Note: See also the O.T. and N.T. bibliographical guides listed in chapters 21 and 22, and also items #193-217 (Bible), #242-244 (O.T.), and #279-286 (N.T.) in Bollier, *The Literature of Theology* (A6).

** CRITICISM AND INTERPRETATION

AA7   *Elenchus Bibliographicus Biblicus*. Rome: Pontifical Biblical Institute Press, 1920-84. Annual.

AA8   *Elenchus of Biblica, 1985- .* Rome: Pontifical Biblical Institute Press, 1988- . Annual.

Vols. 1-48 (1920-1967) issued as part of *Biblica*.   The most extensive bibliography for biblical studies. Published annually, usually 2-3 years after the date of the material included.   Covers over 1,100 journals as well as books, dissertations, etc., in the field. Classified subject arrangement; see the table of contents at the back of each volume. Includes indexes of authors and subjects, Hebrew words, Greek words, and words in other languages. No abstracts. While the index goes back to 1920, it was not so extensive then and its structure and indexing were poor. From 1960 to 1966 supplements to this bibliography were published in *Verbum Domini.* Note the title change beginning in 1988. This is a must tool for extensive biblical studies research.

AA9 *Internationale Zeitschriftenschau für Bibelwissenschaft und Grenzgebiete: International Review of Biblical Studies, 1951/52- .* Dusseldorf: Patmos, 1952- . Annual.

"IZBG." Not as extensive as EBB, but does include abstracts (usually in German) of each item indexed and has an arrangement that is easier to use. Covers articles in over 400 periodicals, plus festschriften, reports, and book reviews. Classified subject arrangement, use the table of contents at the back of each volume. Author index.

AA10 *Bibliographie Biblique; Biblical Bibliography ... 1930-1970.* Paul-Émile Langevin. Québec: Presses de l'Univ. Laval, 1972.

Indexes the biblical studies articles in 70 Catholic journals (from 1930 to 1970) as well as 286 Catholic books. Classified subject arrangement with five major sections: Introduction, O.T., N.T., Jesus Christ, and Biblical Themes. The introduction, table of contents (at the back of the book), subject headings, and subject heading index are repeated in French, English, German, Italian, and Spanish. Indexed by author.

AA11 *Bibliographie Biblique; Biblical Bibliography II, 1930-1975.* Paul-Émile Langevin. Québec: Presses de l'Univ. Laval, 1978.

A companion volume to the above, with the same format. Updates the 70 Catholic journals for 1971-1975, and indexes 50 other major non-Catholic biblical studies journals for 1920-1975. Indexes 1,094 additional monograph works, analyzing 812 of them chapter by chapter.

AA12 *Bibliographie Biblique; Biblical Bibliography III.* Paul-Émile Langevin. Québec: Presses de l'Univer. Laval, 1986.

Updates vols. 1 and 2 by continuing the indexing of the 120 journals for the years 1976-1983, by indexing 43 additional journals from 1930 to 1983, and by indexing essays found in 450 multi-author works. Used together, these three volumes are an important starting point for bibliography compilation.

AA13 *Catalogue de la Bibliothèque de l'École Biblique et Archéologique Francaise.* 13 vols. Boston: G. K. Hall, 1975.

"Catalog of the Library of the French Biblical and Archeological School, Jerusalem, Israel." Contains reproductions of 215,000 catalog cards representing author and subject entries for over 50,000 books and the articles in 300 journals in the library. Material on particular Bible passages is listed directly under the name of the biblical book, arranged by chapter and verse. One of the world's best biblical collections, the library covers the biblical sciences, Palestinology, epigraphy, etc. As the center for study of the Dead Sea Scrolls, the Institute's library holds all significant materials on that topic.

AA14 *L'Année philologique: bibliographie critique et analytique de l'antiquité gréco-latine.* Paris: Société d'édition "Les Belles Lettres," 1924- . Annual.
Covers antiquity in general but contains material on the O.T., N.T., early church history, and other related areas. Entries are arranged topically (see table of contents) and often includes brief annotations. Indexed by ancient names, collective titles, geographical locations, and authors.

AA15 *The Near East/Biblical Periodical Index, 1960-1969.* John M. Elliott, comp. Naperville, IL: NEBPI Press, 1981.
An index of 35 major journals in the field covering 1960-1969. A classified subject arrangement is used (with geographical and topical divisions) and subject and place name indexes are also provided. The geographical access offered will be of some use, but this work duplicates indexing available elsewhere.

AA16 *Articles on Antiquity in Festschriften: the Ancient East, the Old Testament, Greece, Rome, Roman Law, Byzantium; An Index.* Dorothy Rounds. Cambridge: Harvard University Press, 1962.
In part, a supplement to Metzger (see AC10). Contains, in a single alphabet, an author and subject index to the articles in 1,178 festschriften published before 1955. Bibliographical entries for the festschriften themselves are also included in the main listing.

** VERSIONS

AA17 *The Bible: Texts and Translations of the Bible and the Apocrypha and Their Books from the National Union Catalog, Pre-1956 Imprints.* 5 vols. London: Mansell, 1980.
Separate release of the Bible volumes from Pre-56 (J1). The first four volumes list over 63,000 books, both texts of the Bible and commentaries that include the text (but Bible-related materials without the text are usually excluded). Arranged by Bible "uniform title" main entry. Vol. 5 is an 18,000 entry index of the first 4 volumes -- by editor, translator, and variant titles. It is not part of the Pre-56 set, but most of the same cross-references are found scattered in the other Pre-56 volumes. This index is available separately and even those who have access to the full Pre-56 set will find it helpful.

AA18 *The Bible: British Library General Catalogue of Printed Books to 1975.* 5 vols. Munich: Saur, 1981.
A separate release of the Bible volumes from the new cumulative edition of the British Museum catalog.

AA19 *Historical Catalogue of the Printed Editions of Holy Scripture in the Library of the British and Foreign Bible Society.* T. H. Darlow and H. F. Moule. 2 vols. in 4. London: the Bible House, 1903-1911.
Lists all Bibles in that library up to about 1900.   Vol. 1 lists 1,410 English-language editions, arranged by publication date.   It has indexes by translator, revisor, and editor; printer, publisher, etc.; and place of publication, printing, etc. Vol. 2, published in three parts, first lists polyglot editions, then those in all other languages, A to Z. Under each language, the 8,438 entries are arranged by date of publication. Indexed by languages and dialects; translator, revisor, etc.; printer, publisher, etc.; place of printing or publication; and general subjects. This index, at the end of vol. 2, also includes indexing of vol. 1 as well. The major bibliography of Bible editions up to 1900. Herbert (AA20) updates vol. 1. Separate updated supplements for some of the other languages have also been published.

AA20 *Historical Catalogue of Printed Editions of the English Bible, 1525-1961.* A.S. Herbert. Revised and expanded from the edition of T.H. Darlow and H.F. Moule, 1903. New York: American Bible Society, 1968.
Updates and expands vol. 1 of Darlow and Moule (AA21), covering up to 1961 and adding entries for editions in other libraries.   Includes 2,524 entries in publication date order.   Indexed by: translator, revisor, editor, etc.; printer and publisher; place of printing and publication; and general subjects.

AA21 *The English Bible in America: a Bibliography of Editions of the Bible and the New Testament Published in America, 1777-1957.* Margaret T. Hills. New York: American Bible Society, 1961.
Includes English-language Bibles printed in the U.S. and Canada. Based on the holdings of the A.B.S. library, but checked against other lists.   Listed chronologically by publication date. Brief annotations; locations of some copies indicated. Includes six indexes: geographical location of printers and publishers; names of publishers and printers; translators, revisors, and translations; editors and commentators; edition titles; and a general index.

Note: See also items #160-180 (a selective annotated list of English versions), in John Bollier, *The Literature of Theology* (A6).

** SPECIAL TOPICS

AA22 *Bibliography of Holy Land Sites: Compiled in Honor of Dr. Nelson Glueck.* Eleanor K. Vogel. Cincinnati: Hebrew Union College--Jewish Institute of Religion, 1974.
Reprint from the 1971 issue (vol. 42) of the *Hebrew Union College Annual.* A 96-page bibliography, arranged alphabetically by place name, of materials about

200 archeological excavation sites in the Holy Land. Includes cross-references from alternative names.

AA23 *Bibliography of Holy Land Sites Part II (1970-1981)*. Eleanor Vogel and Brooks Holtzclaw. Cincinnati: Hebrew Union College--Jewish Institute of Religion, 1982.
Supplement to the above. Reprint from the 1981 issue (vol. 52) of the *Hebrew Union College Annual.*

AA24 *Jerusalem, the Holy City: a Bibliography*. James D. Purvis. Metuchen, NJ: American Theological Library Association and Scarecrow Press, 1988.
A classified bibliography of 5,827 entries, covering "all aspects of Jerusalem and its history, from ancient to modern times." 40 chapters are included under eight parts. Part one lists general studies on Jerusalem, and parts two through eight cover chronological periods. Author and subject indexes.

AA25 *Bibliographie der Hermeneutik und ihrer Anwendungsbereiche seit Schleiermacher*. Norbert Henrichs. Düsseldorf: Philosophia Verlag, 1968.
A lengthy classified bibliography on modern hermeneutics. Two major sections: general hermeneutics (including the philosophical, psychological, and epistemological discussions); and special hermeneutics -- see esp. section 1, "Theologische Hermeneutik," which has nearly 200 pages. Subject and person indexes.

AA26 *The Bible as Literature: a Selective Bibliography*. John H. Gottcent. New York: G.K. Hall, 1979.
A selective annotated bibliography of materials on "the treatment of the Bible or any of its parts in the way critics and teachers of literature treat secular literary works." Covers primarily 1950 to mid-1978, listing only English-language materials. Includes books, articles, and dissertations. Arranged by the portion of the Bible covered, subdivided by subject. Author and limited subject index.

AA27 *The Bible on Film: a Checklist, 1897-1980*. Richard H. Campbell and Michael R. Pitts. Metuchen, NJ: Scarecrow Press, 1981.
A list of movies which are based on the Bible, giving as much technical information as possible as well as a synopsis of the film's plot. Tries to include all movies but only selected TV programs. Chronological arrangement with a title index.

** THE DEAD SEA SCROLLS

AA28 *The Dead Sea Scrolls: Major Publications and Tools for Study.* Joseph A.
     Fitzmyer. Rev. ed. Atlanta: Scholars Press, 1990.
A very helpful guide to the primary sources (the published texts of the DSS) and
to secondary materials. Topical arrangement, some entries have brief annotations.
Includes indexes by modern author and by biblical passage.

AA29 *Bibliography of the Dead Sea Scrolls 1948-1957.* William S. LaSor.
     Pasadena, CA: Fuller Theological Seminary Library, 1958.
Lists about 3,000 books, periodical articles, etc., arranged by a detailed subject
classification (see pp. 4-6). Includes author index. Fairly comprehensive for the
period covered.

AA30 *A Classified Bibliography of the Finds in the Desert of Judah 1958-1969.*
     B. Jongeling. Leiden: Brill, 1971.
Intended to be a continuation of LaSor's bibliography. Lists a large number of
books and periodical articles in many languages. Entries listed under 13 broad
subject headings, subarranged by author. Includes author index.

AA31 *Bibliographie zu den Handschriften vom Toten Meer.* Christoph Burchard.
     2 vols. Berlin: A. Töpelmann, 1957-1965.
A very extensive list of about 4,500 books and periodical articles on the Dead Sea
Scrolls. Vol. 1 covers 1948-1956, vol. 2 covers 1956-1962. This bibliography is
continued in *Revue de Qumran.* Both volumes are arranged the same: 3 major
sections listing Roman, Greek, and Hebrew alphabet materials, each subarranged
by author. At the back of each volume is a classified subject index.

AA32 *Bibliography of Hebrew Publications on the Dead Sea Scrolls, 1948-1964.*
     Michael Yizhar. Cambridge: Harvard, 1967.
As title indicates, limited to Hebrew-language articles and books. Lists 703 items
in a classified subject arrangement. Author and subject indexes.

CHAPTER 21
BIBLICAL STUDIES, O.T.: BIBLIOGRAPHIES / INDEXES

** BIBLIOGRAPHICAL GUIDES

AB1 *Old Testament Commentary Survey.* Tremper Longman III. Grand Rapids: Baker, 1991.
Book-by-book evaluations of O.T. commentaries, with critical annotations. Each work is rated on a one to five star scale and also categorized for its most appropriate audience: laypeople, ministers, or scholars. Additional chapters discuss one-volume commentaries and commentary sets, as well as other O.T. tools such as histories, introductions, theologies, grammars, atlases, etc. Balanced conservative perspective.

AB2 *Old Testament Books for Pastor and Teacher.* Brevard S. Childs. Philadelphia: Westminster, 1977.
A good prose discussion of the various O.T. study tools by a leading American OT scholar. Directed toward the needs of the pastor and teacher, Childs offers critical evaluation of major tools. The largest part of the book (54 pages) discusses commentaries. A bibliography at the back gives full information for the books cited in short form in the text.

AB3 *Old Testament Exegesis: a Primer for Students and Pastors.* Douglas K. Stuart. 2nd ed., rev. and enl. Philadelphia: Westminster Press, 1984.
Part 1 of this helpful book is a 12-step outline for students explaining how to do complete exegesis of a passage. Part 2 contains a series of examples illustrating these steps. Part 3 is a shorter and more limited guide for pastors. Part 4 is a classified and annotated bibliography of over 200 reference works useful in the task.

** O.T. PROPER

AB4 *Old Testament Abstracts.* Washington, DC: Catholic University of America, 1978- . 3x a year.
The major indexing and abstracting tool for O.T. studies, similar in purpose and content to *New Testament Abstracts*. Includes abstracts (in English) of periodical articles in over 200 scholarly journals from many countries. Also includes a section of brief "Book Notices." Abstracts are grouped by broad subject classifications. The third issue of each year has cumulative author, Bible-passage, and semitic-word indexes. Good coverage, but only since 1978.

AB5   *An Index to English Periodical Literature on the Old Testament and Ancient Near Eastern Studies.* William G. Hupper. Metuchen, NJ: Scarecrow Press, 1987-

Vols. 1-4 of the projected 7 vol. work published so far. An index of English language articles "from over 600 journals which have reference to the Ancient Near East generally, the Old Testament, Intertestamental Literature, Rabbinic Studies, the Dead Sea Scrolls, and ancient contemporary languages and literature." Coverage through 1970. Vol. 1 includes "Bibliographical Articles" and begins "Ancient Near Eastern Civilization -- General Studies," which is continued in vols. 2 and 3. Vol. 4 covers "Critical Studies of the O.T.", textual and literary studies, including general works and specific works arranged by O.T. book. Vol. 5 will be devoted to exegetical studies. Within each subheading, works are listed chronologically. Each vol. includes detailed table of contents, but no indexes.

AB6   *Booklist, 1946- .* London: Society for Old Testament Study, 1946- .

Lists only books. The annual booklist contains critical reviews (about 150 words each) of the important O.T. books published in the preceding year. The reviews are signed and arranged by broad subject areas. Author index.

AB7   *Eleven Years of Bible Bibliography, 1946-1956.* Edited by H. H. Rowley for the Society for Old Testament Study. Indian Hills, CO: Falcon's Wing Press, 1957.

AB8   *A Decade of Bible Bibliography, 1957-1966.* Edited by G. W. Anderson for the Society for Old Testament Study. Oxford: Blackwell, 1967.

AB9   *Bible Bibliography, 1967-1973: Old Testament.* Society for Old Testament Study. Oxford: Blackwell, 1974.

These cumulative volumes reprint the annual lists (the reviews are not newly interfiled by subject) and provide a cumulative author index and a cumulative table of contents.

AB10   *Old Testament Dissertations, 1928-1958.* Martin J. Buss. Ann Arbor: University Microfilms, [1962?].

A privately printed list of O.T. dissertations. Arranged by author. Useful if *Comprehensive Dissertation Index* (P5 - P7) is not available.

AB11   *Exégèse practique des petits prophètes postexiliens: bibliographie commentée, 950 titres.* Robert North. Rome: Biblico, 1969.

Covers Haggai, Zechariah, Joel, Jonah, and Malachi. The largest part of this work (about 150 pp.) is a passage-by-passage discussion of some of the problems of interpretation, with reference to works in the bibliography. This section is followed by a bibliography of 950 books, journal articles, etc., arranged by author. The bibliography entry also gives the location in the essay where the item is discussed. Includes indexes by subject/persons, and by scripture passages cited.

** RELATED AREAS

AB12 *Catalog of the Oriental Institute Library, University of Chicago.* 16 vols. Boston: G. K. Hall, 1970.
Contains "all useful material on every aspect of the Near East." Includes 284,000 cards for 50,000 volumes and 220 journals; strengths in Assyriology, Egyptology, and Islam. Includes all entry (author, title, and subject) cards, authority cards, series cards, and journal cards (which analyze the articles in relevant journals by subject and author).

AB13 *Catalog of the Middle Eastern Collection, formerly the Oriental Institute Library: First Supplement.* Boston: G.K. Hall, 1977.
Supplements the above. Now contains almost exclusively only main-entry (usually author) cards. Scope is somewhat broadened to all aspects of Middle East topics.

AB14 *A Basic Bibliography for the Study of the Semitic Languages.* J. H. Hospers, ed. 2 vols. Leiden: Brill, 1973-1974.
Vol. 1 forms the bulk of this work, covering most of the languages; vol. 2 is restricted to material on the various facets of the Arabic language. A lengthy bibliography of materials on the semitic languages. Arranged topically by language with numerous subdivisions. Indexed by author.

AB15 *A Bibliography of Targum Literature.* Bernard Grossfeld. Cincinnati: Hebrew Union College Press, 1972.
Lists over 1,000 items arranged by ten major subject areas, subdivided by type of publication (books, chapters in books, articles in periodicals). Part 10 lists book reviews. Includes both texts of the targums and materials about them. Author/editor index.

AB16 *A Bibliography of Targum Literature, Volume II.* Bernard Grossfeld. Cincinnati: Hebrew Union College Press, 1977.
Supplements the above work with 1,800 additional entries. Same basic subject and type-of-publication organization. In addition, this volume includes a section listing dissertations and theses and a brief specific subject index.

AB17 *A Bibliography of Targum Literature, Volume III.* Bernard Grossfield. New York: Hermon, 1990.
A continuation of AB15 - AB16, with about 1,000 additional entries.

AB18   *A Classified Bibliography of the Septuagint.* Sebastian P. Brock, Charles
        T. Fritsch, and Sidney Jellicoe. Leiden: Brill, 1973.
Covers 1900-1969, although "exceptional" earlier materials are included.   See
preface for the specific limitations of coverage.   Includes some book reviews.
Entries are arranged by a detailed subject classification, with cross-references and
an author index.   Very useful for Septuagintal studies.

** BIBLIOGRAPHICAL GUIDES

AC1 *New Testament Commentary Survey.* D. A. Carson. 3rd ed. Grand
Rapids: Baker, 1986.
A bibliographic essay listing, evaluating, and discussing N.T. commentaries from
a scholarly evangelical viewpoint. General comments on a number of commentary
sets are followed with a book-by-book analysis. The final page lists "some best
buys'" as a summary. Very helpful and relatively up-to-date.

AC2 *New Testament Books for Pastor and Teacher.* Ralph P. Martin.
Philadelphia: Westminster Press, 1984.
A critical discussion of N.T. study tools by a professor at Fuller Theological
Seminary, following the format of Childs on the O.T. (AB2). Like Childs, Martin
devotes most of this work to evaluating commentaries. The bibliography at the
back is a guide to the works cited in short form in the text.

AC3 *New Testament Exegesis: a Handbook for Students and Pastors.* Gordon
D. Fee. Philadelphia: Westminster, 1983.
Major parts include an outline for students explaining how to do complete
exegesis of a N.T. passage; a detailed guide to the components of exegesis; a short
guide for sermon exegesis; and a classified and annotated bibliography of
reference works useful in the task. Has author and Scripture-passage indexes.

AC4 *A Bibliographical Guide to New Testament Research.* R. T. France. 3rd
ed. Sheffield, England: J.S.O.T. Press, 1979.
Like Scholer (below), also includes listings for O.T., inter-testamental, early
church, and other background tools. Concentrates more on background information
and reference works -- no commentary listings. Some annotations and discussion,
British orientation. Includes a list of 49 periodicals of particular importance in
N.T. research.

AC5 *A Basic Bibliographic Guide for New Testament Exegesis.* David M.
Scholer. 2nd ed. Grand Rapids: Eerdmans, 1973.
This and France (above) complement one another. Scholer provides better
coverage of the central topics of N.T. study. Entries are topically arranged, and
include some annotation and discussion. The final section lists 3 to 5 "best"
commentaries on each N.T. book. Author index.

AC6   *The Bible Book: Resources for Reading the New Testament.* Erasmus
        Hort. New York: Crossroad, 1983.
"A consumer's guide to resources for reading and studying the New Testament."
Examines 750 tools with informative and balanced evaluations. Covers N.T.
introductions, concordances, Greek language tools, dictionaries, atlases, handbooks,
and commentaries (the longest chapter). Many sections distinguish between "the
best" and "the rest." Chapter 10 is a helpful "Wise Buyer's Guide", and a "Quick
Reference Chart" appended. Includes index.

** N.T. PROPER

AC7   *New Testament Abstracts: a Record of Current Periodical Literature.*
        Cambridge, MA: Weston College School of Theology, 1956- . 3x a year.
Provides brief English-language abstracts of articles on the N.T. and related areas,
as well as brief "book notices." Uses a broad classified subject arrangement.
Now indexes over 500 journals and lists over 500 books per year.   Author,
biblical-reference, book review, and book notice indexes are included in the 3rd
issue of each year. A cumulative author and biblical-reference index is available
for 1956-1971. Vols. 1-13 also contain a "biographical notes" section on N.T.
scholars. Extremely valuable -- the major indexing tool for N.T. studies.

AC8   *An Exegetical Bibliography of the New Testament.* Gunter Wagner, ed.
        Macon, GA: Mercer University Press, 1983-
Three volumes (Matthew and Mark; Luke and Acts; John and 1, 2, 3 John)
published thus far. Makes available in book form series 1 and 2 of the card
bibliography available from the Baptist Theological Seminary, Ruschlish-Zurich.
Lists, book by book, chapter by chapter, periodicals over approximately the past
25 years. A useful tool -- both in card form and in this printed edition.

AC9   *A Bibliography of New Testament Bibliographies.* John C. Hurd Jr. New
        York: Seabury, 1966.
A classified list of bibliographies of literature about the N.T.   Includes
bibliographies that were published within books or as a periodical article, as well
as those published separately. Includes some annotations but no indexes. Note
esp. section IV: "N.T. Scholars: Biographies and Bibliographies."

AC10   *Index of Articles on the New Testament and the Early Church Published
        in Festschriften.* Bruce M. Metzger. Philadelphia: Society of Biblical
        Literature, 1951.
AC11   *Supplement to Index of Articles ... in Festschriften.* Bruce M. Metzger.
        Philadelphia: Society of Biblical Literature, 1955.
Indexes 2,350 articles in 640 festschriften in various languages published before
1951. The entries are arranged in a detailed subject classification (see table of

contents) with an author index. The supplement includes those festschriften published in mid and late 1950. An important tool for access to otherwise little-known material.

AC12 *Annotated Bibliography of the Textual Criticism of the New Testament, 1914-1939.* Bruce M. Metzger. Copenhagen: Munksgaard, 1955.
Includes nearly 1,200 entries for books, dissertations, and articles from 236 periodicals and serials. Classified subject arrangement with good table of contents and author index. Brief descriptive annotations of some entries.

AC13 *A Periodical and Monographic Index to the Literature on the Gospels and Acts: Based on the Files of the École Biblique in Jerusalem.* Pittsburgh: Clifford E. Barbour Library, Pittsburgh Theological Seminary, 1971.
A typewritten listing of the part of the shelflist of the École Biblique library covering the Gospels and Acts. Lists books and the articles from about 80 periodicals. Arranged by biblical passage: book by book, chapter by chapter, etc. No indexes.

AC14 *New Testament Christology: A Critical Assessment and Annotated Bibliography.* Arland J. Huttgren. New York: Greenwood, 1988.
Over 1,900 annotated entries of books and articles, arranged in 49 chapters, including Christological titles, Christology of the New Testament, and Christological themes. An introductory essay describes "Literature and Trends in the Study of N.T. Christology." Author, title, and subject indexes.

AC15 *Index to Periodical Literature on Christ and the Gospels.* Bruce M. Metzger. Leiden: Brill, 1966.
Indexes 10,090 items from 160 journals, covering from the beginning of each journal through 1961. Arranged by detailed subject classification (see the table of contents), with an author index. Pages 112-162 and 208-370 form major parts that cover interpretation of passages in the Gospels. Indispensable for retrospective literature searching in this subject area.

AC16 *The Synoptic Problem: a Bibliography, 1716-1988.* Thomas R.W. Longstaff and Page A. Thomas. Macon, GA: Mercer University Press, 1988.
Includes over 1,700 books, reviews, articles, dissertations, and unpublished material related to the synoptic problem and the general relationships among the synoptic gospels. Three sections: author/title listing, a date-of-publication index, and a key word index. Provides partial library holdings and in some instances lists reviews of some books.

AC17 *The Parables of Jesus: a History of Interpretation and Bibliography.*
     Warren S. Kissinger. Metuchen, NJ: Scarecrow, 1979.
Includes 230 pages on the history of interpretation and 184 pages of a classified
bibliography. Includes name and subject indexes. Well done, and very helpful
when studying this topic.

AC18 *The Sermon on the Mount: a History of Interpretation and Bibliography.*
     Warren S. Kissinger. Metuchen, NJ: Scarecrow, 1975.
Similar in format to the above, with 126 pages on the history of interpretation and
148 pages of bibliography. Name/subject and biblical reference indexes. Very
well done and very helpful.

AC19 *The Gospel of Luke: A Cumulative Bibliography, 1973-1988.* Frans Van
     Segbroeck. Leuven: Leuven University Press/Peeters, 1989.
An alphabetically arranged list of 2,759 works on the gospel of Luke. Includes
books, journal articles, festschriften, etc. Includes only works published, reprinted,
or translated from 1973-1988. Subject and Scripture indexes.

AC20 *St. John's Gospel, 1920-1965.*   Edward Malatesta.   Rome: Pontifical
     Biblical Institute, 1967.
"A Cumulative and Classified Bibliography of Books and Periodical Literature on
the Fourth Gospel." Has over 3100 entries for books, periodical articles, and parts
of books about the fourth gospel. Arranged by a detailed subject classification.
Includes cross-references, author index, and author of book reviews index.
Includes all relevant entries in the *Elenchus Bibliographicus Biblicus* (AA7),
1920-1966, and some additional material as well. Thorough for the period
covered.

AC21 *Johannine Bibliography 1966-1985: A Cumulative Bibliography on the
     Fourth Gospel.* Gilbert Van Belle. Leuven: University Press / Peeters,
     1988.
Continuation of the above work, including 6,300 books, periodical articles, and
parts of books. Arranged under eight headings with cross references.

AC22 *A Classified Bibliography of Literature on the Acts of the Apostles.* A.J.
     Mattill and Mary B. Mattill. Leiden: Brill, 1966.
Extensive coverage of periodical articles and books up through 1961. Arranged by
subject with author index. Includes 6,646 items, indexing over 200 journals as
well as festschriften articles and monographs. Has an extensive chapter-by-chapter
and verse-by-verse section.

AC23 *A Bibliography of the Periodical Literature on the Acts of the Apostles,
      1962-1984.* Watson E. Mills. Leiden: Brill, 1986.
A supplement to the Mattill bibliography (above), listing nearly 1,000 entries for
the years described. Covers only journals articles. Arranged by author.

AC24 *Index to Periodical Literature on the Apostle Paul.* Bruce M. Metzger.
      Grand Rapids: Eerdmans, 1960.
Indexes 2,987 articles from 135 periodicals in 14 languages. Covers from the
beginning of each journal through 1957. Arranged by a detailed classified subject
scheme.   A   major   section   lists   exegetical   articles   book-by-book,
chapter-by-chapter, and verse-by-verse.

AC25 *Paul and His Interpreters.* Gerald R. Borchet. Madison, WI: InterVarsity,
      1985.
A list, with brief annotations, of about 1,000 English-language works on Paul and
Pauline theology, including commentaries on the Pauline epistles.   Subject
arrangement with author index.

** RELATED AREAS

AC26 *Targum and New Testament: a Bibliography, Together with a New
      Testament Index.* Peter Nickels. Rome: Pontifical Biblical Institute, 1967.
Part I, arranged by author, lists books and periodical articles on this topic. Part II
indexes the books and articles by the N.T. passage(s) treated. Each citation in part
II has a brief note explaining the article's relevance for the passage.

AC27 *Targumic Traditions and the New Testament.* J. Terence Forestell. (SBL
      Aramaic Studies, 4) Chico, CA: Scholars Press, 1979.
"An Annotated Bibliography with a New Testament Index."   Intended to
supplement and extend Nickels' work (AC26). The bibliography lists 362 items
in two sections: 1930-1955 and 1956- ; subarranged by author. The "N.T. Index"
gives access to the bibliography by the N.T. texts whose interpretation has been
affected by the item discussed. Also includes a brief subject index and an
appendix listing recent editions and translations of the targums.

AC28 *The Intertestamental Period.* Stephen F. Noll. Madison, WI: InterVarsity,
      1985.
A short overview of the intertestamental period, and a basic bibliography of about
500 (mostly English-language) works on the history, language, literature, and
theology of the era. Author index.

AC29 *Bibliographie zur jüdisch-hellenistischen und intertestamentarischen Literatur, 1900-1970.* G. Delling. 2., überarb. und bis 1970 fortgef. Aufl. Berlin: Akademie-Verlag, 1975.

A revision and expansion of the 1st ed. (1969). A bibliography of over 2,500 items in classified subject order. Covers Apocrypha, Pseudepigrapha, Philo, Josephus, etc. Excludes Dead Sea Scrolls and Rabbinics. A large section lists items by apocryphal or pseudepigraphic text treated. Author index.

AC30 *The Pseudepigrapha and Modern Research, with a Supplement.* James H. Charlesworth. Chico: Scholars Press, 1981.

A bibliographical report on the current state of study of the pseudepigrapha. Excludes pre-1960 materials, material on Qumran, and material on the N.T. apocrypha (see preface). A 1,618-item list covers 1960-1976 and a 750-item supplement brings it up to 1979. Arranged topically -- each section includes a critical and descriptive bibliographical essay followed by a bibliography. Author index.

AC31 *The New Testament Apocrypha and Pseudepigrapha: a Guide to Publications, with Excurses on Apocalypses.* James H. Charlesworth with James R. Mueller.   Metuchen, NJ: American Theological Library Association, 1987.

A companion to the above, listing 5,000 citations to primary and secondary literature on NT apocrypha and pseudepigrapha. Arranged in 5 broad sections: general studies, apocalyptic literature, apocryphal acts, canon, and fragments of unknown works.   Then lists citations under 99 major writings or cycles of writings, with brief annotations. Author index.

AC32 *Nag Hammadi Bibliography, 1948-1969.* David M. Scholer. Leiden: Brill, 1971.

Includes all types of published materials, listing 2,425 items; intends to be exhaustive.   This bibliography is continued by the annual Nag Hammadi bibliography in *Novum Testamentum.* Under each book included, reviews of that book are noted.   Classified subject arrangement.   Particularly valuable is the extensive listing of the published texts of each tractate in the Nag Hammadi corpus and the publications about each tractate. Author index.

AC33 *Bibliographie zu Flavius Josephus.* Heinz Schreckenberg. Leiden: Brill, 1968.

Lists materials by and about Josephus published between 1470 and 1968. Entries are arranged by year of publication.   Beside each entry, one or more "subject code" numbers are given, see p. xvii for their meanings.   Includes author, Josephus'-works-references, and Greek-word indexes.   Fairly complete, but difficult to use for material on specific subjects -- you must scan the pages looking for the correct "subject code."

AC34 *Bibliographie zu Flavius Josephus: Supplementband mit Gesamtregister.*
         Heinz Schreckenberg. Leiden: Brill, 1979.
Updates and supplements the above for 1967 to early 1979. The major portion lists materials in a single alphabet, arranged by author. As in the above work, "subject codes" are indicated. Part II of this work indexes the editions and translations of Josephus' works listed in both volumes, citing the editor and the page number where the full bibliographical entry is found. Includes an alphabetical author index for both volumes.

AC35 *Josephus and Modern Scholarship, 1937-1980.* Louis H. Feldman. Berlin:
         de Gruyter, 1984.
A comprehensive and critical bibliography for the years described. 4,000 entries are arranged in 429 sections within 29 broad chapters. In each section, a bibliography is followed by an essay with well-written critical notes. Its annotations and subject arrangement make it more useful than Schreckenberg (AC33 - AC34). Includes detailed table of contents and three indexes: references, words, and modern scholars.

** GENERAL COVERAGE -- MULTI-VOLUME

AD1   *International Standard Bible Encyclopedia.* Geoffrey Bromiley, ed. Full
      rev. ed. 4 vols. Grand Rapids: Eerdmans, 1979-1988.
A "new, or at least a completely reconstructed," edition of the earlier "ISBE"
(1930). Articles represent an attitude "of a reasonable conservatism," and the
evangelical scholars who have contributed represent a variety of denominations
and countries. Its purpose is "to define, identify, and explain terms and topics that
are of interest for those studying the Bible." A mixture of short unsigned articles
and longer signed articles with selected bibliographies is used.

AD2   *Interpreter's Dictionary of the Bible.* 4 vols. New York: Abingdon, 1962.
      "An Illustrated Encyclopedia Identifying and Explaining all Proper Names
and Significant Terms and Subjects in the Holy Scripture, including the
Apocrypha; with Attention to Archaeological Discussions and Researches into the
Life and Faith of Ancient Times" (Subtitle). Generally considered the best Bible
encyclopedia available today. 250 scholars contributed the articles (most are
signed), which have selective bibliographies and numerous illustrations. Moderate
to extreme liberal viewpoint in most articles. A basic place to begin research on
a biblical topic.

AD3   *Interpreter's Dictionary of the Bible: Supplementary Volume.* Nashville:
      Abingdon, 1976.
Updates the articles in the original volumes and adds new articles on important
topics. Includes cross-references to articles in the main volumes.

AD4   *The Illustrated Bible Dictionary.* 3 vols. Wheaton, IL: Tyndale House,
      1980.
A revised and newly illustrated edition of the *New Bible Dictionary* (1962). Has
over 2,000 entries by 165 leading biblical scholars with about 1,600 carefully
chosen illustrations and selective bibliographies. Excellent layout and typography,
with a comprehensive system of marginal references and cross-references. Vol.
3 includes a 6,000-entry index.

AD5   *Baker Encyclopedia of the Bible.* Walter A. Elwell, gen. ed. 2 vols.
      Grand Rapids: Baker, 1988.
5,700 mostly signed articles by 200 international evangelical scholars. Offers
mini-commentaries on each biblical book, articles on theological topics, life and

times of the biblical world, biographies of biblical figures, and geographical and archeological information. Black and white illustrations, some bibiographies and cross-references. Represents the latest in evangelical scholarship.

AD6   *Zondervan Pictorial Encyclopedia of the Bible.* Merrill C. Tenney, ed. 5 vols. Grand Rapids: Zondervan, 1975.
Written by evangelicals, but other viewpoints are generally represented. Has received mixed reviews -- the quality of some articles is questionable. One place to come for an evangelical viewpoint on biblical topics. Brief bibliographies are included with most articles. The 7,500 signed articles cover all places, objects, persons, customs, events, and teachings of the Bible. Well illustrated.

AD7   *Dictionnaire de la Bible.* Fulcran Grégoire Vigouroux, ed. 5 vols. in 10. Paris: Letouzey, 1907-1912.
AD8   *Dictionnaire de la Bible: Supplément.* L. Pirot, ed. Paris: Letouzey, 1928-

"Contenant tous les noms de personnes, de lieux, de plantes, d'animaux mentionnés dans les Saintes Écritures, les questions théologiques, archéologiques, scientifiques, critiques relatives a l'Ancien et au Nouveau Testament et des notices sur les commentateurs anciens et modernes." Eleven volumes in supplement thus far. The most extensive Bible encyclopedia, covering all topics named in the subtitle. Includes long signed articles by French Catholic scholars. Bibliographies and illustrations accompany each article. Note that this work includes biographical material about Bible commentators -- ancient and modern, regardless of religion. The supplement, not yet complete, stresses theological questions.

AD9   *Dictionary of the Bible: Dealing with its Language, Literature, and Contents, Including the Biblical Theology.* Ed. by James Hasting. 4 vols. and Supplement. New York: Scribners, 1898-1904.
An older standard work with long signed articles and bibliographies. More moderate viewpoint than Cheyne (AD10). Still valuable for its scholarly articles and representation of early 20th century biblical scholarship. The supplementary 5th volume includes 37 additional articles, maps, and indexes of: authors and their articles; subjects; Scripture texts; Greek and Hebrew terms; illustrations, and the maps.

AD10   *Encyclopaedia Biblica.* Ed. by T. K. Cheyne and J. S. Black. 4 vols. New York: Macmillan, 1899-1903.
"A Critical Dictionary of Literary, Political, and Religious History, the Archaeology, Geography, and Natural History of the Bible." Intended for the scholar and advanced student, its standpoint is that of the "advanced higher criticism" of the late l9th century. It is dedicated to W. Robertson Smith. Long signed articles with bibliographies by specialists.

** GENERAL COVERAGE--ONE VOLUME

Used primarily for quick reference to find answers to specific questions.   Thus, only English-language and relatively current titles are listed here.

AD11 *Harper's Bible Dictionary.* Paul J. Achtemeier, gen. ed.   San Francisco: Harper & Row, 1985.
A totally revised edition with all new articles, illustrations, and maps.   Produced in cooperation with the Society of Biblical Literature with 179 scholars from seven countries contributing articles on biblical archaeology, geography, chronology, etc.   3,700 entries, with photographs, maps, drawings, charts, and a pronounciation guide.   Longer articles have bibliographies.

AD12 *The Eerdmans Bible Dictionary.*   Allen C. Myers, ed.   Grand Rapids: Eerdmans, 1987.
An expanded and updated translation of *Bijbelse Encyclopedie* (1975).   Contains over 5,000 unsigned articles on biblical books, persons, places, etc.   Some longer articles have bibliographies.

AD13 *The New International Dictionary of the Bible.*   J. D. Douglas, revision editor, Merrill C. Tenney, general editor.   Pictorial ed.   Grand Rapids: Zondervan, 1987.
Revision of the *Zondervan Pictorial Bible Dictionary* (1963).   A good, single-volume Bible encyclopedia with 5,400 entries, 1,000 illustrations, and 167 maps. Written by 65 conservative evangelical scholars.   Includes index to maps.

AD14 *New Westminster Dictionary of the Bible.*   Henry S. Gehman, ed. Philadelphia: Westminster Press, 1970.
A thorough reworking and updating of the 1st ed. (1944).   Useful for pastors, students, and laymen; Protestant viewpoint.   Includes about 4,000 brief entries, indicates pronunciations where necessary, but has no bibliographies.

AD15 *Dictionary of the Bible.*   James Hastings. rev. ed.   Rev. by F. C. Grant and H. H. Rowley.   New York: Scribner, 1963.
A total revision of the 1st ed. done by Hastings in 1909.   Includes contributions by 150 American and British biblical scholars.   Protestant viewpoint, based on the Revised Standard Version.   Has short signed articles without bibliographies.

AD16 *Catholic Biblical Encyclopedia.*   John E. Steinmueller and Kathryn Sullivan, comps.   2 vols. in 1.   New York: Wagner, 1956.
The first Catholic Bible encyclopedia in English.   Intended for the educated layman.   Includes material on geographical, biographical, archeological, and

dogmatic subjects. Represents the more traditional, pre-Vatican II Catholic scholarship.

AD17 *Encyclopedic Dictionary of the Bible.* Louis F. Hartman, trans. New
York: McGraw-Hill, 1963.
"A Translation and Adaptation of A. van den Born's *Bijbels woordenboek* (2nd rev. ed., 1954-1957)." A "free adaption" of the Dutch original. Represents modern Catholic scholarship. Signed articles, with short bibliographies. The bibliographies have been updated and expanded, with English titles substituted wherever possible.

** ARCHEOLOGY

See also the topic "Atlases" in chapter 25.

AD18 *Archaeological Encyclopedia of the Holy Land.* Edited by Avraham
Negev. Rev. ed. Nashville: Thomas Nelson, 1986.
Brief articles on "the majority of the geographical names mentioned in the Bible, both places in the Holy Land and countries and cities in other parts of the Middle East, identifying them as far as possible, describing the excavations that have been carried out at or near them, and analysing the importance of the finds they have yielded." Written by 32 archeologists. No bibliographies. Gives references to the Bible, Josephus, and other early writers.

AD19 *New International Dictionary of Biblical Archaeology.* E. M. Blaiklock
and R. K. Harrison, gen. eds. Grand Rapids: Zondervan, 1983.
About 800 signed articles by 20 scholars on a wide range of topics related to Biblical archeology, including archaeological sites and ancient customs. Some articles have bibliographies. Illustrations, color plates and maps (with a map index) are added features that make this a valuable tool for layman and specialist.

AD20 *Encyclopedia of Archaeological Excavations in the Holy Land.* English ed.
4 vols. Englewood Cliffs, NJ: Prentice-Hall, 1975-1978.
Intended as a "summary of excavation work in Israel," this edition covers work done through 1971. Includes, under the name commonly used in scholarly circles, articles on nearly 200 sites, each describing the history, excavations, and discoveries at that location. Vol. 4 has indexes of names and of places for the entire work.

** NEW TESTAMENT

AD21 *Dictionary of Christ and the Gospels.* Ed. by James Hastings. 2 vols. New York: Scribner's, 1906-1908.
A complement to his *Dictionary of the Bible* (AD15), this work is intended to cover everything relating to Christ and the Gospels in the Bible and in world literature. Includes long signed articles with good bibliographies. Indexed by subject and by Greek terms. Dated but still useful.

AD22 *Dictionary of the Apostolic Church.* Ed. by James Hastings. 2 vols. New York: Scribner's, 1916.
Designed to complement the above work. Covers the history of the early church from Christ's ascension to the end of the first century. Long signed articles with bibliographies. Includes indexes. Dated but still useful.

Note: The above two works were reprinted in 1973 by Baker Book House as a 4-volume set under the title: *Dictionary of the New Testament.*

AD23 *Dictionary of the New Testament.* Xavier Leon-Dufour. New York: Harper, 1980.
Translation of *Dictionnaire du Nouveau Testament.* A compact, scholarly dictionary of about 1,000 N.T. terms needing historical, theological, literary, and/or archeological explanation, as well as important terms in N.T. study today. Provides, with each entry, a listing of relevant biblical references. Has an excellent system of cross-references to other relevant articles in the dictionary, and an index of Greek words cited in the dictionary.

** SPECIAL TOPICS

AD24 *A Dictionary of Biblical Interpretation.* R. J. Coggins and J. L. Houlden, eds. Philadelphia: Trinity Press International, 1990.
350 signed articles, with bibliographies, from 150 contributors, intended to introduce issues of biblical interpretation to general readers. Explains topics used in contemporary scholarship, including influential figures, schools of interpretation, Biblical books and figures, and major terms. A useful tool, although the selection of topics and quality of the entries are uneven. Includes subject and Scripture indexes.

AD25 *Harper's Encyclopedia of Bible Life.* Madeleine S. Miller and J. Lane Miller. 3rd rev. ed. Rev. by Boyce M. Bennett and David H. Scott. New York: Harper & Row, 1978.
Classified subject arrangement covering the world of the Bible; how the people of the Bible lived; and how the people of the Bible worked. The appendix

includes a selected bibliography, scriptural reference index, and name and subject index. Has illustrations and maps.

AD26 *Encyclopedia of Biblical Prophecy: The Complete Guide to Scriptural Predictions and Their Fulfillment.* J. Barton Payne. New York: Harper & Row, 1973.

Includes a long introduction followed by a listing of scriptural predictions (in canonical order) with accompanying summaries and comments on their meaning and fulfillments. Has five indexes and an 8-page bibliography. Evangelical Christian viewpoint.

** OLD AND NEW TESTAMENTS

AE1   *A Companion to the Bible.* Jean Jacques von Allmen, ed. New York:
      Oxford University Press, 1958.
A translation of *Vocabulaire biblique* (Delachaux & Niestlé, 2nd ed., 1956). Well-
known in Europe, written by French and Swiss Protestant scholars. Popular level
but helpful. A dictionary of 350 important biblical words, with the emphasis on
their theology rather than linguistic backgrounds.

AE2   *Sacramentum Verbi: an Encyclopedia of Biblical Theology.* Johannes B.
      Bauer, ed. 3 vols. New York: Herder & Herder, 1970.
Translation of the *Bibeltheologisches Wörterbuch* (3rd ed., 1977). Reprinted in
1981 in 1 vol. by Crossroad (New York) under the title *Encyclopedia of Biblical
Theology.* Includes long signed articles with bibliographies by 53 European
Catholic biblical scholars. Termed "an outstanding example of the renewal in
Catholic biblical scholarship." Vol. 3 includes a supplementary bibliography, an
analytic index of the articles, a biblical reference index, and a Greek and Hebrew
word index.

AE3   *Dictionary of Biblical Theology.* Xavier Leon-Dufour, ed. 2nd rev. and
      enl. ed. Trans. by P. J. Cahill. New York: Seabury, 1973.
Translation of *Vocabulaire de theologie biblique* (2nd ed., Paris: Ed. du Cerf,
1968). Intended primarily for Roman Catholic laity and clergy, it is "theological
and pastoral in approach." Arranged by broad topics, with extensive discussion
and bibliographical references. Many cross-references, analytical table of contents.

AE4   *A Theological Word Book of the Bible.* Alan Richardson, ed. New York:
      Macmillan, 1951.
Includes biblical words of "theological" interest, and aims "to elucidate the
distinctive meanings of the keywords of the Bible." Words are listed in the
English form found in the 1885 English Revised Version, with the Greek or
Hebrew words given in transliteration at the top of each article. The clear, short,
and well-organized articles are by 31 primarily British and Protestant scholars.
Many short bibliographies are included. Useful, especially to the "English-only"
user, for its summaries of the theological import of biblical words.

** OLD TESTAMENT

AE5   *Theological Dictionary of the Old Testament.* G. Johannes Botterweck and
        Helmer Ringgren, eds. Grand Rapids: Eerdmans, 1974- .

Known as "TDOT" or the "OT Kittel." Six volumes (--Yatar I) of a projected
12-volume set published thus far. A translation of *Theologisches Wörterbuch zum
Alten Testament*, vols. 1 and 2 were issued in two editions due to translation
problems: 1st ed., 1974-75; rev. ed. 1977. Includes extensive, well-documented
article on "theologically significant" Old Testament words, including information
drawn from other Near Eastern languages.

AE6   *Theologisches Handwörterbuch zum Alten Testament.* Ernst Jenni. Unter
        Mitarbeit von Claus Westermann. 2 vols. Munchen: Kaiser, 1971-1975.

Known as "THAT." A more compact and briefer wordbook than TDOT. Shorter,
more "cryptic" entries, with numerous bibliographical and biblical references.
Signed articles by O.T. scholars. Indexed by Hebrew words, by German words,
and by the authors cited. A useful complement to TDOT.

AE7   *Theological Wordbook of the Old Testament.* Edited by R. Laird Harris,
        Gleason L. Archer, and Bruce K. Waltke. 2 vols. Chicago: Moody Press,
        1980.

Has over 1,400 articles by 43 scholars that discuss every Hebrew word of
theological significance in the O.T. Also provides the definitions of all other
words. Articles stress theological, not linguistic, understanding and include
bibliographies. For the English-only user, a cross-index from the "Hebrew word
number" in *Strong's Concordance* (AF1) to entries in this wordbook is appended.

AE8   *Nelson's Expository Dictionary of the Old Testament.* Merrill F. Unger
        and William White. Nashville: Nelson, 1980.

Explains the root, use, and theological importance of 500 significant O.T. words,
arranged by their English-language equivalents. Includes cross-index from
alternative English words and phrases. Should be very helpful, especially for
those who know little or no Hebrew.

** NEW TESTAMENT

AE9   *Theological Dictionary of the New Testament.* Edited by G. Kittel and G.
        Friedrich. 10 vols. Grand Rapids: Eerdmans, 1964-76.

Known as "Kittel" or "TDNT." Translation of the *Theologisches Wörterbuch zum
Neuen Testament*, which began publication in 1932. Contributors are almost all
German biblical scholars. Older articles are somewhat dated, and the English
edition does not update the German bibliography. The long, scholarly, and
well-documented articles analyze the background and usage of many N.T. words.

Indispensable for N.T. research. Vol. 10, the Index, includes indexes for English key words, Greek words, Hebrew and Aramaic words, biblical references, and for contributors. The index also has brief biographical information on the contributors and a short "Pre-History of the TDNT." Note: The 10th volume of the German edition is different and includes different indexes and additional bibliographical information.

AE10 *Theological Dictionary of the New Testament.* G. Kittel and G. Friedrich. eds.; abridged and trans. by Geoffrey Bromiley. Grand Rapids: Eerdmans, 1985.

A one-volume abridgement of the above. All of the original entries are included, but details and documentation (footnotes and bibliography) are omitted. For each entry there is a cross-reference to its treatment in the larger work. An affordable alternative to the ten-volume set.

AE11 *The New International Dictionary of New Testament Theology.* Edited by Colin Brown. 3 vols. Grand Rapids: Zondervan, 1975-78.

Translated, with additions and revisions from the German *Theologisches Begriffslexikon zum Neuen Testament.* More concise, up-to-date, and conservative than the TDNT but not as extensive. Articles are arranged under English key words; vols. 1 and 2 have their own indexes of Hebrew and Aramaic words; Greek words; and English words. Vol. 3 has cumulative indexes for all three volumes. The large bibliographies have been updated and enlarged from those of the German edition. A necessary complement to the TDNT.

AE12 *Scripture Index to the New International Dictionary of New Testament Theology.* David Townsley and Russell Bjork. Grand Rapids: Zondervan, 1983.

Intended to be "as inclusive as possible", this work indexes both primary and secondary citations of Scripture passages from NIDNTT (above). Also contains an "Index to Selected Extrabiblical Literature," including O.T. Apocrypha and Pseudepigrapha, Dead Sea Scrolls, Jewish Hellenistic writings, early Christian literature, and Rabbinic writings.

AE13 *Christian Words.* Nigel Turner. Edinburgh: T & T Clark, 1980.

"This book . . . is but a sample of the speciality of Biblical and Christian language. By 'Christian words' I have in mind Greek terms which so far as I know the first believers devised for themselves. . . . the improvised 'Biblical' words in both LXX and NT." Words are arranged by their English translation, with Greek words given immediately below the English. An index by Greek words is included. For each word, the secular Greek and biblical Greek meanings are given. Indicates the applicable biblical references and scholarly literature for each word.

CHAPTER 25
BIBLICAL STUDIES: OTHER TOOLS

** CONCORDANCES AND TOPICAL BIBLES

A few of the more widely used and important concordances and topical Bibles are listed below. Only concordances including both the Old Testament and the New Testament are listed. See the bibliographical guides listed in Chapter 20 for listings of concordances to the Old and New Testament and to their Greek and Hebrew texts. Also, some of the CD-ROM tools listed in chapter 19 function as biblical concordances.

Concordances arrange the words in the Bible alphabetically so that a user can find a particular verse by referring to one or more of the key words in it or can find where a given word occurs in a given translation.

Topical Bibles arrange small portions of the biblical text under specific topical headings so that the user can find the texts that relate to a given topic or theme even though the topic or theme itself may not be among the words used in the text.

AF1   *The Exhaustive Concordance of the Bible.* James Strong. New York: Abingdon, 1890.
Many editions and reprints have been published. The most complete English concordance of the King James Version, covering *all* words (occurrences of 47 of the most common, e.g. "the" and "and," are listed in an appendix). Totals about 400,000 entries. Under each English word, a single list of all its occurrences is given. Along side each occurrence, an entry number indicates the Greek or Hebrew word being translated. The entry numbers refer to the numbered Hebrew and Chaldee dictionary and the biblical Greek dictionary at the back of the concordance.

AF2   *Analytical Concordance to the Bible.* Robert Young. New York: Funk & Wagnalls, 1881.
Many editions and reprints have been published. Later editions include a variety of supplementary articles about the Bible. Includes 311,000 entries under the English words of the King James Version, subarranging the entries by the Greek and/or Hebrew word(s) being translated. Also includes a list of names of persons and places. At the back is an "index lexicon" which lists the Hebrew and Greek words of the original text, gives their meaning, and indicates the English word(s) used to translate each and the number of times it is used.

AF3   *Harper's Topical Concordance.* Charles R. Joy. Rev. & enl. ed. New York: Harper, 1962.
Lists over 30,000 verses under 2,800 topical headings. Not truly a concordance -- rather, it is a topical Bible for the person looking for biblical texts on a particular topic. A list of cross-references is appended to the main list.

AF4   *Nave's Topical Bible: a Digest of the Holy Scripture.* Orville Nave. New York: International Bible Agency, 1897.
Reprinted numerous times under various titles, this is the most widely known topical Bible. Lists more than 100,000 references to Scripture under 20,000 topics and subtopics. Each entry tries to briefly bring together all that the Bible contains on a particular topic.

AF5   *The Zondervan Topical Bible.* Edward Viening. Grand Rapids: Zondervan, 1969.
Although it does not say so, this work is based on *Nave's Topical Bible*, but is slightly revised and reorganized. Slightly preferable to Nave's.

** ATLASES

Only a few of the many available are listed below. See AD18 - AD20 for encyclopedias on biblical archeology.

AF6   *The Harper Atlas of the Bible.* Ed. by James B. Pritchard. New York: Harper & Row, 1987.
Covers historical eras -- OT, intertestamental, and NT -- with full color photographs, drawings, and 134 maps, accompanied by an extensive, readable text. Uses a new method of projecting maps, replacing a "flat projection with a more readable one" that depicts the curvature of the earth's surface. Includes extensive chronology, glossary, and a name-place index. A high quality, visually attractive, and up-to-date atlas.

AF7   *The Macmillan Bible Atlas.* Yohanan Aharoni and Michael Avi-Yonah. Rev. ed. New York: Macmillan, 1977.
One of the better Bible atlases, emphasizes the Holy Land. Contains over 250 maps arranged chronologically, covering from the Caananite period up to the 2nd Jewish revolt. Includes explanatory text, bibliographical references, and an index/gazetteer.

AF8   *Moody Atlas of Bible Lands.* Barry J. Beitzel. Chicago: Moody Press, 1985.
Arranged in three sections: physical geography, historical geography, and a survey on the history of biblical map-making. Three indexes (map citation index,

Scripture index, and index to extra-biblical literature) and a time line. Altogether includes 95 color maps. A good technical reference atlas, with a balanced conservative approach. No gazetteer.

AF9   *Zondervan NIV Atlas of the Bible.* Carl Rasmussen. Grand Rapids: Zondervan, 1989.
Designed for the non-specialist, a conservative commentary with good color photographs and high-quality maps. Divided into geographical and historical sections. Text discussion not well-coordinated with maps. Extensive gazetteer.

AF10   *Atlas of Israel: Cartography, Physical Geography, Human and Economic Geography, History.* Jerusalem: Survey of Israel, Minister of Labor; Amsterdam: Elsevier, 1970.
An extensive atlas of Israel useful for the study of the Bible. Includes maps covering geology, climate, botany, zoology, land use, history, etc. Covers both the current times and the past. Originally published in Hebrew in the early 1960s. Includes explanatory text and selective bibliographies.

** MISCELLANEOUS

AF11   *Handbook of Biblical Chronology.* Jack Finegan. Princeton, NJ: Princeton University Press, 1964.
"Principles of Time Reckoning in the Ancient World and Problems of Chronology in the Bible." Part 1 covers the calendars of Egypt, Babylon, Israel, etc., as well as early Christian chronologies. Part 2 is a discussion of some of the major problems of biblical chronology. Includes full footnoting and bibliographies. Indexed by Scripture references and by subject. Very helpful book.

AF12   *The Cambridge History of the Bible.* 3 vols. New York: Cambridge University Press, 1963-1970.
Editors: v. 1 -- P. R. Ackroyd and C. F. Evans; v. 2 -- G. W. H. Lampe; v. 3 -- S. L. Greenslade. Volumes were published in reverse order. Gives "accounts of the texts and versions of the Bible used in the West, of its multiplication in manuscript and print, and its circulation; of attitudes toward its authority and exegesis; and of its place in the life of the Western church." Has well-done bibliographies for each chapter, and each volume has bibliographical appendices. Good indexes and plates. Material is written by a wide range of scholars. A good source for a brief summary and further bibliography on these topics.

AF13   *A Cumulative Index to New Testament Greek Grammars.* Timothy Owings. Grand Rapids: Baker, 1983.
An index to the citations of biblical passages in eight N.T. Greek grammars: Blass, Debrunner and Funk; Brooks and Winbery; Dana and Mantey; Moule

(*Idiom Book*);   Moulton, Howard and Turner; Robertson; Robertson and Davis; and Zerwick.   Useful for exegetical study.

AF14   *A Student's Dictionary for Biblical and Theological Studies.*   F.B. Huey
        and Bruce Corley.   Grand Rapids: Academie Books, 1983.
A helpful list of about 1,400 terms related to O.T. and N.T. studies.   Brief and simple definitions with examples.   Cross references to related terms.   An excellent guide to technical vocabulary of Biblical studies for the beginning student.

AF15   *Who's Who in Biblical Studies and Archaeology.*   1st ed.   Washington,
        DC: Biblical Archaeology Society, 1986.
"A compilation of men and women of superior achievement and status who are devoting their professional lives to helping the world better understand the Bible" -- introdution.   Planned to be a biannual, the 1986-87 edition contains 1,500 entries.   Arranged alphabetically, with indexes by eight specializations and by geographic location.   Includes standard biographical data, such as education, family, publications, address, etc.

CHAPTER 26
CHURCH HISTORY: GENERAL COVERAGE

** GENERAL HISTORY -- BIBLIOGRAPHIES, GUIDES, INDEXES

BA1   *The Historian's Handbook: a Descriptive Guide to Reference Works.*
Helen J. Poulton. Norman, OK: Univ. of Oklahoma Press, 1972.
"Surveys a wide variety of the major reference works in all fields of history," as
well as relevant general and related-discipline tools. A good basic introduction
to the reference tools of historical study. No distinct church history section. Lists
about 1,000 items with running commentary, emphasis on American studies.
Includes a general index and an index of titles.

BA2   *Guide to Historical Literature.* American Historical Association. New
York: Macmillan, 1961.
A selective, briefly annotated bibliography of about 20,000 items, emphasizing
English-language materials. Items listed include important periodical articles.
Arranged by time period, then geographical area, then by subject. See esp. pp.
65-74, "Christianity," but also be certain to use the extensive subject index to
locate many other pertinent items. Includes author index. A valuable tool.

BA3   *International Bibliography of Historical Sciences.* Edited for the
International Committee of Historical Sciences, 1926- . Oxford: Oxford
University Press, 1930- . Annual.
Publisher varies. Vol. 15, to cover 1940-46, never published. An extensive,
useful, and important bibliography of historical publications, including periodical
articles. Classified arrangement by time period and geographical location.
Includes author/proper name index and geographical index.

** CHURCH HISTORY -- BIBLIOGRAPHIES, GUIDES, INDEXES

BA4   *The History of the Church: a Select Bibliography.* Owen Chadwick. 3rd
ed. London: Historical Association, 1973.
A valuable selective bibliography arranged by subject. Lists both reference works
and major works in the field, giving brief annotations for many of them. An
excellent beginning point for research, but lacks both subject and author indexes.
Stronger on the Reformation and the British churches, weak on American church
history.

BA5   *A Bibliographical Guide to the History of Christianity.* Shirley Jackson
        Case, ed. Chicago: University of Chicago, 1931.
An extensive and still useful, although somewhat dated, annotated bibliography.
Entries are arranged by broad geographical areas, then by time period or topical
subjects. Lists over 2,500 books and periodical articles. Somewhat difficult to
use due to its limited subject index and its lack of a table of contents.

BA6   *Bibliographical Introduction to Church History.* Karel Blockx. Leuven:
        Katholieke Universiteit, 1982.
An unannotated list arranged in six sections: encyclopedias and dictionaries,
handbooks, bibliographies, primary sources, atlases, and periodicals and series.
European emphasis. Includes a detailed table of contents and an author index, but
its lack of a subject or title index limits its usefulness.

BA7   "Bibliographie" in *Revue d'histoire ecclésiastique.* Louvain: Université
        catholique de Louvain, 1900- . 3x a year.
Now issued as a separately paged section of the journal. An extensive
bibliography, this is the major indexing work for church history. Indexes over
900 periodicals and also lists numerous books and other types of printed material.
Entries are arranged by a detailed subject scheme (see the table of contents which
appears at the end of the last issue for each year). Difficult to search
retrospectively since there are now over 240 separate issues of the bibliography
which are *not* cumulated in any way. Includes author index.

Note: There is no other periodical index devoted to church history in general.
You will need to use either one of the more specialized indexes listed below, one
of the general or humanities indexes (chapter 11), or one of the general
religious/theological indexes. For English-language materials, *Religion Index One*
(M8) and the *Catholic Periodical and Literature Index* (M11) are particularly
helpful.

See also the chapter, "Church History: Bibliographies", in G. E. Gorman and Lyn
Gorman, *Theological and Religious Reference Materials*, vol. 2 (A8).

** CHURCH HISTORY -- ENCYCLOPEDIAS

There is a fine line between what is a "theological" encyclopedia and what is a
"church history" encyclopedia. Listed here are some of those encyclopedias
oriented more obviously to church history. Remember though that the theological
encyclopedias (listed in Chapter 3) also include a great deal of church history
material.

BA8   *Oxford Dictionary of the Christian Church.*   F. L. Cross and E. A.
       Livingstone, eds. 2nd ed. New York: Oxford University Press, 1974.
First published in 1957, this is the standard one-volume reference work for church
history. Its broad coverage includes many biographies, as well as definitions of
ecclesiastical terms and customs. Includes about 6,000 entries, most with good
and often extensive bibliographies. Emphasis on Christianity in Western Europe,
especially Great Britain, stressing the Anglican and Catholic churches. Relatively
poor coverage of American Christianity.

BA9   *The New International Dictionary of the Christian Church.* J. D. Douglas,
       ed. Rev. ed. Grand Rapids: Zondervan, 1978.
Similar in scope to the Oxford work, but about two-thirds as long and with much
less extensive bibliographies. Offers better coverage of North American and
world Christianity.   Has over 4,800 brief signed articles which include
bibliographies, written by 150 contributors from the perspective of evangelical
Protestantism. 2nd ed. is not substantially different from the first.

BA10 *Westminster Dictionary of Church History.*   Jerald C. Brauer, ed.
       Philadelphia: Westminster, 1971.
Offers brief unsigned articles "concerning the major men, events, facts, and
movements in the history of Christianity." Emphasizes modern church history and
the American scene. Some articles have brief bibliographies.

BA11 *Corpus Dictionary of Western Churches.*   Thomas C. O'Brien, ed.
       Washington, DC: Corpus, 1970.
Primarily by Catholic scholars, but ecumenically oriented. The 2,300 concise
unsigned articles are "a convenient source of biographies, beliefs, practices, and
history of the churches of Western Christendom," stressing the North American
church.

BA12 *The Wycliffe Biographical Dictionary of the Church.* By Elgin Moyer,
       revised and enlarged by Earle E. Cairns. Chicago: Moody Press, 1982.
Previous edition (1968) titled *Who Was Who in Church History.* Offers brief
information on 2,000 individuals in church history, stressing evangelicals and
black leaders of the United States and Africa. Now includes a "Chronological
Index and Outline of Church History" which lists, with very brief biographical
information, the names of individuals from each time period that are in this
dictionary.   Some entries are inaccurate, but helpful for information on
lesser-known evangelicals and fundamentalists not listed elsewhere.

BA13 *Dictionnaire d'histoire et de géographie ecclésiastiques.* Paris: Letouzey, 1912-

21 vols. (--Gregoire) published thus far. Covers the history of the Roman Catholic Church from the beginning to the present and other churches as they affect the Roman Catholic Church. Has good signed articles with bibliographies. Especially good coverage of the Byzantine period, medieval theology, and Catholic biography and ecclesiastical data.

BA14 *Biographisch-Bibliographisches Kirchenlexikon.* Bearb. und hrsg. von Friedrich W. Bautz. Hamm (Westf.): Bautz, 1970- .

To be four volumes; vol. 1 (Aadlers--Faustus) now complete and some additional fascicles have been published. Intends to include biographies of "the major figures who were influential in any of the manifold aspects of the Christian churches." Each biography also includes a bibliography of materials by and about the individual. If completed as planned, this could be a significant tool.

** CHURCH HISTORY -- MAJOR WORKS

BA15 *History of the Church.* Hubert Jedin and J. Dolan, eds. Trans. from the 3rd rev. German ed. 10 vols. New York: Crossroad, 1980-1981.

Translation of the *Handbuch der Kirchengeschichte* (1962-1979). Vols. 1, 3, and 4 originally published by Herder and Herder (1965-1970) under the title, *Handbook of Church History.* Vols. 1-5 also published by Seabury in 1980. A long scholarly history of the church from a Catholic perspective. Each volume is indexed separately and includes bibliographies for each chapter.

BA16 *A History of Christianity.* Kenneth Scott Latourette. Rev. ed. 2 vols. New York: Harper & Row, 1975.

A successful attempt to summarize all of church history (totals over 1,500 pages in length) by a major church historian. Each chapter has selected bibliographies, and the detailed index includes over 6,000 entries. First published in 1954. The rev. ed. includes a "Supplementary Bibliography" (found just before the index) listing additional books published since 1950, and a chapter 62, "The World Christian Movement, 1950-1975." The supplementary bibliographies and the 62nd chapter are by Ralph Winter.

BA17 *History of the Christian Church.* Philip Schaff. 7 vols. in 8. New York: Scribner, 1882-1910.

An older, extensive, detailed, and documented history by a major church historian. While now dated, it still offers a wealth of information. Includes bibliographies and a name/subject index in each volume.

** CHURCH HISTORY--ATLASES

BA18 *Atlas zur Kirchengeschichte: die christlichen Kirchen in Geschichte und Gegenwart.* Hrsg. von Hubert Jedin, Kenneth Latourette, und Jochen Martin. Freiburg: Herder, 1970.

An excellent and detailed atlas, useful whether or not one reads German. Contains 257 colored maps and charts covering most aspects of church history, with 80 pages of documented text and commentary on those maps and charts. A very detailed (36 six-column pages) index/gazetteer gives good access to the maps and text. Finally, bibliographical references are given for each map and chart at the end of the commentary on the map or chart.

BA19 *The Macmillan Atlas History of Christianity.* Franklin H. Littel. New York: Macmillan, 1976.

Not as detailed or as extensive as the above work. Includes 197 maps with text. Emphasis on the intellectual, ethical, and moral development of Christianity in relation to times and places. Has name and subject index.

CHAPTER 27
ANCIENT CHURCH HISTORY AND PATRISTICS

** BIBLIOGRAPHICAL GUIDES / HANDBOOKS

BB1   *Patrology.* Berthold Altaner. 2nd ed. Trans. by Hilda C. Graef. New
       York: Herder and Herder, 1960.
A handbook briefly summarizing the lives, writings, and teachings of the church
fathers up to 636 (West) and 749 (East). Gives extensive bibliographies, with
descriptive commentary, of works by and about each person. Catholic orientation.
Patristic name and title index. The 8th German edition (*Patrologie*, 8. Aufl. von
Alfred Stuiber, Freiburg: Herder, 1978) has updated bibliographies.

BB2   *Patrology.* Johannes Quasten. 4 vols. Westminster, MD: Newman Press,
       1951-1988.
Similar to Altaner (above) but with more extensive treatment of each person.
Bibliographies are less cryptic, more extensive, and better arranged. Extensive
name and subject indexes in each volume. Four volumes have been published (v.
1 -- The Beginnings of Patristic Literature; v. 2 -- The Ante-Nicene Literature
after Ireneaus; v. 3 -- The Golden Age of Greek Patristric Literature; v. 4 -- The
Golden Age of Latin Patristic Literature). This work and (where Quasten is
incomplete) Altaner's are indispensable for patristic studies.

BB3   *Patrology: the Lives and Works of the Fathers of the Church.* Otto
       Bardenhewer. Trans. from the 2nd German ed. St. Louis: Herder, 1908.
Dated and intended primarily for Catholic seminarians, but still helpful. For each
person it gives a biographical sketch, a statement on his writings and theology,
and a bibliography of works by and about the individual. Includes index.

BB4   *Pre-Nicene Syrian Christianity: a Bibliographic Survey.* Robert L.
       Sample. Evanston, IL: Garrett-Evangelical Theological Seminary Library,
       1977.
A classified and selectively annotated bibliography of "modern scholarly works
on the various facets of Syrian Christianity." Covers up to the council of Nicea
in 325.

** BIBLIOGRAPHIES / INDEXES

BB5   *A Bibliography of Bibliographies on Patristics.* J. L. Stewardson.
       Evanston, IL: Garrett Theological Seminary Library, 1967.
"The purpose of this bibliography is to list and describe as completely as time and
resources permit the main bibliographical sources for the field of patristics." Lists

195 books and periodical articles, arranged in 14 major sections. Includes fairly lengthy annotations. Somewhat helpful, especially in explaining the usefulness of some of the more esoteric tools. No indexes.

BB6   *Bibliographia Patristica; Internationale patristische Bibliographie, v. 1- , 1956- .* Wilhelm Schneemelcher, ed. Berlin: de Gruyter, 1959- . Annual.

Published biannually as "v. 12/13, 1967/1968," etc. since 1967. Somewhat slow in appearing. An extensive bibliography of books, journal articles, etc. on patristics, covering up to A.D. 657 (West) and 787 (East). Entries are arranged by subject with a detailed table of contents and an author index. Includes a major section arranged by the names of the church fathers, a section on patristic biblical exegesis, and a listing of reviews of relevant books. No annotations.

BB7   *Bulletin de théologie ancienne et médiévale.* Louvain: Abbaye du Mont César, 1929- . Annual.

Frequency varies. A detailed and critical bibliography of materials on ancient and medieval theology, listing works in many languages. Includes name, doctrine, and manuscript indexes.

** ENCYCLOPEDIAS

BB8   *Encyclopedia of Early Christianity.* Everett Ferguson, ed. New York: Garland, 1990.

A comprehensive treatment of the development of Christianity from the life of Christ to 600 A.D. Nearly 1,000 signed entries from 135 contributors describe persons, places, doctrines, practices, art, liturgy, heresies, and schisms of the early church. Articles are non-technical and designed for general readers, and are accompanied by good bibliographies. Extensive index.

BB9   *Pauly's Real-Encyclopädie der classischen Altertumswissenschaft.* August Friedrich von Pauly. Stuttgart: Druckenmüller, 1893- .

Publisher varies. Known as "Pauly-Wissowa." A major authoritative German work covering classical history, antiquities, literature, biography, and all other aspects of the period. Now includes over 80 physical volumes. The overall arrangement and alphabetizing are complex, with a number of series and supplements. Includes signed articles with extensive bibliographies, written by specialists on each topic.

BB10   *Dictionnaire d'archéologie chrétienne et de liturgie.* Fernand Cabrol and Henri Leclercq. Publié sous la direction de Henri Marrou. 15 vols. in 30. Paris: Letouzey, 1907-1953.

An important scholarly work on all aspects of ancient Christianity down to the time of Charlemagne. Lengthy documented articles with major bibliographies appended.   Covers the architecture, art, ceremonies, customs, epigraphy, iconography, institutions, liturgy, numismatics, rites, symbols, etc., of the early church.

BB11 *Reallexikon für Antike und Christentum; Sachwörterbuch zur Auseinandersetzung des Christentums mit der antiken Welt.* Theodor Klauser, ed.   In Verbindung mit Franz J. Dölger & Hans Lietzmann. Stuttgart: Hiersemann, 1950- .
Up to Bd. 13 (--Heilgotter). A basic German work on Christianity and the ancient world, covering up to the 6th century A.D.   Includes long signed articles by specialists with selected bibliographies. Began publishing supplementary volumes in 1985.

BB12 *Dictionary of Christian Antiquities.* William Smith and Samuel Cheethan. 2 vols. Boston: Little, 1876-1880.
Intended to complement the *Dictionary of Christian Biography* (BB13 below), it excludes biography but treats subjects connected with the organization of the church (e.g. officers, architecture, music, discipline, sacred days). Covers down to the time of Charlemagne (ca. A.D. 800). Contains long, signed articles with bibliographies. Not up-to-date but still helpful.

BB13 *Dictionary of Christian Biography, Literature, Sects and Doctrines.* William Smith and Henry Wace, eds.   4 vols.   London: Murray, 1877-1887.
Covers down to the time of Charlemagne (ca. A.D. 800). Its object is "to supply an adequate account, based upon original authorities, of all persons connected with the history of the church within the period treated concerning whom anything is known, of the literature connected with them, and the controversies respecting doctrine or discipline in which they were engaged."   Includes long, valuable, signed articles with good bibliographies. While 100 years old, often the only or major source for information on minor figures in church history. Special attention is given to names and subjects in the church history of the British Isles.

BB14 *Dictionary of Christian Biography and Literature to the End of the Sixth Century, A.D., with an Account of the Principal Sects and Heresies.* Henry Wace and William Piercy. Boston: Little, 1911.
An abridgement of Smith and Wace (above) by cutting off two centuries and by omitting many insignificant names included in the original work. Does include more recent bibliographical entries.

** PATRISTIC WRITINGS -- BIBLIOGRAPHIES

BB15 *Clavis patrum latinorum: qua in novum corpus Christianorum edendum*
      optimas quasque scriptorum recensiones a Tertulliano ad Bedam. Eligius
      Dekkers. Ed. altera, aucta et emendata. Steenbrugis: In Abbatia Sancti
      Petri, 1961.

An extensive index to the published texts of the Latin church fathers -- whether
in books, sets, or periodicals. Arranged chronologically by the date of the person.
Includes indexes by personal names and works, by subject, and by first lines.

BB16 *Clavis patrum graecorum.* Mauritius Geerard, ed. 5 vols. Turnhout:
      Brepols, 1974-1987.

Subtitle: "Qua optimae quaeque scriptorum patrum graecorum recensiones a
primaeuis saeculis usque ad octavum commode recluduntur." Arranged
chronologically by when the Greek church father lived. Each entry includes a brief
bibliography of material about the person and then lists each of his works with
bibliographies of published texts. Notes in the margins indicate where the texts
can be found in Migne's *Patrologiae.* An appendix cross-indexes Migne volume
and page numbers to the entry numbers in this work. Also has alphabetical index
of persons included.

BB17 *The Literatures of the World in English Translation.* Vol. I: *The Greek*
      and Latin Literatures. George B. Parks and Ruth Z. Temple. New York:
      Ungar, 1968.

Valuable in patristics for its fairly complete (up to 1968) listings of translations of
the Greek and Latin writings of the church. See pp. 54-58, 138-145, and 243-268
which cover Christian literature. Also use the index to locate additional listings
for individual authors. Helpful for its author-by-author analysis of the contents
of translation sets which are not indexed elsewhere and/or analyzed in the card
catalog; as well as for its listings of individually published translations.

** PATRISTIC WRITINGS -- LEXICONS AND CONCORDANCES

BB18 *A Patristic Greek Lexicon.* G. W. H. Lampe. Oxford: Clarendon Press,
      1961.

"The object of this work is primarily to interpret the theological and ecclesiastical
vocabulary of the Greek Christian authors from Clement of Rome to Theodore of
Studium" (preface). Helpful for the study and reading of the Greek Fathers.
Excludes the common meanings of words given in Liddell-Scott-Jones, and usages
found in the LXX and N.T. biblical materials. Includes some bibliography and
cites numerous examples of use as well as analyzing meanings.

BB19 *Biblia Patristica: Index des citations et allusions Bibliques dans la littérature patristique.* 3 vol. Paris: Éditions du Centre national de la recherche scientifique, 1975-1980.

Vol. 1 covers up to Clement of Alexandria and Tertullian; vol. 2 covers the third century except for Origen; vol. 3 indexes Origen. Gives, in Bible passage order, the locations in the patristic writings where the Bible is used. Each location is identified by the patristic work's name and the book, chapter, paragraph, page, and line (as applicable). The exact edition of each patristic work indexed is listed in the introductory material. Based on an extensive new project to identify and index all such usages.

BB20 *Biblia Patristica: Supplement, Philo d'Alexandrie.* Paris: Éditions du Centre national de la recherche scientifique, 1982.

Supplement to the above, indexing the biblical citations from Philo of Alexandria.

BB21 *Clavis patrum apostolicorum: catalogum vocum in libris patrum qui dicuntur apostolici non raro occurrentium.* Henricus Kraft. München: Kösel, 1963.

Lists the Greek and Latin words that appear in the writings of the apostolic fathers; gives a brief (German or Latin) definition, and a list of where that word occurs. Thus serves as a limited lexicon and concordance to the very early patristic writings. Arranged in 2 sections: Greek words (about 470 pages) and Latin words (about 30 pages). Supersedes E. J. Goodspeed, *Index Patristicus sive Clavis Patrum Apostolicorum Operum* (Leipzig: Hinrichs', 1907).

BB22 *Voces: eine Bibliographie zu Wörtern und Begriffen aus der Patristik (1918-1978).* Hermann Josef Sieben. Berlin: de Gruyter, 1980.

Arranged in two sections: Greek words and Latin words. In each section words are listed alphabetically, and under each word are bibliographical citations to articles and/or books discussing patristic usage of that word. Indexed by the patristic authors referred to and by the modern authors cited.

** OTHER

BB23 *Atlas of the Early Christian World.* Frederik van der Meer and Christine Mohrmann. Trans. and ed. by Mary F. Hedlund and H.H. Rowley. London: Nelson, 1958.

Translation of the *Atlas van de oudchristelijke wereld* (Amsterdam, 1958). Covers down to the 7th century. Has 42 six-color maps with commentary. More extensive is the section with 620 plates and commentary on the sculpture, architecture, cities, mosaics, etc., of early Christianity. Includes a geographical index to the plates and maps, and an index to author and "things" mentioned in the text. Particularly helpful for locating early cities, etc., by their old names.

CHAPTER 28
MEDIEVAL CHURCH HISTORY

There are few specialized tools for the study of medieval church history. What is listed below is, for the most part, a highly selective list of some general tools for the study of medieval history. Those working extensively in this area will need to consult the bibliographical guides listed below for more information.

** BIBLIOGRAPHIES / INDEXES

BC1 *Medieval Studies: a Bibliographical Guide.* Everett U. Crosby et al. New York: Garland, 1983.
An annotated guide to the major primary and secondary works on medieval history and culture. About 9,00 entries are arranged in 138 sections. An author/editor index and a small topical index are included.

BC2 *Guide to the Sources of Medieval History.* R. C. van Caenegem. With the collaboration of F. L. Ganshof. Amsterdam: North Holland, 1978.
Revised and enlarged ed. of a guide earlier done in German (1964) and Dutch (1962). Five major sections: the sources of medieval history; archives and libraries (where source material can be found); great collections and repertories of sources; reference works; and bibliographical introduction to the auxiliary historical sciences. Each section explains its topic in some detail, listing and describing the many materials available for medieval studies. Good table of contents. Name and limited title index.

BC3 *A Guide to the Study of Medieval History.* Louis John Paetow. Rev. ed. New York: F.S. Crofts, 1931.
An older (but still useful), standard, scholarly guide for medieval studies. Classed arrangement, listing original source materials and secondary works in the field. Has annotated entries and each section has an explanatory introduction. Complete index of authors, editors, titles of large collections, and subjects. Critical and scholarly, but now dated.

BC4 *Literature of Medieval History 1930-1975: a Supplement to Louis John Paetow's "A Guide to the Study of Medieval History."* Gray Cowan Boyce. 5 vols. Millwood, NY: Kraus, 1981.
An extensive supplement to Paetow listing over 55,000 works on all aspects of medieval life and culture. Classified subject arrangement. Part 1 is a listing of reference works for the study of medieval history. Author and subject-name indexes.

BC5   *Serial Bibliographies for Medieval Studies.* Richard H. Rouse. Berkeley: Univ. of California Press, 1969.

Lists 283 serials (i.e. continuing publications) with bibliographies of help in medieval studies. Entries are arranged topically and include annotations. Has title and editor indexes.

BC6   *Dictionary Catalogue of the Library of the Pontifical Institute of Medieval Studies, Toronto, Canada.* 5 vols. Boston: G. K. Hall, 1972.

Includes nearly 90,000 author, title, and subject catalog cards of the library. A strong source of information on the medieval period.

BC7   *Dictionary Catalogue of the Library of the Pontifical Institute of Medieval Studies, Toronto, Canada. Supplement.* Boston: G. K. Hall, 1979- .

Updates the above work with new entries.

BC8   *Répertoire des sources historiques du moyen age.* Cyr Ulysse J. Chevalier. Nouv. éd. refondue, corr. et augm. 2 volumes in 4. Paris: Picard, 1894-1907.

An important bibliography indexing a large amount of the source material and secondary literature of medieval history. Two major parts: Bio-bibliographie -- which lists individuals from the period (by the French form of name) and gives brief biographical data and references to materials about them; and Topobibliographie -- which is a similar list for places and topics.

Note: See also the *Bulletin de théologie ancienne et médiévale* (BB7 above), which indexes material on medieval theology.

** MAJOR WORKS

BC9   *Cambridge Mediaeval History.* 8 vols. Cambridge, Eng.: University Press, 1911-36.

2nd ed., 1966- in progress. An extensive and authoritative work by specialists in the field. Covers from A.D. 324 up to the Renaissance.

BC10 *Dictionary of the Middle Ages.* 13 vols. Joseph R. Strayer, ed. in chief. New York: Scribner, 1982-1989.

5,000 articles written by 1,300 scholars. Intends to cover every aspect of medieval life in Western Europe, Islam, Byzantium, and the Slavic world from A.D. 500 to 1500. Includes illustrations, maps, and bibliographies (chiefly limited to English-language works). While the scholarship is routine but acceptable, this is the only multi-volume English-language work covering all aspects of the Middle Ages. Volume 13 is an index.

** SPECIAL TOPICS

BC11 *Medieval Heresies: a Bibliography, 1960-1979.* Carl T. Berkhout and Jeffrey B. Russell, eds. Toronto: Pontifical Institute of Mediaeval Studies, 1981.

Lists over 2,000 books and articles on the social, popular heresies of western Europe from 700 to 1500. Doctrinal heresies are covered if they produced a popular following. Classified arrangement with author, subject and manuscript indexes. Includes material on pre-Luther reform movements.

BC12 *Medieval Monasticism: a Select Bibliography.* Giles Constable. Toronto: University of Toronto Press, 1976.

Intended "to provide a guide to the secondary literature of Christian monasticism from its origins to the end of the Middle Ages." A valuable, selected, classified bibliography of about 1,000 items in French, German, English, Italian, Latin, and Spanish.

BC13 *The Crusade: Historiography and Bibliography.* Aziz S. Atiya. Bloomington, IN: Indiana University Press, 1962.

A classified bibliography of the source material and of the secondary material in periodicals and books. Includes non-English materials. Also has a chapter on the historiography of the Crusades.

CHAPTER 29
THE REFORMATION

** GENERAL -- BIBLIOGRAPHICAL GUIDES

BD1   *Reformation Europe: a Guide to Research.* Steven Ozment, ed. St. Louis:
Center for Reformation Research, 1982.
Includes 16 essays on different aspects of Reformation studies by major scholars.
Each essay summarizes the present state of research in that field, identifies the
keys issues which scholars are addressing, and identifies major resources for study
of that field. A selected bibliography follows each essay. Includes name index.

BD2   *Contemporary Research on the Sixteenth Century Reformation.* B.J. van
der Walt.   Potchefstroom, South Africa: Potchefstroomse Univ. for
Christian Higher Education, 1979.
A brief survey of current-day research activity, country-by-country. Includes
numerous bibliographical entries.

BD3   "A Bibliographical Guide to the Study of the Reformation. Part 1:
Beginnings." A. Skevington Wood. *Themelios* 2 (Jan. 1977): 52-57.
"... Part 2: Development." A. Skevington Wood. *Themelios* 3 (Jan. 1978):
24-27.
A good basic bibliographical survey of the literature on the Reformation. Suggests
a few of the better English-language works in each area. Needs to be
supplemented, but a good starting point.

BD4   *Bibliography of the Continental Reformation: Materials Available in
English.* Roland H. Bainton and Eric W. Gritsch. 2nd rev. & enl. ed.
Hamden, CT: Archon, 1972.
1st ed. (1935) much less extensive.   Provides good coverage with a topical
arrangement. No indexes, but has a detailed table of contents. Most entries have
brief annotations. Includes many periodical articles, and has a large section on the
individual reformers.   Intended to supplement Read (BD16 below) and
Schottenloher (BD13 below).

** GENERAL -- BIBLIOGRAPHIES / INDEXES

BD5   *Bibliographie de la Reförme, 1450-1648.* International Committee of
Historical Sciences; Commission internationale d'histoire ecclésiastique
comparée. Leiden: Brill, 1958- .
Lists books, dissertations, and articles published between 1940 and 1955 (1960 for
fascicles 6 and 7). Subdivided into fascicles by the country where the material

was published. Each fascicle includes indexes of authors, subjects, etc., but no overall index exists. Fascicle 8, published in 1982, lists additional materials published in 1956-1975 (Belgium and Luxembourg) or 1956-1976 (Netherlands). The Netherlands portion (1,526 items) continues the policy of listing materials about the Reformation *published* in that country -- regardless of the specific topic addressed. However, the Belgium and Luxembourg portion (1,527 items) lists only materials *about* the Reformation *in those countries* -- regardless of where the material was published. Supplement coverage of parts of fasc. 1 and fasc. 2. Still arranged by author with subject index.

BD6   *Microform Holdings from All Periods: a General Finding List.* 8 vols. St. Louis: Center for Reformation Research, 1977-1979.

The Center, which has major holdings on microform of some 10,000 printed works from the Reformation period, will lend microform copies of its holdings to researchers. This work lists all those printed works held except for the Newberry French political pamphlets (indexed elsewhere) and works listed in earlier numbers (2, 3, 6, and 7) of the series *Sixteenth Century Bibliography* (see BD7 below). Entries are arranged by author, subarranged by title and then by publication date. A valuable bibliographic tool for Reformation research, particularly since copies of works listed here can generally be borrowed from the Center.

BD7   *Sixteenth Century Bibliography*, v. 1- . St. Louis: Center for Reformation Research, 1975- .

A series of small separately published bibliographies covering many topics of Reformation studies. All are well done, many are annotated. For a listing of those available, consult the card catalog in your library. Several of these are listed individually below.

BD8   *Archiv für Reformationsgeschichte: Beiheft, Literaturbericht; Archive for Reformation History: Supplement, Literature Review.* Gutersloher: Mohn, 1972- . Annual.

Provides, since 1972, fairly comprehensive coverage of literature on the Reformation, covering 1450-1650 in Eastern Europe, Western Europe, and the British Isles. Detailed subject arrangement (see table of contents) but no indexes. A volume of cumulative indexes of authors, names, and places for vols. 1-5 was published in 1978. The editorial apparatus is in German, the critical and descriptive annotations are in German, English, or French.

BD9   *Bibliographie internationale de l'Humanisme et de la Renaissance, 1965- .* Geneva: Droz, 1966- . Annual.

An extensive bibliography of the literature on all aspects of life in the 15th and 16th centuries. An important scholarly tool for the study of the Reformation and its setting. Classified subject arrangement with two major sections: materials on individuals, arranged by name of the person (e.g. Calvin, Bucer); and materials on subjects (see esp. part II, "Religion et vie religieuse"). Author index.

** GENERAL -- OTHER WORKS

BD10 *Augsburg Historical Atlas of Christianity in the Middle Ages and Reformation.* Charles S. Anderson. Minneapolis: Augsburg, 1967.
Designed to be a "working atlas for the study of Medieval and Reformation Church History," this work illustrates that history with maps and texts from Gregory the Great (590 A.D.) to the Peace of Westphalia (1648 A.D.). Has 32 colored maps with texts. Two indexes: of the plates by place and subject, of the text by subject.

BD11 *The Reformation.* Edited by G.R. Elton. Cambridge: Cambridge Univ. Press, 1958.
Vol. 2 of the *New Cambridge Modern History.* A well-received, carefully structured set of essays by authorities in the field, both church and "secular" historians.

BD12 *Contemporaries of Erasmus: a Biographical Register of the Renaissance and Reformation.* Peter G. Bietenholz, ed.; Thomas B. Deutscher, assoc. ed. 3 vol. Toronto: University of Toronto Press, 1985- .
An ambitious project containing biographical sketches of the more than 1,900 persons referred to in the collected works of Erasmus (University of Toronto Press edition). For some obscure persons, no more information is given beyond what is found in Erasmus' works. Included with each entry is a partial list of where the individuals are mentioned in Erasmus' works.

** IN GERMANY AND SWITZERLAND

BD13 *Bibliographie zur deutschen Geschichte im Zeitalter der Glaubensspaltung: 1517-1585.* Karl Schottenlohrer. 7 vols. Leipzig: Hiersemann, 1933-1940; Supplement, 1966.
A very comprehensive bibliography (primarily of German materials) of books and periodical articles published up through 1960. Detailed subject arrangement with extensive indexes. Contents: v. 1-2 -- Personen, A-Z; v. 3 -- Reich und Kaiser, Teritorien und Landesherren; v. 4 -- Gesamtdarstellungen der Reformationszeit, Stoffe; v. 5 -- Nachträge und Ergänzungen Zeittafel; v. 6 -- Verfasser- und Titelverzeichnis; and v. 7 -- Das Schrifttum von 1938 bis 1960 [i.e., Supplement].

BD14 *Early Sixteenth Century Roman Catholic Theologians and the German Reformation; a Finding List of CRR Holdings.* St. Louis: Center for Reformation Research, 1975.

Lists the microfilm holdings at the Center of early (1520-1550) anti-Reformation writings by 21 Catholic theologians. For each theologian, a brief vita is given, followed by a listing of available writings (in publication date order). The Center will lend copies of its holdings to researchers.

BD15 *Evangelical Theologians of Wurttemberg in the Sixteenth Century: a Finding List of CRR Holdings.* St. Louis: Center for Reformation Research, 1975.

Lists the microfilm holdings at the Center of the writings of five major theologians from Wurttemberg (Jacob Andreae, Johannes Brenz, Jakob Heerbrand, Lucas Osiander, and Dietrich Schnepf) and of the official publications by Wurttemberg (a center of Lutheran thought in the 16th century). Under each author, works are listed by date of publication.

** IN GREAT BRITAIN

BD16 *Bibliography of British History, Tudor Period, 1485-1603.* Conyers Read, ed. 2nd ed. Oxford: University Press, 1959.

A selective 6,543-item bibliography of pamphlets, books, periodical articles, etc., up to Jan. 1957. Strong on church history, but covers all aspects of the history of the period. Stresses English-language materials. Includes some annotations, detailed table of contents, author/subject index.

BD17 *Bibliography of British History, Stuart Period, 1603-1714.* Godfrey Davies. 2nd ed., edited by Mary F. Keeler. Oxford: Clarendon Press, 1970.

Complements the above, covering another century. This work includes 4,350 items, arranged topically. Detailed table of contents, includes an author and subject index. Some annotations are included.

BD18 *The Bibliography of the Reform, 1450-1648, Relating to the United Kingdom and Ireland for the Years 1955-1970.* Derek Baker. Oxford: Blackwells, 1975.

Sponsored by the Commission internationale d'histoire ecclésiastique comparée, British subcommission of the International Committee of Historical Sciences. Serves as a complement to BD5 (above) for materials on the Reformation in Great Britain. In three major sections: England and Wales, Scotland, and Ireland. Subdivided by type of material (book, periodical article, review, thesis) and then listed alphabetically by author. Given this arrangement and no subject index, subject access is difficult. No author index.

BD19 *Catalogue of the McAlpin Collection of British History and Theology.*
    Compiled and edited by Charles R. Gillett. 5 vols. New York: Union
    Theological Seminary, 1927-1930.
Includes over 15,000 titles published between 1501 and 1700 that were in the
collection through 1926. Arranged by date of publication, then by author. Vol.
5 is an author index. Especially important for its listing of pre-1700 publications.

BD20 *Catalogue of the McAlpin Collection of British History and Theology;*
    Acquisitions, 1924-1978. New York: G. K. Hall, 1979.
Supplement to the above. Lists over 3,000 additional titles. Unlike the main set
above, this work reproduces the author, title, and subject cards for each title,
arranged in a single alphabet.

BD21 *Early Nonconformity, 1566-1800: a Catalogue of Books in Dr. William's*
    Library, London. 12 vols. Boston: G.K. Hall, 1968.
The collection consists of books on early nonconformity in Great Britain and
Ireland that were printed between 1566 and 1800. The 12 volumes form three
distinct subsets, each reproducing catalog cards for the same books in different
ways: author arrangement (5 vols., 32,200 cards); subject arrangement (5 vols.,
33,500 cards); date of publication arrangement (2 vols., 14,300 cards).

BD22 *The Sources and Literature of Scottish Church History.* Malcolm B.
    Macgregor. Glasgow: J. McCallum, 1934.
A classified and briefly annotated bibliography of primary and secondary material,
with emphasis on the Reformation period. Includes a detailed "chronological
table," a subject index, and an author and "biographical subject" index. Good
coverage of pre-1930 materials.

** LUTHER

There is no major retrospective bibliography devoted to material about Luther.
However, since Schottenloher's bibliography (BD13) includes extensive coverage
of Luther bibliography, as well as related topics, this is not a major problem. In
Schottenloher, see vol. 1, pp. 458-631, and vol. 7, pp. 114-161, for the listing of
materials by and about Luther.

BD23 *Hilfsbuch zum Lutherstudium.* Kurt Aland. Dritte, neubearb. und erw.
    Aufl. Witten: Luther-Verlag, 1970.
An extensive work that lists, indexes, and cross-indexes the various published
editions of Luther's writings. Invaluable for study of the text and/or editions of
Luther's works. Part I is a classified alphabetical list of his works, arranged by
the first significant word in the title of the work. It tells where the work is found
in the modern editions and translations listed in part II (19th and 20th century

editions) and part III (16th-18th century editions).   Parts II and III are cross-indexed to the other parts.

BD24 *Annotated Bibliography of Luther Studies, 1967-1976.* Jack Bigane and Kenneth Hagen. St. Louis: Center for Reformation Research, 1977.

"This bibliography is a scholarly survey of representative and significant literature on Luther to appear during the last decade." Selection is based on a poll of a number of Luther scholars. Lists about 160 items with substantial descriptive annotations. Arranged by author. An appendix lists "Surveys of Modern Research."

BD25 *Annotated Bibliography of Luther Studies, 1977-1983.* Kenneth Hagen and Franz Possett. St. Louis: Center for Reformation Research, 1985.

A continuation of BD24, including "an effort to deal with the mass of [scholarly] literature produced in celebration of Luther's 500th birthday." Lists nearly 200 entries (limited to English and German) with a subject index.

BD26 "Lutherbibliographie 1925- ." In *Lutherjahrbuch.* Göttingen: Vandenhoeck and Ruprecht, 1926- . Annual.

Publisher varies. The bibliographies for 1940-1953 were published as a single listing in the 1957 volume. Now a fairly comprehensive bibliography covering materials by and about Luther and about closely related topics. Includes books, periodical articles, dissertations, etc., as well as a listing of reviews of significant books in Luther studies. Classified subject arrangement with author index.

BD27 *What Luther Says: an Anthology.* Compiled by Ewald M. Plass. 3 vols. St. Louis: Concordia, 1959.

Topically arranges 5,100 passages (translated into English) from Luther's works under 200 subject headings. The source of each quotation in the Weimar, Erlangen, and revised Halle edition is indicated. Has appendixes of biographical sketches of prominent personages mentioned, Luther editions and the reformer's principal writings, and the world of Luther in chronological outline. Also includes indexes of specific subjects and of scripture passages cited.

** CALVIN AND CALVINISM

The first four works form a continuous bibliography of Calviniana up to the present. The other works listed are supplementary bibliographies.

BD28 *Bibliographia Calviniana: Catalogus chronologicus operum Calvini, catalogus systematicus Operum quae sunt de Calvino.* D. Alfredus Erichson. Reprint ed. Nieuwkoop: de Graaf, 1960.

Reprint of vol. 59 of the *Calvini Opera* volumes of the *Corpus Reformatorum.*

Includes two parts: editions of Calvin's works up to 1898 and books about Calvin up to 1898. Entries in part 1 are listed three times, in three different sequences: in order of the edition, in alphabetical order, and in chronological order (includes all known subsequent editions and versions). Part 2 is arranged topically, subdivided geographically. Emphasis on German, Latin, and French materials. Author index.

BD29 *Calvin-Bibliographie, 1901-1959.* Wilhelm Niesel. München: Kaiser, 1961.
A supplement to BD28 up through 1959. Classified arrangement, author index.

BD30 "Calvin Bibliography: 1960-1970" Joseph Tylenda. Ed. by Peter De Klerk. *Calvin Theological Journal* 6 (1971): 156-193.
Supplements the above work through 1970. Includes French, English, German, Dutch, and Italian books and periodical literature, as well as some dissertations. Classified arrangement (an outline is on p. 193). Pages 190-191 list other bibliographies.

BD31 "Calvin Bibliography, 1972- ." Peter De Klerk, ed. *Calvin Theological Journal* 7- (1972-). Annual.
An annually published continuation of the above bibliography. Classified arrangement. Includes books, journal articles, dissertations, encyclopedia articles, parts of books, etc.

BD32 *Living Themes in the Thought of John Calvin: a Bibliographical Study.* Lester R. De Koster. Ph.D. dissertation, University of Michigan, 1964.
An extensive (563 pp.) study of the literature on Calvin. Each chapter covers a different topic and discusses the relevant bibliography. Includes a thematic index and an author index. Very helpful for its thematic approach.

BD33 *A Bibliography of Calviniana 1959-1974.* Dionysius Kempff. Leiden: Brill, 1975.
Updates and supplements Niesel (BD33). Lists over 3,000 titles, divided into four major areas: Calvin's works, general works about Calvin, specialized works about Calvin, and Calvinism and later development. Classified subject arrangement under each topic. Includes author index.

** ZWINGLI

BD34 *Zwingli-Bibliographie: Verzeichnis der gedruckten Schriften von und über Ulrich Zwingli.* Georg Finsler. Zürich: Stiftung von Schnyder von Wartensee, 1897.
Covers up to 1895. Two major parts: writings of Zwingli and writings about

Zwingli. Part 1 lists editions of his works (arranged chronologically) with a title index. Part 2 lists secondary materials by author and has a classified subject index and a date-of-publication index. Includes brief annotations.

BD35 *A Zwingli Bibliography.* H. Wayne Pipkin. Pittsburgh: Clifford E. Barbour Library, Pittsburgh Theological Seminary, 1972.

Designed to extend and supplement the above work. Part 1 lists works about Zwingli alphabetically by author; Part 2 lists new editions and translations of Zwingli's works. Entries include book reviews, as well as items of fiction, drama, poetry, and music. Two indexes: of reviews and of subjects.

BD36 *Huldrych Zwingli im 20. Jahrhundert: Forschungsbericht und annotierte Bibliographie, 1897-1972.* Ulrich Gäbler. Zürich: Theologischer Verlag, 1975.

Designed to complement Finsler (BD34). Part 1 reviews 20th century research on Zwingli. Part 2 lists materials by and about Zwingli. Arranged by year, subdivided into "by" and "about" items, then subarranged by author. Includes 1679 items with brief annotations. Indexed by author, writings, and letters of Zwingli, proper names, and subjects.

** THE RADICAL REFORMATION

BD37 *A Bibliography of Menno Simons, ca. 1496-1561, Dutch Reformer: with a Census of Known Copies.* Irvin B. Horst. Nieuwkoop: de Graaf, 1962.

Lists "all printed books devoted entirely or in part to the writings of Menno Simons." An appendix selectively lists books and pamphlets about him. Arranged by titles of collected works and of individual works. Includes many title page facsimilies and a name index.

BD38 *A Bibliography of Anabaptism, 1520-1630.* Hans J. Hillerbrand. Elkhart, IN: Institute of Mennonite Studies, 1962.

Intends to be exhaustive. Listing about 4500 items, it includes books, periodical articles, parts of books, and dissertations. Uses a detailed subject arrangement deliberately similar to that of Schottenloher (BD13). Has author and short-title index. Gives limited information on the locations of pre-1940 titles; has only a few brief annotations. Coverage of the Mennonites is continued by Springer and Klassen (BE17).

BD39 *A Bibliography of Anabaptism, 1520-1630: a Sequel, 1962-1974.* Hans J. Hillerbrand. St. Louis: Center for Reformation Research, 1975.

Supplement to the above work. Classified subject arrangement with same structure as original work. Lists about 500 items without annotations or index. Excludes material on Thomas Müntzer.

BD40 *Thomas Müntzer: a Bibliography*. Hans J. Hillerbrand. St. Louis: Center
     for Reformation Research, 1976.
Intended to be a comprehensive bibliography of material by and about Müntzer
from the 16th century to the present. Entries divided into four groups: primary
works; general assessments; specific studies; and belles lettres. Within each
section, entries are arranged by date of publication. Includes about 280 books and
periodical articles. Author index.

** SPECIAL TOPICS

BD41 *The Hussite Movement and the Reformation in Bohemia, Moravia and
     Slovakia (1350-1650)*. Jarold K. Zeman. Ann Arbor: Michigan Slavic
     Pub., 1977.
"A Bibliographical Study Guide (with Particular Reference to Resources in North
America)." Published under the auspices of the Center for Reformation Research.
A classified bibliography with brief introductions to each section but no
annotations. Lists most (up to 1972) manuscripts, rare books, microfilms, and
modern critical editions of primary source material. Gives locations of the
materials in N. America. Extensive coverage of materials in English, moderate
coverage of other western European languages, selective for Slavic and eastern
European materials. See especially Part IV, "Aids to Study." Includes
author/editor index.

BD42 *Die Melanchthonforschung im Wandel der Jahrhunderte; ein
     beschreibendes Verzeichnis*. Wilhelm Hammer. 2 vols. Gütersloh: Gerd
     Mohn, 1967-1968.
Lists 4,136 items by and about Melanchthon. Includes all types of printed
material and gives annotations for each item. Arranged by date of publication,
subdivided into "by" and "about" sections. No index.

BD43 *A Bibliography of the Pioneers of the Socinian-Unitarian Movement in
     Modern Christianity in Italy, Switzerland, Germany, Holland*. Earl M.
     Wilbur, comp. Rome: Edizioni di Storia e Letteratura, 1950.
A fairly complete bibliography of periodical and monograph literature on the
topic. Classified arrangement with the table of contents at the back, no indexes.
Some entries have brief annotations.

CHAPTER 30
POST-REFORMATION CHURCH HISTORY

** GENERAL

BE1   *Cambridge Modern History.* 13 vols. and altas. Cambridge, England: University Press, 1902-1912.
Covers from the Renaissance to the present. An extensive authoritative work by specialists in the field. Vol. 13 includes a long general index. Is now being superseded by the following work.

BE2   *New Cambridge Modern History.*   14 vols.   Cambridge, England: University Press, 1957-1979.
Vol. 12 issued in a 1st (1960) and rev. ed. (1968). Similar to the original, but entirely rewritten and updated. Does not include the footnotes or the extensive bibliographies found in its predecessor. For the bibliographies, see Roach (BE3).

BE3   *A Bibliography of Modern History.* John Roach. Cambridge: University Press, 1968.
Intended to serve as the bibliography for the *New Cambridge Modern History.* Arranged in 3 sections by date (1493-1648, 1648-1793, 1793-1945); then by subject within each section. Highly selective -- mainly monographs are listed (few periodical articles are included), emphasis on English and Western European languages. Cutoff date is 1961. Includes personal name and country index.

BE4   *Historical Abstracts, 1775-1945: Bibliography of the World's Periodical Literature.* Santa Barbara, CA: Clio Press, 1955- . Quarterly.
Published in two parts since v. 17 (1971): (A, *Modern History Abstracts, 1775-1914*; and B, *Twentieth Century Abstracts, 1914-*) with the expanded coverage indicated in the new subtitles. Up to 1964 included the U.S. and Canada, since then the U.S. and Canada are excluded and covered in *America: History and Life* (see BF2). Includes English abstracts of articles from over 2000 periodicals, festschriften, proceedings, and transactions. Arranged in classified order, with quarterly, annual, and five-year subject and author indexes.

BE5   *Christianity in a Revolutionary Age: a History of Christianity in the Nineteenth and Twentieth Centuries.* Kenneth Scott Latourette. 5 vols. New York: Harper, 1958-1962.
Covers all aspects of Christianity (Roman Catholic, Orthodox, and Protestant) throughout the world (e.g., organization; devotional life; and social, political, and educational influences) since 1815. Includes numerous footnotes and selected annotated bibliographies. Detailed index in each volume.

** THE ECUMENICAL MOVEMENT

BE6   *A History of the Ecumenical Movement.* Ruth Rouse and Stephen C. Neil, eds. 2nd ed. with rev. bibliography. 2 vols. Philadelphia: Westminster Press, 1967-1970.

A survey covering from the Reformation to 1968, this is an authoritative work with essays by many scholars in the field. Each volume includes an extensive classified bibliography, an analytical subject index, and an author index. Vol. 1 covers 1517-1948, and vol. 2 covers 1948-1968. Vol. 2 was edited by Harold Fey.

BE7   *The Ecumenical Movement in Bibliographical Outline.* Paul A. Crow. New York: Dept. of Faith and Order, National Council of the Churches of Christ, 1965.

A classified but unannotated bibliography, mainly of English-language materials. Intended to update and supplement the earlier bibliographies of Auguste Senaud (*Christian Unity, a Bibliography* [Geneva: World's Committee of Y.M.C.A., 1937]) and Henry R. T. Brandreth (*Unity and Religion, a Bibliography* [London: A & C Black, 1945]).

BE8   *Classified Catalog of the Ecumenical Movement.* 2 vols. Boston: G. K. Hall, 1972.

Includes 25,000 catalog cards, representing about 11,000 titles from the library of the World Council of Churches in Geneva. Arranged by subject using a modified Dewey classification (outlined at the front of the first volume). The catalog includes cards for relevant periodical articles. An extensive collection of ecumenical material, international in scope, primarily English in language. Lists only the printed materials in the collection, not the mss. or mimeographed items. Has an alphabetical index by author and editor.

BE9   *Internationale ökumenische Bibliographie: International Ecumenical Bibliography, 1962/63- .* Mainz: Kaiser, 1967- . Annual.

An important classed bibliography of books and periodical articles that deal with the ecumenical movement, inter-church relations, and controversial theology. Some brief annotations, author index. Includes a section listing book reviews.

BE10   *Ecumenism Around the World: a Directory of Ecumenical Institutes, Centers, and Organizations.* 2nd ed. Rome: the Friars of the Atonement, for Centro pro Unione, 1974.

A directory of over 300 bodies concerned with ecumenism. Arranged by continent and then by country. Indexed by country. Appendix I lists bulletins, newsletters, and reviews which deal with ecumenism.

BE11 *Six Hundred Ecumenical Consultations, 1948-1982.* A. J. Van der Bent.
      Geneva: WCC, 1983.
Brief descriptions and bibliographical data of 633 World Council of
Churches-related ecumenical consultations. Classified according to the subject of
the consultation (faith and witness, justice, education, and other). Within each
section arrangement is chronological. Three indexes: geographical, themes, and
subject. Important resource for ecumenical research.

** DENOMINATIONAL BIBLIOGRAPHIES

Included here are bibliographies that are limited to inclusion of material by and/or
about members of a particular denomination.

BE12 *A Baptist Bibliography: Being a Register of Printed Materials by and
      about Baptists; Including Works Against the Baptists.* Edward C. Starr.
      25 vols. Rochester: American Baptist Historical Society, 1947-1976.
Publisher varies. Lists books by and about Baptists. Arranged alphabetically by
author. Each volume has indexes of co-editors and co-authors, titles, subjects, and
Baptist publishers. No cumulative index. Gives locations of copies of each title.
Supersedes William T. Whitely, *A Baptist Bibliography* (2 vols., London:
Kingsgate Press, 1916-1922).

BE13 *Charismatic Religion in Modern Research: a Bibliography.* Watson
      E. Mills. Macon, GA: Mercer University Press, 1985.
A 2,105-item list with annotations. Charismatic is defined broadly to include
Pentecostals, Neo-pentecostals, and the Jesus Movement. Almost exclusively cites
American works, and includes only a few representative works critical of the
charismatic movement. Prefaced with an introductory essay on the history of the
movement, the bibliography is arranged by author with two indexes: joint author
and subject.

BE14 "Collections toward a Bibliography of Congregationalism." Henry M.
      Dexter. In *The Congregationalism of the Last 300 Years; as Seen in Its
      Literature.* New York: Harper, 1880.
This bibliographical appendix contains 326 pages, has 7,250 entries, and is one of
the most extensive bibliographies on Congregationalism.

BE15 *The Disciples of Christ and American Culture: A Bibliography of Works
      by Disciples of Christ Members, 1866-1984.* Leslie R. Galbraith and
      Heather F. Day. Metuchen, N.J.: Scarecrow Press, 1990.
A list of over 5,200 books, theses, and reports written by members of the
Christian Church (Disciples of Christ) and related bodies. Includes authors from
all professions and disciplines, not only religious writers, from 1866 to 1984.

Works are listed alphabetically by author within 21 subject categories. Author and subject indexes.

BE16 *A Guide to the Study of the Holiness Movement.*   Charles E. Jones. Metuchen, NJ: Scarecrow, 1974.
A major bibliography of material by and about the Holiness churches arranged in six parts: General works; The Holiness Movement (subdivided by specific movements and denominations); The Keswick Movement; The Holiness-Pentecostal Movement; Schools (of the Movement); and Biography. Subarranged in each area by specific subjects. Includes an author and subject index.

BE17 *Mennonite Bibliography, 1631-1961.*   Nelson P. Springer and A. J. Klassen. 2 vols. Scottsdale, PA: Herald Press, 1977.
Designed to supplement Hillerbrand's *Bibliography of Anabaptism, 1520-1630* (BD38). Intends to comprehensively list all types of published materials by and about Mennonites. The 28,000 entries are arranged geographically, then by type of publication or topic. Includes author, subject, and book review indexes. A valuable complement to Hillerbrand's work.

BE18 *United Methodist Studies: Basic Bibliographies.*   Kenneth E. Rowe, ed. Nashville: Abingdon, 1982.
Compiled for the Advisory Committee on United Methodist Studies, Board of Higher Education and Ministry, Division of Ordained Ministry. Designed to provide a selected list of the most important basic resources in United Methodist history, doctrine, and polity. Six basic parts (subarranged topically): General Resources (includes major bibliographies and reference tools); History; Doctrine; Polity; For Children and Youth; and Basic Library for Students. Very useful for study of this denomination.

BE19 *Methodist Union Catalog: Pre-1976 Imprints.*   Metuchen, NJ: Scarecrow, 1975- .
    Six vols. thus far; to be about 20 vols. Will list 50,000 books, pamphlets, and theses by and about Methodists. Gives locations of each work in about 200 U.S., Canadian, and British libraries. Arranged by author. The set will eventually include cumulative title, added-entry, and subject indexes. When complete will replace: Brooks B. Little, *Methodist Union Catalog of History, Biography, Disciplines, and Hymnals* (Prelim. ed. Lake Junaluska, NC: Assoc. of Methodist Hist. Soc., 1967).

BE20 *A Guide to the Study of the Pentecostal Movement.* Charles Edwin Jones.
 2 vols. Metuchen, NJ: Scarecrow Press, 1983.

A nearly 10,000-item list of literature, schools, and people related to Pentecostalism. Pt. 1 is a bibliography on the movement as a whole; pt. 2 classes works according to doctrinal tradition; pt. 3 is a list of schools with related bibliography; and pt. 4 lists nearly 4,000 individuals with related bibliography. An extensive index provides subject access.

Note: For a bibliography on the Brethren tradition see the extensive bibliography in vol. 3 of the *Brethren Encyclopedia* (C23).

CHAPTER 31
AMERICAN CHURCH HISTORY

** GENERAL AMERICAN HISTORY

BF1   *Harvard Guide to American History.* Frank Freidel. rev. ed. 2 vols.
        Cambridge: Harvard University Press, 1974.
The major selective bibliographical guide for American history. Vol. 1 arranged
topically, vol. 2 chronologically.   Vol. 1 also includes some valuable
methodological essays. See esp. chapter 24 (1:512-530), "Religion," which has
seven major topical sections. The 7th section lists material by denomination or
religious group. Be sure to read "How to Use the Guide to Locate Historical
Materials" found on the inside cover, and to use the separate name and subject
indexes to find additional material.

BF2   *America: History and Life: A Guide to Periodical Literature.*   Santa
        Barbara: Clio Press, 1964- . Quarterly.
Covers the history of the U.S. and Canada. Abstracts articles from more than
2,000 periodicals, festschriften, proceedings, and annuals from many countries.
Since 1974, published in 4 parts: A. Article abstract and citations (Spring,
Summer, and Fall); B. Book reviews (Spring and Fall); C. American history
bibliography (annual, includes all materials in A and B, as well as dissertations);
and D. Annual index. Five-year indexes are also published.

** BIBLIOGRAPHICAL GUIDES / BIBLIOGRAPHIES

BF3   *American Religion and Philosophy: A Guide to Information Sources.*
        Ernest R. Sandeen and Frederick Hale. Detroit: Gale, 1978.
Contains 1,639 entries with brief descriptive and critical annotations. Entries are
arranged topically in some detail, with a functional overall structure. Separate
author, title, and subject indexes. Does not supersede the bibliography below but
is easier to use and more up-to-date.

BF4   *A Critical Bibliography of Religion in America.* Nelson R. Burr. 2 vols.
        Princeton: Princeton University Press, 1961.
Published as vol. 4, parts 1-5 of *Religion in American Life.* A valuable and
comprehensive bibliography of "select titles which seemed to be essential and
illustrative of movements and influences" covering all religions in America.
Arranged by subject with citations in a running commentary that also incorporates
historical and critical notes. Extensive table of contents but no subject index.
Author index is included.

BF5   *Religion in American Life: Resources.* Anne T. Fraker, ed. Urbana, Ill.:
University of Illinois Press, 1989.
A guide to the most significant articles and books (mostly written over the last 50
years) on the role of religion in American culture. Extensive (page-long)
annotations by 40 contributors describe 116 books and 121 articles, providing
descriptive and critical discussions of each source, as well as help for further
study. A good first source for information on American religion. Author and title
indexes, but no subject index.

BF6   *Religion in American Life.* Nelson R. Burr. New York: Appleton-
Century-Crofts, 1971.
A very selective classified bibliography with brief annotations listing books,
journal articles, dissertations, etc. Emphasis on 20th century research and the
sociological aspects of American religion. Author index.

BF7   *Source Book and Bibliographical Guide for American Church History.*
Peter G. Mode. Menasha, WI: Banta, 1921.
An older but still useful tool. Includes 29 chapters, each with a bibliography and
selected source documents. Covers from the 17th to the early 20th century. The
bibliographies are actually short bibliographical essays which discuss the relevant
bibliography for each chapter. Subject index.

** MAJOR WORKS

BF8   *Dictionary of Christianity in America.* Daniel G. Reid, coordinating ed.
Downers Grove, Ill.: InterVarsity Press, 1990.
An objective and thorough treatment of all aspects of American religion, giving
"comprehensive attention to the evangelical tradition in America." An initial essay
surveying the history of Christianity in America is followed by over 2,400 signed
articles from 400 contributors, including biographies, events, movements, ideas,
and denominations. Predominantly historical in focus, but covers some
contemporary movements and individuals as well. Includes bibliographies and
extensive cross-references.

BF9   *Encyclopedia of the American Religious Experience.* Charles H. Lippy and
Peter W. Williams, eds. 3 vols. New York: Scribner's, 1987.
105 lengthy thematic essays (arranged in nine parts) with extensive bibliographies
written by some of the leading scholars on American religion. Interdenominational and interdisciplinary, each essay is written with a view "to the
significance of the subject in the development of American society and culture."
A valuable summary of the current scholarship on American religion. Includes
cross-references and a detailed index.

BF10 *A Religious History of the American People.* Sidney E. Ahlstrom. New Haven: Yale University Press, 1972.
A major comprehensive survey by a leading church historian. Includes nearly 1,100 pages of text, an extensive classified bibliography, and a detailed index. An authoritative work, useful (through the index) for reference consultation.

BF11 *A History of the Churches in the United States and Canada.* Robert T. Handy. Oxford: Clarendon Press, 1976.
About half the size of Ahlstrom, but oriented toward the institutional, rather than the cultural and intellectual, aspects of American religious history. Gives particularly good coverage to Canada. Includes an excellent bibliographical essay and a detailed subject index.

** ATLASES

BF12 *Historical Atlas of Religion in America.* Edwin S. Gaustad. Rev. ed. New York: Harper & Row, 1976.
1st ed. published in 1961. Uses maps, tables, and charts with accompanying text to show the expansion and development of churches and their membership in America. Covers 1650 through the early 1970s with 70 maps and 60 charts and tables. Indexed by place, religious bodies, names, and subjects. Helpful for an overview of the development of a religious group and for demographical and geographical information on religion.

BF13 *Atlas of Religious Change in America; 1952-1971.* Peter L. Halvorson and William M. Newman. Washington, DC: Glenmary Research Center, 1978.
Consists primarily of 144 maps in 36 sets of 4 maps each. Also contains an introduction and brief commentaries on each set of maps. Each set gives, for a denomination or group of churches, maps of county-by-county data on: 1952 adherents; 1971 adherents; percentage of change in 1952-1971; and "shift-share, 1952-1971." (The 36th set is for "all denominations.")

** SPECIAL TOPICS

BF14 *Black Holiness: a Guide to the Study of Black Participation in Wesleyan Perfectionist and Glossolalic Pentecostal Movements.* Charles Edwin Jones. Metuchen, NJ: Scarecrow Press, 1987.
A bibliographical guide to the role of blacks in the Wesleyan and Pentecostal traditions, mostly in North America, but also in Africa, the West Indies, and the U.K. In six sections: part 1 covers general aspects, parts 2 and 3 are classified by doctrinal emphasis, part 4 treats leader-centered bodies, part 5 lists black schools with information and bibliographies, and part 6 is a bibliography of prominent individuals. Index to organizations, subjects, and names.

BF15 *A Guide to American Catholic History.* John T. Ellis and Robert Trisco.
2nd ed., rev. and enlarged. Santa Barbara, CA: ABC-Clio, 1982.
A classified list, with critical annotations, of material on American Catholic
history. Includes author, title, and subject indexes. Revises many of the 800
entries found in the 1st edition (Bruce, 1959) and adds 489 new entries. The
section on "Manuscript Depositories" found in the first edition has been
eliminated. For other reference works on American Catholic church history, see
McCabe, *Critical Guide to Catholic Reference Books* (A7 above).

BF16 *Twentieth-Century Evangelicalism: A Guide to the Sources.*   Edith L.
Blumhofer, Joel A. Carpenter. New York: Garland, 1990.
A timely guide to an expanding field.   Section one is a guide to sources on
American evangelicalism, including libraries, archives, periodicals, publishers, etc.
Sections two through six are bibliographies of books, chapters, and articles
arranged under 22 topics, both historical and topical, with critical annotations.
Altogether lists over 1,500 citations. Author, organizational, and subject indexes.

BF17 *A Bibliography of American Presbyterianism During the Colonial Period.*
Leonard J. Trinterud. Philadelphia: Presbyterian Historical Society, 1968.
Intended "to identify the printed sources available for the study of American
Presbyterianism in the Colonial Period, or, more precisely, up to that year in
which each particular Presbyterian body terminated its colonial pattern by some
form of reorganization prior to 1800." Material is arranged by the 12 distinctive
bodies covered, subarranged by author. Lists only American imprints. Includes
author and major cross-reference indexes.

BF18 *Annals of the American Pulpit.* William Buell Sprague. 9 vols. New
York: Carter, 1859-69.
"Commemorative Notices of Distinguished American Clergymen of Various
Denominations, from the Earliest Settlement of the Country to the Close of the
Year 1855, with Historical Introductions." Provides biographical information on
many individuals not listed elsewhere. Divided into sections and volumes by
denomination. Within each section, the individuals are listed by when they began
their ministry.   Includes a 2-5 page sketch of each individual with (where
applicable) a bibliography of materials by that person. Has a name index for each
denomination but no cumulative index.

BF19 *American Puritan Studies: an Annotated Bibliography of Dissertations,
1882-1981.* Michael S. Montgomery. Westport, CT: Greenwood, 1984.
Lists 940 doctoral dissertations in chronological order in order to provide "a sense
of the historical development of American Puritan Studies." Most of the extensive
abstracts are excerpts from *Dissertation Abstracts International.* Includes four
indexes: author, short title, institution, and subject.

BF20 *Encyclopedia of Religion in the South.* Samuel S. Hill. Macon, GA: Mercer University Press, 1984.

Signed articles with bibliographies provide a wealth of material on the religious history of 16 southern states. Inclusive of Judaism and Christianity, with entries on denominations, doctrines, significant people, places, and events. Includes index.

BF21 *Women in American Religious History: An Annotated Bibliography and Guide to Sources.* Dorothy C. Bass and Sandra Hughes Boyd. Boston: G.K. Hall, 1986.

A guide to research tools for the study of the role of women in American religion, arranged in seven sections: general works, Protestantism, Catholicism, Judaism, Afro-American religion, Native American religion, and alternative religious movements. Altogether, the work annotates 568 entries, with helpful cross-references. Author and editor indexes.

** BIBLIOGRAPHIES

CA1　*Theology Primer: Resources for the Theological Student.*　John Jefferson
　　　　Davis.　Grand Rapids: Baker, 1981.
A basic guide to the study of systematic theology, emphasizing modern
developments.　Includes a glossary of theological terms, brief biographies of
modern theologians, two introductory essays, and a classified annotated
bibliography with about 400 entries.　The bibliography lists reference works,
major systematic theologies, and works on each major loci of theology.　No
indexes.

CA2　"Systematic Theology [a Bibliography]."　Jack Cottrell.　*Seminary Review*
　　　　26 (March 1980): 9-34.
Lists about 300 books with brief annotations.　Codes are given to indicate
usefulness and theological viewpoint.　Conservative evangelical perspective, but
many books from other positions are included.　Classed subject arrangement under
25 headings.

CA3　*Bibliography of Systematic Theology for Theological Students.*　Princeton,
　　　　NJ: Princeton Theological Seminary Library, 1949.
Now somewhat dated but still of use.　Intended to be "a convenient hand list of
the most important works of theological study."　Not annotated.　Classified subject
arrangement.

Note: See also the chapter, "Systematic/Doctrinal Theology and Ethics:
Bibliographies", in G. E. Gorman and Lyn Gorman, *Theological and Religious
Reference Materials*, vol. 2 (A8).

No periodical index is devoted exclusively to systematic theology.　However, of
the general religious/theological indexes, the "Elenchus Bibliographicus" in
Ephemerides Theologicae Lovanienses (M12) has the most extensive coverage.

** ENCYCLOPEDIAS -- PROTESTANT

There is a fine line between what is a "general theological" encyclopedia and what
is a "systematic theology" encyclopedia.　Thus, the general theological
encyclopedias in Chapter 3 include much material on dogmatic theology.　Listed
here are those works more closely confined to explaining the terms of systematic
theology.

CA4   *New Dictionary of Theology.* Sinclair B. Ferguson, David F. Wright, J. I.
       Packer, eds. Downers Grove, IL: InterVarsity Press, 1988.
Over 630 entries from 205 international scholars. Includes biographies and
biblical, systematic, and historical perspectives. Selective bibliographies and
extensive cross-references. A good, concise, and up-to-date dictionary for both
general readers and specialists.

CA5   *Evangelical Dictionary of Theology.* Walter A. Elwell, ed. Grand Rapids:
       Baker, 1984.
Successor to *Baker's Dictionary of Theology* (1961). 1,200 articles, some with
bibliographies, from 200 contributors (mostly American and British), representing
a variety of evangelical viewpoints. Includes entries on the Bible, church history,
and biographies, but the stress in each entry is on the "theological dimension" of
the subject.

CA6   *The Westminster Dictionary of Christian Theology.* Alan Richardson and
       John Bowden, eds. Philadelphia: Westminster Press, 1983.
A major revision of the 1969 edition. Like the earlier edition, focus is on
"theological thinking" rather than on historical events. Biographical entries have
been dropped (although there is a name index). The 175 contributors are more
international than the mainly British earlier edition, and the 600 articles focus on
contemporary developments, such as non-Christian religions and political theology.

CA7   *Beacon Dictionary of Theology.* Richard S. Taylor, ed. Kansas City, MO:
       Beacon Press, 1983.
Nearly 1,000 signed articles from 157 contributors, designed for pastors, students,
and laypersons, with bibliographies and extensive cross-references. The viewpoint
is "unabashedly evangelical and just as unabashedly Wesleyan."

** ENCYCLOPEDIAS--CATHOLIC

CA8   *Sacramentum Mundi: an Encyclopedia of Theology.* Karl Rahner, ed. 6
       vols. New York: Herder, 1968-70.
A very important work for the study of Catholic theology, now published in six
languages. Post-Vatican II viewpoint. Has over 1,000 lengthy articles by over
600 Catholic scholars from many countries. Most articles have bibliographies and
vol. 6 includes a a short general index.

CA9   *Dictionary of Theology.* Karl Rahner and Herbert Vorgrimler. 2nd ed.
       NY: Crossroad, 1981.
A "thoroughly revised and augmented English edition." Similar in scope, purpose,
and quality to the first edition, but all articles have been revised, some new ones
added, and some old ones dropped. "Contains revised versions of the major

articles ... from *Sacramentum Mundi*, together with a large number of articles translated from the major German works *Lexikon für Theologie und Kirche* and *Theologisches Taschenlexikon*, and entirely new articles on topics of major importance written for the occasion." Intended for the student and layperson; no bibliographies.

CA10 *The New Dictionary of Theology.* ed. by Joseph A. Komonchak, et al. Wilmington, Del.: Michael Glazier, 1987.
Attempts to "take stock of the remarkable developments in the church and in theology since the Second Vatican Council" (preface). About 380 articles by Roman Catholic scholars, but intended for an ecumenical audience. The articles range in length: a few are single sentence definitions, but most are very extensive, signed articles with bibliographies. Cross references, but no index.

** THE CREEDS

CA11 *The Creeds of Christendom: with an History and Critical Notes.* Phillip Schaff. 6th ed. 3 vols. New York: Harper, 1919.
Vol. 1 contains essays on the history of creeds, church by church, with many bibliographies. Vol. 2 contains the creeds of the Greek and Latin churches. Vol. 3 includes the creeds of the Evangelical Protestant churches. Each creed is given in its original language with an accompanying English translation. Each volume has an index of subjects.

CA12 *A History of Creeds and Confessions of Faith in Christendom and Beyond.* William A. Curtis. Edinburgh: Clark, 1911.
A major survey of the creeds, with extensive representative quotes. Includes bibliographies, an index, and appendices containing historical tables.

CA13 *The Encyclopedia of American Religions: Religious Creeds.* J. Gordon Melton, ed. 1st ed. Detroit: Gale, 1988.
Contains 450 creedal statements of Christian, Jewish, and other faiths in the United States and Canada. Ch. 1 lists ancient creeds, and chs. 2-23 arrange creeds under broad religious families. For foreign language creeds a contemporary English translation was chosen. Includes some historical notes, but no theological exposition or textual analysis. Indexed by creed/organization name and keyword.

** SPECIAL TOPICS

CA14 *A Bibliographic History of Dispensationalism.* Arnold D. Ehlert. Grand Rapids: Baker, 1965.
Intended "to provide a basis for the study of the doctrinal history of the subject of ages and dispensations." Consists primarily of a well done bibliographical

essay discussing the literature. At the end is an "additional bibliography" (that lists only material not discussed in the text) and an index of authors cited in the essay.

CA15 *A Bibliography of Baptist Writings on Baptism, 1900-1968.* Athol Gill. Ruschlikon-Zürich: Baptist Theological Seminary, 1969.
A classified bibliography of 1,250 books and periodical articles on baptism and its various aspects. Has author index and an index of book reviews.

CA16 *Bibliotheca Trinitariorum.* Erwin Schadel, ed. 2 vols. Munich: K.G. Saur, 1984-1988.
Vol. 1 is an alphabetical listing of 4,712 entries, covering every relevant book, article, or pamphlet published from 2nd century to the present on the doctrine of the Trinity. There are some annotations on content and viewpoint (written in German). The introduction is published in six languages. Vol. 2 contains fives indexes and a supplementary list of 967 additional entries.

CA17 *Black Theology: a Critical Assessment and Annotated Bibliography.* James H. Evans, Jr. New York: Greenwood Press, 1987.
An annotated bibliography in three sections: "Origin and Development of Black Theology" (the longest section); "Liberation, Feminism, and Marxism"; and "Cultural and Global Discourse." Within each section works are listed by author. Includes only English-language published works. Most of the 461 entires were published from 1968 to 1985. An introductory essay offers a critical assessment of black theology. Indexes: names, titles, and subjects.

CA18 *Glossolalia: A Bibliography.* Watson E. Mills. New York: Edwin Mellen Press, 1985.
Aims to "identify the more significant works in glossolalia, examining the various approaches taken to speaking in tongues." A bibliographical essay, describing historical, psychological, sociological, and biblical studies is followed by an unannotated list of 1,158 books, articles, theses, and dissertations. Subject index and a very brief Scripture index.

CA19 *The Holy Spirit: A Bibliography.* Watson E. Mills. Peabody, Mass.: Hendrickson, 1988.
A 2,098-entry unannotated bibliography of studies (mostly in English) related to the person and work of the Holy Spirit. Books, articles, and dissertations are included. A good bibliographical starting point for the field. There is a subject and a very brief Scripture index.

CA20 *Index to Literature on Barth, Bonhoeffer and Bultmann.* Manfred Kwiran.
        Basel: F. Reinhardt, 1977.
An extensive bibliography (5,645 items) of the secondary literature on three major
theologians of the 20th century. Includes books, periodical articles, theses, and
dissertations. Divided into three major sections, one for each theologian. Within
each section are found: a brief vita for the man; a listing of the secondary
literature, arranged alphabetically by author; an index by persons; an index by
subjects; and an index which lists the major works of the individual and indicates
which entries in the bibliography discuss those works.

CA21 *Jesus Christ Our Lord: an English Bibliography of Christology Comprising
        Over Five Thousand Titles Annotated and Classified.* Samuel G. Ayres.
        New York: Armstrong, 1906.
Includes over 5,000 books on Christ, arranged topically under about 70 headings.
Each section has a brief introduction and short list of recommended titles,
followed by an extensive bibliography in author order. Includes subject and
author indexes. Dated but valuable for its pre-1905 inclusiveness.

CA22 *The Literature of the Doctrine of a Future Life.* Ezra Abbot. New York:
        Waddleton, 1871.
"A catalogue of works relating to the nature, origin, and destiny of the soul; the
titles classified, and arranged chronologically, with notes, and indexes of authors
and subjects." Originally an appendix to: William Alger, *Critical History of the
Doctrine of a Future Life* (1860). An extensive (234 p.) classified bibliography
with brief annotations. Has author and subject indexes. Covers the older
literature on this subject extensively, including all types of printed material.
Valuable for historical study of this topic.

Note: On third world theology in general, and liberation theology in particular,
see Chapter 37.

CHAPTER 33
CHRISTIAN ETHICS

** BIBLIOGRAPHIES

There is no important or extensive bibliography for Christian ethics as such. A few of the more recent and helpful of a number of specialized bibliographies are listed below.

However, both the general theological bibliographies and periodical indexes (See Chapters 8 and 12) and the general philosophical bibliographies and indexes (see Chapter 34) have reasonable coverage of the bibliography of Christian ethics.

CB1 "Ethics [a Bibliography]" Jack Cottrell. *Seminary Review* 26 (March 1980): 35-51.
Lists about 200 books with brief annotations. Codes are given to indicate usefulness and theological viewpoint. Conservative evangelical perspective, but many books from other positions are included. Covers ethics in general, Christian ethics, and specific issues in ethics. Classified subject arrangement under 11 headings.

CB2 "Bibliographie" in *Zeitschrift für evangelische Ethik*, 1957- . Quarterly.
Covers all aspects of Christian ethics including politics, the family, anthropology, psychology, medicine, etc. Up to 1968, it included both books and periodical articles, since then only books are listed. Primarily German material, but books in other languages, esp. English, are included.

CB3 "A Critical Bibliography of Recent Discussions of Religious Ethics by Philosophers." Glen Garber. *Journal of Religious Ethics* 2 (1974): 53-80.
A bibliographical essay on "religious ethics in recent Anglo-American philosophical literature, organized in terms of a critical analysis of the main lines of argument." Emphasis on metaethics. The essay is followed by an alphabetical bibliography of all works discussed.

CB4 *Selected Bibliography on Moral Education.* Bruce B. Suttle. Parkland College, Champaign, IL: the author, 1980.
A helpful 46-page unannotated bibliography. Arranged by publication format, *not* by subject. Includes a section on "Sources with Major Bibliographies" on the topic.

** DICTIONARIES AND ENCYCLOPEDIAS

CB5   *The Westminster Dictionary of Christian Ethics.* James F. Childress and
         John McQuarrie, eds. Philadelphia: Westminster Press, 1986.
A new edition, two-thirds of which is new material. Consists of 620 entries (most
with bibliographies) from 167 contributors. Presents "various perspectives" from
"a wide range of religious traditions and academic disciplines" on the major issues
in ethics and morality.

CB6   *Concise Dictionary of Christian Ethics.* Bernhard Stoeckle, ed. New
         York: Seabury, 1979.
Has over 100 central articles plus supplementary definitions, written by 30 leading
moral theologians. Attempts to provide the latest information available for ethical
decision-making in a Christian context. Includes short bibliographies.

CB7   *Baker's Dictionary of Christian Ethics.* Carl F. H. Henry, ed. Grand
         Rapids: Baker, 1973.
Contains moderate length essays and numerous short entries on all aspects of
Christian ethics by 263 well-known evangelical scholars. All articles are signed
but only occasionally have bibliographies, and those are short.

CB8   *Encyclopedia of Morals.* Vergilius Ferm, ed. New York: Philosophical
         Library, 1956.
Covers both ethical theory and moral behavior. Has moderate length articles,
most with bibliographies. Also has numerous cross-references and a personal
name index.

CB9   *Evangelisches Soziallexikon.* Begr. von Friedrich Karrenberg. 7. Aufl.
         Stuttgart: Kreuz, 1980.
Includes numerous signed articles by over 230 contributors on a wide variety of
social and ethical topics. Protestant German viewpoint. Most articles have
bibliographies. This work is well cross-indexed and also has a subject index.

** BIOETHICS

CB10 *Bioethics: a Guide to Information Sources.* Doris M. Goldstein, ed.
         Detroit: Gale Research, 1982.
An extensive well-annotated bibliography of about 1,000 items on "the study of
ethical issues arising in medicine and the life sciences," primarily material from
1973-1981. Classified arrangement with an author/title/subject index. Also
includes information on "Organizations, Programs, and Library Collections" and
lists 55 other bibliographies on bioethics.

CB11 *Bibliography of Bioethics*. Leroy Walters, ed. Washington, DC: Kennedy
        Institute of Ethics (Georgetown University), 1975- . Annual.
Vols. 1-6 published at irregular intervals by Gale Research Co., vols. 7-9 by The
Free Press. Each document listed includes full bibliographical information as well
as a list of subject terms summarizing the item. Each volume has 6 sections:
introduction; a list of journals cited; the bioethics thesaurus; subject entry section;
title index; and author index. Read the introduction in order to use this work
effectively.

CB12 *Encyclopedia of Bioethics*. Warren T. Reich, ed. in chief. 4 vols. New
        York: Free Press, 1978.
A widely acclaimed major work in the field, dealing with the major issues in the
area as well as specifics. The 300 articles, each with a bibliography, include the
latest scholarship and give thorough coverage to this topic. Fully cross-referenced
and indexed. Indispensable when working in bioethics.

** SPECIFIC ISSUES

CB13 *Abortion: an Annotated Indexed Bibliography*. Maureen Muldoon. New
        York: E. Mellen Press, 1980.
Includes 3,400 North American English-language items, primarily from
1970-1980. Lists other bibliographies; studies of the ethical, theological, medical,
social, and legal aspects of abortion; and studies on abortion in various states and
countries. Arranged by author with a classified subject index at the front of the
volume. Some entries have brief annotations.

CB14 "Christianity and Apartheid: an Introductory Bibliography."   Irving
        Hexham. *Reformed Journal* 30 (April 1980): S2-S11.
Published as special supplementary pages at the center of the journal.   An
excellent bibliographical essay with sections including basic works about South
Africa, Christianity and race relations with particular reference to South Africa,
background studies, journals, and works in Afrikaans.

CB15 *Hunger, Food, and Poverty: A Bibliography and List of Resource
        Organizations*. Clinton E. Stockwell, comp. Chicago: Urban Church
        Resource Center and the Seminary Consortium for Urban Pastoral
        Education, 1982.
Includes: a bibliography of about 110 books and periodical articles (arranged by
author, no annotations or subject classification); a list of organizations active in
this area; and a list of "other resources, organizational and audio visual." Useful
as a raw list of resources, but provides no help in evaluating them.

CB16 *A Search for Environmental Ethics: an Initial Bibliography.*   Mary
      Anglemyer, Eleanor Seagreaves, and Catherina LeMaistre. Washington,
      DC: Smithsonian Inst. Press, 1980.
A selective annotated bibliography of about 400 books and articles on ethics and
the natural environment.   Covers English-language material from 1945-1979.
Arranged by author with subject and name indexes.   Includes a good number of
works from a religious, usually Christian, perspective.

** GENERAL PHILOSOPHY--BIBLIOGRAPHICAL GUIDES

CC1 *The Philosopher's Guide to Sources, Research Tools, Professional Life, and Related Fields.* Richard T. De George. Lawrence, KS: Regents Press of Kansas, 1980.
Arranged in three major parts: an introduction to the research and reference tools in philosophy (contents of this section are arranged by subject and type of tool; also includes lists of philosophical journals, associations, research centers, etc.); a survey of general reference tools; and basic research and reference tools in fields related to philosophy. Each bibliographical entry has a brief annotation.

CC2 *Philosophy: a Guide to the Reference Literature.* Hans E. Bynagle. Littleton, CO: Libraries Unlimited, 1986.
Focusing on current, English-language reference works, this is less extensive than De George (above). But the 421 works listed are accompanied with extensive annotations. After an introductory chapter with an overview of main philosophical traditions, 13 chapters are arranged by type of reference sources (dictionaries, bibliographies, concordances, journals, etc.). Subject access is provided through the subject index; there is also an author-title index.

CC3 *A Bibliographical Survey for a Foundation in Philosophy.* Francis Elliott Jordak. Washington, DC: University Press of America, 1978.
An extensive classified bibliography designed to direct the user to the best available works. The first 16 pages list reference tools; the rest of the book lists important works on various topics in philosophy (e.g. the major philosophers, logic, ethics, oriental philosophy, etc.). Most entries include descriptive and critical annotations. The "index" is actually a detailed table of contents. A helpful guide.

CC4 *The History of Ideas: a Bibliographical Introduction.* Jeremy L. Tobey. Santa Barbara, CA: Clio, 1975- .
Two vols. thus far. "This bibliography surveys the most important bibliographical guides and writings on the history of philosophy, science, aesthetics, and religious thought." The books are discussed in the well-organized and carefully written bibliographical essay. Full bibliographical citations are given in the index/bibliography at the end of each volume. See vol. 1, pp. 160-74 and vol. 2, pp. 146-182 for coverage of Christianity.

** GENERAL PHILOSOPHY -- BIBLIOGRAPHIES / INDEXES

CC5   *A Bibliography of Philosophical Bibliographies.*   Herbert Guerry. Westport, CT: Greenwood Press, 1977.
A bibliography of over 2,400 other bibliographies that cover philosophy in general or specific topics. Arranged in two major A to Z sections: bibliographies of individual philosophers, listed alphabetically by the name of the philosopher, and bibliographies on specific philosophical subjects arranged alphabetically by specific subject. Author index.

CC6   *Dissertations in Philosophy Accepted at American Universities, 1861-1975.* Thomas C. Bechtle and Mary F. Riley. New York: Garland, 1978.
Lists over 7,500 doctoral dissertations done in North American universities. Arranged by author with a detailed subject index.

CC7   *The Philosopher's Index: an International Index to Philosophical Periodicals.* Bowling Green, OH: Philosophical Documentation Center, Bowling Green State University, 1967- Quarterly.
Annual cumulations. Indexes all the major English-language philosophy journals and selected foreign-language titles. An important tool. Now includes two major sections: a subject index and an author listing with the full bibliographic entries and abstracts. A third section indexes book reviews found in the journals.

CC8   *The Philosopher's Index: a Retrospective Index to U. S. Publications from 1940.* 3 vols. Bowling Green, OH: Philosophical Documentation Center, Bowling Green State University, 1978.
Indexes about 6,000 books from 1940 to 1976 and about 15,000 periodicals articles from 1940 to 1966. Note the limitation to U.S. publications. Vols. 1 and 2 are a listing by specific subject; vol. 3 is a listing by author.

CC9   *The Philosopher's Index: a Retrospective Index to non-U.S. English Language Publications from 1940.* 3 vols. Bowling Green, OH: Philosophical Documentation Center, Bowling Green State University, 1980.
Indexes about 5,000 books from 1940 to 1978 and about 12,000 journal articles from 1940 to 1966. Vols. 1 and 2 are a listing by specific subject; vol. 3 is a listing by author.

** GENERAL PHILOSOPHY -- ENCYCLOPEDIAS

CC10   *Encyclopedia of Philosophy.* Edited by Paul Edwards. 8 vols. New York: Macmillan, 1967.
The major English-language work in the field, this work covers the whole of philosophy. A good starting point when researching a topic in philosophy. Over

1,400 articles are generally on broad subject areas -- you must use the index to find specific topics. The long signed articles include bibliographies, many with annotations.

CC11 *Dictionary of the History of Ideas: Studies of Selected Pivotal Ideas.*
      Philip P. Wiener, ed. 5 vols. New York: Scribners, 1973-74.
Includes over 300 long signed articles covering a wide range of topics in intellectual history. Concentrates on concepts which can be traced historically. Includes bibliographies, a good index, and an analytical table of contents.

CC12 *Dictionary of Philosophy and Psychology, Including Many of the Principal
      Conceptions of Ethics, Logic, Aesthetics, Philosophy of Religion.* James
      M. Baldwin, ed. 3 vols. in 4. New York: Macmillan, 1901-1905.
The first two volumes are an A-Z sequence of articles on philosophy. Articles are generally fairly short summaries of a topic. Vol. 3, which is bound in two parts, is an extensive bibliography of philosophy and psychology. The first encyclopedia of philosophy in English, this work is now largely superseded by *The Encyclopedia of Philosophy* (CC10), but is still of historical importance.

** GENERAL PHILOSOPHY -- OTHER

CC13 *Directory of American Philosophers, 1990-91.* Archie J. Bahm, Richard
      H. Lineback, and Mary M. Shurts, eds. 15th ed. Bowling Green, OH:
      Philosophical Documentation Center, Bowling Green State University,
      1990.
New edition published every two years. Arranged by country (U.S. or Canada), then by state or province, then by institution. Under each institution is a list of its philosophy faculty members. Includes name indexes to philosophers and institutions.

CC14 *International Directory of Philosophy and Philosophers, 1990-92.* Ramona
      Cromier and Richard H. Lineback, eds. 7th ed. Bowling Green, OH:
      Philosophical Documentation Center, Bowling Green State University,
      1990.
Provides up-to-date information on worldwide philosophical activities. Part I gives brief information on international philosophical organizations. Part II is arranged by country. Under each country, brief information is given about its universities and colleges, institutions and research, associations and societies, journals, and publishers of interest to philosophers. Indexed by the names of societies, philosophers, universities, centers and institutions, journals, and publishers.

** PHILOSOPHY OF RELIGION, APOLOGETICS

CC15 *A Selective Bibliography for Christian Apologetics.* Clark H. Pinnock.
Madison, WI: Theological Students Fellowship, [1974?].
A classified bibliography of about 150 items divided into nine subject areas,
prepared by a leading evangelical theologian. A minimum of bibliographical
information is given and only a few entries have brief annotations. "An asterisk
indicates primary books of particular value" in each subject area.

CC16 *Philosophy of Religion: an Annotated Bibliography of Twentieth-Century
Writings in English.* William J. Wainwright. New York: Garland, 1978.
Contains 1,135 entries with fairly long descriptive and critical annotations.
Addressed primarily to those working in the analytic tradition and interested in
"the solution of philosophical problems," not systems or history. "Items have been
included which either make a significant contribution to our understanding of the
relevant problem or have proved to be influential." Thus, it is highly selective;
only works by analytic philosophers are included.

CC17 *A Bibliography of Christian Philosophy and Contemporary Issues.* George
F. McLean. New York: Ungar, 1967.
A selective bibliography of books and periodical articles, 1937 to 1966, on
Christian philosophical perspectives. Wide coverage with emphasis on Catholic
authors.   Topical arrangement, author index.   Topics covered: Christian
Philosophy, Contemporary Philosophies, Philosophy and Technology, Philosophy
of Man and God, The Problem of God in a Secular Culture, Religious Knowledge
and Language, Moral Philosophy, and Teaching Philosophy.

CHAPTER 35
PRACTICAL THEOLOGY

** GENERAL WORKS

DA1   *Resources for Christian Leaders: a Guide for Churches, Denominations, Missions, Service Agencies.* Edward R. Dayton. 8th ed. Monrovia, CA: Missions Advanced Research & Communication Center, 1985.

Like the previous editions, about half of this book is a selective, classified, annotated bibliography of books to help the Christian leader. Includes both works from a Christian perspective (marked with a *) and helpful "secular" works. The rest of the book lists other resources (computers, newsletters, magazines, calendars, workbooks, cassettes, films, management and technical associations, training seminars, resource centers, directories). Has author, title, and publisher indexes.

DA2   *Répertoire bibliographique des institutions chrétiennes, 1967-   .* Strasbourg: Centre de recherche et de documentation des institutions chrétiennes, 1968- . Semiannual.

English name: *Repertory of Christian Institutions.* Published annually 1967-1976. "RIC" is a computer-produced continuing bibliography of materials on the life and work of the church. Includes books and periodical articles in five languages with international and ecumenical coverage. The arrangement and structure of this index is somewhat unusual -- be sure to read its preface for use information. Provides good subject access but has no author indexing.

DA3   *RIC [Répertoire bibliographique des institutions chrétiennes]. Supplement 1- .* Strasbourg: Cerdic, 1973- .

An on-going series of computer-compiled bibliographies on various special topics of concern to the church today. Various formats are used, see the preface of each work for a clear explanation of its use. In general, the more recent ones have better coverage and easier to use formats. Topics covered include abortion, baptism, church and state, the ecumenical movement, liberation theology, marriage and divorce, etc.

DA4   *The Westminster Dictionary of Christian Spirituality.* Gordon S. Wakeman. Philadelphia: Westminster Press, 1983.

Intended to provide "direct access to the whole development and present state" of Christian spirituality. About 150 international scholars have contributed over 350 articles representing international and ecumenical perspectives. Many biographical entries among the signed articles. Bibliographies are appended to most articles.

DA5   *Baker's Dictionary of Practical Theology.* Ralph G. Turnbull, ed. Grand Rapids: Baker, 1967.
Intended to be "a source book for pastors and students." Ten major topical sections: preaching, homiletics, hermeneutics, evangelism and missions, counseling, administration, pastoral, stewardship, worship, and education. Under each heading are a number of essays on aspects of the topic, complete with bibliographies. Indexed by subject and by persons. Conservative and American orientation.

** CHURCH AND SOCIETY

DA6   *Sociological Abstracts.* San Diego: Sociological Abstracts, 1952-   . Bimonthly.
Sixth issue is cumulative index for the year. The major American abstracting and indexing tool in sociology. Classified arrangement. Indexes and abstracts a large number of U.S. and foreign periodicals, covering a wide range of sociological research. See U12 for an online version of this index.

DA7   *Issues in the Sociology of Religion: a Bibliography.* Anthony J. Blasi. New York: Garland, 1987.
A classified list of about 3,600 works (books, articles, and significant dissertations and theses), organized in three chapters: structures, processes, and disciplinary conceptualizations. Includes literature up to 1984. Introductory annotations begin each chapter, section, and subsection. Author and subject indexes.

DA8   *The Sociology of Religion: a Bibliographical Survey.* Roger Homan. New York: Greenwood, 1987.
Over 1,000 annotated entries classified in 24 chapters. Limited to books and journal articles, mostly published within the last 20 years. Author, subject, and title indexes.

DA9   *Religion and Society in North America: an Annotated Bibliography.* Robert Brunkow, ed. Santa Barbara, CA: ABC-Clio Information Services, 1983.
A 4,304-entry bibliography of articles on the interaction of religious belief and social behavior, drawn from 600 journals, most of which were published between 1973 and 1980. Entries are classified either by social or denominational headings. Signed annotations were written by a international group of scholars. Includes a very extensive subject index and an author index.

DA10 *Social Scientific Studies of Religion: a Bibliography.* Morris I. Berkowitz and J. Edmund Johnson. Pittsburgh: University of Pittsburgh Press, 1967.
A classified bibliography of over 6,000 items. Emphasis on recent

English-language works that relate religion to social science variables. Author index.

DA11 *Church and Social Action: A Critical Assessment and Bibliographical Survey.* Roger T. Wolcott and Dorita F. Bolger. Westport, Conn.: Greenwood Press, 1990.
An introductory survey on "The Study of Church and Social Action" is followed by an annotated bibliography of 748 books and articles on "religiously-inspired" efforts "to bring about changes in surrounding social systems." Includes studies by social scientists, not theologians. Classified into comparative studies and historical studies. Author, title, and subject indexes.

** CHURCH AND STATE

DA12 *Church and State in America: a Bibliographical Guide.* 2 vols. John F. Wilson, ed. New York: Greenwood Press, 1986-1987.
Vol. 1 -- The colonial and Early National Periods; v. 2 -- The Civil War to the Present Day. Each volume has 11 bibliographic essays (with about 250 entries each); most of them cover historical periods, but there are also essays on education, law, and women. An excellent starting point not only for the church-state debate but also for study of the broader issues of American religion and culture. Author/subject index.

DA13 *Church-State Relations: an Annotated Bibliography.* Albert J. Menendez. New York: Garland, 1976.
"Includes only English language, full-length books which treat the subject in some depth or completeness." Emphasis on the situation in the U.S. and Great Britain. Classified arrangement, brief annotations, author index.

DA14 *Law and Theology: an Annotated Bibliography.* Lynn Robert Buzzard. Oak Park, IL: Christian Legal Society, 1979.
Lists books and periodical articles which are of major importance when exploring legal-theological questions. Selections are limited to English-language material and materials of particular interest to the Judeo-Christian tradition. Includes moderate-length descriptive annotations. Arranged by author, limited subject index. Also has a list of additional works that "may be appropriate to the purpose of this volume."

DA15 *Religious Conflict in America: a Bibliography.* Albert J. Menendez. New York: Garland, 1985.
A selective list of "the major writings which deal with with religious conflict and hostility through three centuries" in the United States. Of the nearly 1,400 entries most deal with current issues. Arranged in 17 sections. The first seven are on

chronological periods, followed by four sections on religion and presidential elections, and then six sections on special topics. Each section consists of an unannotated list preceded by a short bibliographical essay which points out the most important works. Author index.

DA16 *Religious Liberty: International Bibliography 1918-1978.* Andrea Gianna. (RIC Supplement, 47-49). Strasbourg: Cerdic, 1980.
Lists books and periodical articles "on religious liberty treated under juridical, sociological or historical aspects. Works that are specifically theological have been left out." A wide variety of countries and languages are represented in the material. Classified subject arrangement with a detailed table of contents at the back of the volume. Pp. 112-114 list other bibliographies on this topic.

DA17 *Bibliography of Doctoral Dissertations on Politics and Religion, Undertaken in American and Canadian Universities (1940-1962).* George R. LaNoue. New York: National Council of Churches, 1963.
Lists 649 dissertations on the topic in a simple classified arrangement. No annotations or indexes are included. Citations give author, title, area of concentration, school granting, and year granted for each item.

DA18 *School Prayer and Other Religious Issues in American Public Education: a Bibliography.* Albert J. Menendez. New York: Garland, 1985.
A reasonably up-to-date list of 1,600 books, articles, and theses on issues related to religion and public education in America. Arranged according to 21 different topics, with an attempt to represent all sides in controversial issues. Brief essays precede each unannotated list, pointing users to more important works. Author and subject indexes.

** URBAN MINISTRY

DA19 *Abstract Service.* Chicago: Institute on the Church in Urban-Industrial Society, 1970- . Monthly.
Now prepared by the ICUIS and published by the Urban-Rural Mission Office, Commission on World Mission and Evangelism, World Council of Churches. Indexes and abstracts material on the urban church, church ministries to minorities, etc. Also provides information on where copies of the abstracted items may be obtained. An annual author, title, and subject index is available.

DA20 *Forming a Theology of Urban-Industrial Mission.* Chicago: Institute on the Church in Urban-Industrial Society, 1975.
A classified annotated bibliography of materials treating the theology of the church's mission in modern urban society. Author index. Also lists addresses of sources of the materials listed.

DA21 *A General Bibliography for Urban Ministry.* David J. Frenchak and
Clinton E. Stockwell. Chicago: Urban Church Resource Center and the
Seminary Consortium for Urban Pastoral Education, 1982.
A bibliography of about 400 items, arranged in two sections (books and periodical
articles) by author. No annotations or subject classification. Useful as a raw list
of "significant" material, but provides no help in evaluating that material.

DA22 *Mission Beyond Survival: The Task for the Urban Church in the Eighties.*
Chicago: Institute on the Church in Urban-Industrial Society, 1980.
A classified annotated bibliography of materials about the church's mission in the
city. Fairly long descriptive annotations.

** OTHER AREAS

DA23 *Rural Church in America, a Century of Writings: A Bibliography.* Gary
A. Goreham. New York: Garland, 1990.
An extensive collection of 2,188 books, articles, theses, government publications,
reports, and newspaper articles on the topic. Arranged by type of publication,
subarranged by author. Author and subject indexes.

DA24 *Readings for Town and Country Church Workers: An Annotated
Bibliography.* David M. Byers and Bernard Quinn. Washington, DC:
Glenmary Research Center, 1974.
"An attempt to bring together recent material of significant value on the peoples,
places, problems, and prospects of rural America." A highly selective list of 425
primarily non-religious items which will provide a background for church work
in rural areas. Has descriptive and critical annotations. Indexed by author and by
particular states discussed in the various materials.

DA25 *Resource Book on Aging.* M. A. Suseelan, ed. New York: United Church
Board for Homeland Ministries, 1981.
Produced by the United Church of Christ, this work both describes the aging and
lists numerous resources for working with the aging. Major sections are:
Theological Perspectives on Aging; Description of the Aging, Services to the
Aging, and Additional Resources on Aging (organizations, bibliographies, etc.).

DA26 *Religion & Aging: An Annotated Bibliography.* Vincent John Fecher. San
Antonio: Trinity University Press, 1982.
Lists with good descriptive annotations 473 books, dissertations, and articles
(primarily English-language) on the religious aspects of life after age 60.
Arranged under four major headings with useful subject and author indexes. A
supplement at the back lists (without annotations) 11 "unlocated titles" and 20
"new titles." A primary bibliographical tool for study of this topic.

CHAPTER 36
PASTORAL PSYCHOLOGY AND COUNSELING

** GENERAL WORKS

DB1 *Dictionary of Pastoral Care and Counseling.* Rodney J. Hunter, ed. Nashville: Abingdon Press, 1990.
A comprehensive guide to almost every topic related to pastoral care and counseling, designed for "a wide range of religious caregivers," from professional specialists to laypeople. 1,200 articles, some very extensive, from 600 Protestant, Catholic, Orthodox, and Jewish contributors. Includes biographies, psychological theories, doctrinal issues, historical studies, illness and disorders, and legal and practical issues. Bibliographies and extensive cross-references.

DB2 *A Dictionary of Pastoral Care.* Alastair V. Campbell, ed. New York: Crossroad, 1987.
An interdenominational (mostly Christian, but some Jewish) and interdisciplinary approach to pastoral care, with topics both theoretical and practical. Far less extensive than Hunter (above), includes 300 entries by 185 authors, most accompanied by bibliographies.

** PSYCHOLOGY -- SURVEYS / GUIDES

DB3 *Library Use: A Handbook for Psychology.* Jeffrey G. Reed and Pam M. Baxter. Washington: American Psychological Association, 1983.
Both a guide to library use and an introduction to psychological literature, intended for the college students. Eleven chapters cover topics such as selecting research topics, finding books in libraries, using *Psychological Abstracts*, computer searches, and miscellaneous sources. Detailed table of contents and index. A good tool for any beginning researcher: its explanations of library search strategies are valuable beyond the study of psychology.

DB4 *Humanistic Psychology: a Guide to Information Sources.* Gloria B. Gottsegen and Abbey J. Gottsegen. Detroit: Gale, 1980.
Lists English-language books about alternatives to behaviorism and psychoanalysis, giving brief annotations. Has author, title, and subject indexes. Topics covered include humanistic psychology's historical, philosophical, and theoretical origins; texts; affective education; encounter, sensitivity, and T-groups; experiential techniques and activities; industrial and organization applications; general applied settings; interpersonal behavior reference sources; periodicals; and organizations and associations.

DB5   *American Handbook of Psychiatry.* 2nd ed. 6 vols. Edited by Silvano Arieti, et al. New York: Basic Books, 1974-75.
An extensive guide by leading authorities in the field. Each essay is accompanied by a bibliography. Each volume has name and subject indexes. Contents: v. 1 -- Foundations of Psychiatry; v. 2 -- Child and Adolescent Psychiatry, Sociocultural and Community Psychiatry; v. 3 -- Adult Clinical Psychiatry; v. 4 -- Organic Disorders and Psychosomatic Medicine; v. 5 -- Treatment; and v. 6 -- New Frontiers.

DB6   *Basic Handbook of Child Psychiatry.* Joseph D. Noshpitz, ed. 4 vols. New York: Basic Books, 1979-1980.
An extensive survey of and guide to child psychiatry containing essays by 250 authorities in the field. Each essay includes a bibliography. Each volume has a name and subject index. Contents: v.1 -- Development; v.2 -- Disturbances of Development; v.3 -- Therapeutic Interventions; and v.4 -- Prevention and Current Issues.

** PSYCHOLOGY -- INDEXES

DB7   *Psychological Abstracts.* Washington, DC: American Psychological Association, 1927- . Monthly.
The major indexing and abstracting work in the field. Includes new books, journal articles, and reports, each with a signed abstract. Classified arrangement in 17 major sections, some subdivided. Includes author and subject indexes that are cumulated annually. Indispensable.

DB8   *Psychological Abstracts.* Cumulated Subject Index to "Psychological Abstracts," 1927-1960. 2 vols. Boston: G.K. Hall, 1966.
DB9   *Psychological Abstracts. Cumulated Subject Index to "Psychological Abstracts," Supplement, 1961-65.* Boston: G.K. Hall, 1968.
DB10   *Psychological Abstracts. Cumulated Subject Index to "Psychological Abstracts," Supplement, 1966-68.* 2 vols. Boston: G.K. Hall, 1971.
The original set plus its two supplements include over 650,000 entries. A detailed alphabetical subject index to the first 34 years of *Psychological Abstracts.* Gives reference to the year and the number of the relevant abstracts.

DB11   *Author Index to "Psychological Index," 1894-1935, and "Psychological Abstracts," 1927-1958.* Columbia University. Psychological Library. 5 vols. Boston: G.K. Hall, 1960.
DB12   *Psychological Abstracts: Cumulative Author Index, Supplement, 1959-63.* Boston: G.K. Hall, 1965.
DB13   *Psychological Abstracts: Cumulative Author Index, Supplement, 1964-68.* 2 vols. Boston: G.K. Hall, 1970.

The original volumes plus the supplements include nearly 450,000 entries. Together, they provide easier multiple-year author access to the bulk of *Psychological Abstracts*.

** PSYCHOLOGY -- BIBLIOGRAPHIES

DB14 *Eminent Contributors to Psychology*. Robert I. Watson. 2 vols. New York: Springer, 1974-76.
An extensive bibliography arranged by the name of 500 individuals from 1600 to 1967 who contributed to psychology, although they were not necessarily psychologists. Vol. 1 lists materials written by the individuals (about 12,000 items), vol. 2 lists materials about them (about 50,000 items).

DB15 *International Bibliography of Research in Marriage and the Family*. Edited by Joan Aldous, Reuben Hill, and Nancy Dahl. 2 vols. Minneapolis: Dist. by the Univ. of Minnesota Press for the Minnesota Family Study Center and the Institute of Life Insurance, 1967-1974.
Vol. 1 covers the literature of 1900 to 1964, vol. 2 covers that of 1965-1972. Together, these list over 18,000 articles from major journals in the field of marital and family relations. Includes author, title, and key-word-in-title indexing.

DB16 *Inventory of Marriage and Family Literature, vol. 3- , 1973- *. Beverly Hills, CA: Sage Publications, 1975- . Annual.
Vols. 3 and 4 published by Univ. of Minnesota Press. Vols. 3-5 cover two-year periods; now published annually listing over 3,000 articles from about 800 journals. Divided into 3 portions: the Subject Index (that lists the articles under 120 headings); the Author Index (that includes the author's current address); and the Key-Word-in-Title Index. A useful bibliography on all aspects of this topic.

DB17 *Counseling: a Bibliography (with Annotations)*. Ruth St. John Freeman and Harrop A. Freeman. New York: Scarecrow, 1964.
Has nine major sections, one of which is "Religion (Clergy)." Uses a strange indexing system, so be sure to read the preface. Covers 1950 to 1964.

** PSYCHOLOGY -- ENCYCLOPEDIAS

DB18 *Encyclopedia of Psychology*. Raymond J. Corsini, ed. 4 vols. New York: Wiley, 1984.
An authoritative work consisting of 2,100 entries ranging from short biographies to long articles on major subjects. All fields of psychology are covered by the 500 contributors, all specialists in their fields. The consulting editors are all former presidents of the American Psychological Association. Vol. 4 includes a 15,000 item bibliography and author and subject indexes.

DB19 *International Encyclopedia of Psychiatry, Psychology, Psychoanalysis & Neurology.* Edited by B. B. Wolman. 12 vols. New York: Van Nostrand Reinhold, 1977.
A major new international encyclopedia intended to give "an authoritative, complete, and up-to-date description of research, theory, and practice in sciences and professions dealing with man's mind and its ills." Definitely aimed at professionals and graduate students. Includes over 1,900 articles by over 1,500 specialists. All articles are signed, most have bibliographies. Vol. 12 includes: a complete list of all articles, a name index, and an extensive subject index.

DB20 *International Encyclopedia of Psychiatry, Psychology, Psychoanalysis & Neurology: Progress Volume 1- .* New York: Aesculapius Publishers, 1983- .
Summarizes the most recent and spectacular developments in the research, theory, and practice of every field covered by the Encyclopedia. The first volume includes 136 articles. Additional volumes forthcoming.

DB21 *Baker Encyclopedia of Psychology.* David G. Benner, ed. Grand Rapids: Baker, 1985.
1,050 signed articles by evangelical scholars covering the entire field of psychology from a Christian perspective. Dictionary arrangement, with a "Category Index" that guides the user to articles under 12 broad categories. Includes 100 biographical entries. Some articles have bibliographies.

** PASTORAL PSYCHOLOGY / COUNSELING

DB22 "Bibliographies of Psychology/Religion Studies." G. Allison Stokes. *Religious Studies Review* 4 (1978): 273-279.
An annotated list of 34 past bibliographies on the subject. Helpful for its list of past bibliographies (particularly those that are part of larger works).

DB23 *Psychology of Religion: a Guide to Information Sources.* Donald Capps, Lewis Rambo, and Paul Ransohoff. Detroit: Gale, 1976.
See especially section G, "Directional Dimension of Religion." A classified bibliography with author, title, and subject indexes. Includes only post-1950 items, no unpublished materials, and very few foreign titles.

DB24 *Annotated Bibliography in Religion and Psychology.* William W. Meissner. New York: Academy of Religion and Mental Health, 1961.
An older but still important annotated bibliography of over 2,900 books and journal articles on the topic. Author index. Entries are listed under one of 47 subject categories. Covers up through 1960.

DB25 *Pastoral Care and Counseling Abstracts.* 7 vols. National Clearinghouse, Joint Council on Research in Pastoral Care and Counseling, 1972-1978.

DB26 *Abstracts of Research in Pastoral Care and Counseling.* National Clearinghouse, Joint Council on Research in Pastoral Care and Counseling, 1979- . Annual.

Lists known published, unpublished, and in-progress research for the year. Gives abstracts in a classified arrangement. Abstracts vary considerably in quality and length. Author index. A cumulative index to vols. 1-15 is found in vol. 15 (1987).

DB27 *Psychological Studies of Clergymen: Abstracts of Research.* Robert J. Menges and James E. Dittes. New York: Nelson, 1965.

Lists over 700 books, articles, reports, etc., in a classified and annotated bibliography. Covers, for the most part, only 1955-1965. Indexed by author, instruments and methods, samples, and subjects.

DB28 *Psychoanalysis and Religion: a Bibliography.* Benjamin Beit-Hallahmi. Norwood, PA: Norwood Editions, 1978.

A selective bibliography of about 800 books (primarily in English, a few in French) judged to be "attempts to relate religion and psychoanalysis in a meaningful way." Arranged in two major sections: a classified subject arrangement under 39 subject headings, and the same articles in author order. Note especially subject section 39: "Psychoanalytic Influences on Pastoral Counseling."

DB29 *Religion and Mental Health: A Bibliography.* Florence A. Summerlin, ed. Washington, DC: Alcohol, Drug Abuse, and Mental Health Administration [and] the National Institute of Mental Health, 1981.

A classified bibliography listing over 1,800 books, articles, reports, dissertations, etc. published since 1970. Includes abstracts of each item, an author index, and an extensive key-title-word specific subject index. A well-done and important bibliography for study of this topic.

DB30 *Psychology and Theology in Western Thought, 1672-1965: a Historical and Annotated Bibliography.* Hendrika Vende Kemp. In collaboration with H. Newton Malony. Millwood, N.Y.: Kraus International, 1984.

A 1,047-item list of works related to the integration of theology and psychology. Arranged in seven sections with four indexes: name, institution, title, and subject. Within each section works are listed chronologically. The well-worded annotations describe the theological and psychological orientation of each work.

DB31 *Directory, American Association of Pastoral Counselors.* Washington, DC: the Association, 1979- .

Published at irregular intervals. The main portion of this work is an alphabetical list of members which gives the exact name, academic degrees, full address, phone number, relation to the AAPC, and church affiliation of each. Also has a directory of institutional members, a list of affiliate members, and a geographical directory for the U.S. and Canada.

CHAPTER 37
MISSIONS, THE THIRD WORLD CHURCH

** BIBLIOGRAPHIES / INDEXES

DC1 "Bibliography of World Mission and Evangelism." In *The International Review of Mission*, 1912-   . Quarterly.
Title varies, previously titled "International Missionary Bibliography." Appears in each issue of the journal. Includes about 1,000 books, dissertations, and articles a year. Arranged by a fairly detailed classed system, using eight main sections. A good way to keep current on missions bibliography.

DC2 *Bibliografia missionaria.* Rome: Pontificia Universita' Urbaniana, 1933-   . Annual.
Publisher varies; first few issues covered several years. Four-year cumulated indexes are available. A continuing bibliography of Catholic missions; includes some Protestant material. Classified arrangement with author and subject indexes.

DC3 "Selected Annotated Bibliography on Missiology." Norman E. Thomas, gen ed. In *Missiology* 14 (1986) - 19 (1991). Quarterly.
A five-year project planned to be completed in 1991 and eventually published in book form. Lists books and articles related to missiology published since 1960, classed into 20 categories, including special topics and geographical areas. Each quarterly bibliography includes about 30 entries with brief annotations.

DC4 *Dictionary Catalog of the Missionary Research Library, New York.* 17 vols. Boston: G. K. Hall, 1968.
A major resource of the study of missions. Now located at Union Theological Seminary in New York, this collection began as a result of action of the 1910 Edinburgh world missionary conference. This printed catalog includes 273,000 author, title, and subject cards (in a single A-Z sequence) which represent about 100,000 titles. Includes cards for about 800 mission periodicals (in vol. 17), as well as for reports of missions, pamphlets, etc.

DC5 *Bibliotheca Missionum.* Robert Streit. 30 vols. Freiburg: Herder, 1916-1974.
Imprint varies. The monumental Catholic bibliography of the literature on missions, covering from the 16th century to the present. Estimated to contain entries for more than 60,000 items. Arranged first by country, then by year, then by author. Each volume has author, person, subject, and place indexes. Appendix 2 lists 701 relevant periodicals. Gives, for each entry: full bibliographical information, a critical annotation, and some locations in European libraries.

** BIBLIOGRAPHIES -- SPECIAL TOPICS

DC6   *Theology in Context.* Aachen, West Germany: Institute of Missiology
        Missio, 1984- . Semiannual.
English edition of *Theologie im Kontext.* An annotated index of about 70 major
journals published in Africa, Asia, Oceania, and Latin America, arranged
geographically. Each issue also includes half-to-full page summaries of some
articles that are "especially typical" of third world theology and reports of recent
third world theological conferences. Indexes by author and keyword.

DC7   *Christian Faith Amidst Religious Pluralism: an Introductory Bibliography.*
        Donald G. Dawe, ed. Richmond, VA: Union Theological Seminary in
        Virginia, 1980.
A bibliography of English-language books and non-print materials, arranged by
broad subject categories with an author index. Covers the history,
phenomenology, philosophy, and theology of religion, the relationship of
Christianity with other religions (in general and with specific religions), the
theology and practice of mission, third world theology, etc. "Prepared to facilitate
and enlarge the scope of the Christian search for faithfulness in relating to other
religions." Not annotated.

DC8   *Author and Added Entry Catalog of the American Missionary Association
        Archives, with References to Schools and Mission Stations.* Amistad
        Research Center. 3 vols. Westport, CT: Greenwood, 1970.
A major archival collection which, along with the missions materials, includes
substantial material for the study of Black history and the abolition movement.
The archives includes over 105,000 items, primarily letters. The last volume has
an index of "References to schools and mission stations."

DC9   *Bibliography of the Theology of Missions in the Twentieth Century.*
        Gerald H. Anderson. 3rd ed., rev. and enl. New York: Missionary
        Research Library, 1966.
A bibliography of about 1,000 items, stressing the Protestant and Anglican
literature, with representative Catholic works. Divided topically into four major
sections: biblical studies; historical studies; Christianity and other faiths; and
theory of missions. Arranged by author within each section. Indexed by names
and by corporate/conference names.

DC10 *Bibliography of Third World Missions with Emphasis on Asia.* Marlin L.
        Nelson. Pasadena, CA: Fuller Theological Seminary, 1976.
A helpful introduction to the topic with about 300 briefly annotated items.
Includes books, articles, and theses. Items are coded "most important,"
"important," and "informative."

DC11 *Bible and Mission: a Partially Annotated Bibliography, 1960-1980.* Ed.
        by M. R. Spindler with P. R. Middelkoop. Leiden: Interuniversitair
        Instituut voor Missiologie en Oecumenica, 1981.
An inventory of biblical studies materials, published since 1960, of relevance to
the study of missions. Lists 1,069 books and periodical articles in English,
French, and German. Arranged topically under 31 subject headings with an author
index. Some entries have brief annotations. Particularly useful for those studying
the biblical basis of missions.

DC12 *The Composite Bibliography of Church Growth.* Kent R. Hunter.
        Corunna, IN: Church Growth Analysis and Learning Center, 1982.
An unannotated list of about 270 books, periodicals, cassettes, and films related
to the church growth movement.

Note: The *International Bulletin of Missionary Research* (formerly the *Occasional
Bulletin of Missionary Research*, and the *Occasional Bulletin from the Missionary
Research Library*) often publishes helpful bibliographies on many aspects of
missions research.

** BIBLIOGRAPHIES -- THESES / DISSERTATIONS

DC13 *United States Doctoral Dissertations in Third World Studies, 1869-1978.*
        Michael Sims. Waltham, MA: Crossroads Press, 1980.
Lists about 19,000 dissertations done at U.S. universities between 1869 and 1978
on topics pertaining to the Third World (Africa, Latin America, Asia, and the
Middle East). Arranged geographically by region and country, then alphabetically
by author. Includes extensive indexes of: topical subjects, personal names, place
names, languages, and ethnic groups.

DC14 "Doctoral Dissertations on Mission, 1945-1981." Ernest Theodore
        Bachman. *International Bulletin of Missionary Research* 7 (July 1983):
        97-134.
A 934-item unannotated bibliography of doctoral dissertations representing 145
institutions. Excludes D.Min. and D.Miss. theses. Listed by author and each
entry includes title, degree, year, and institution. There is a subject index.
Updated regularly in IBMR.

DC15 *Missiological Abstracts: the School of World Mission, Fuller Theological
        Seminary, 1966-1984.* Pasadena, CA: Fuller Theological Seminary, 1984.
Lists 453 theses and dissertations from Fuller's SWM. Classified by geographical
area with short, 2-3 sentence annotations. UMI order numbers accompany those
entries available from University Microfilms. Three indexes: author, title, and key
word and phrases.

DC16 *Studies in Missions: an Index of Theses on Missions*. Monrovia, CA: Missions Advanced Research & Communication Center, 1974.
Lists 200 graduate theses from 21 schools, including Fuller Seminary, Wheaton College, and Trinity Evangelical Divinity School. Gives an abstract of each; has author and key-word title indexing.

** ENCYCLOPEDIAS AND DIRECTORIES -- GENERAL

DC17 *Concise Dictionary of the Christian World Mission*. Stephen Neill, Gerald H. Anderson, and John Goodwin, eds. Nashville: Abingdon, 1971.
An international and ecumenical dictionary covering from 1492 to the present. Covers all aspects of the extension of the church and its evangelistic work. The brief articles are signed and include bibliographies. Entries for persons and organizations are included. A valuable, if brief tool.

DC18 *The Encyclopedia of Modern Christian Missions: the Agencies*. Burton L. Goddard, et al., eds. Camden, NJ: Nelson, 1967.
Prepared by the Gordon Divinity School faculty. Gives primary coverage to Protestant missions with survey articles on missions in other traditions. Focuses on mission organizations, describing their history, activities, organization, etc. Most of the 1,400 articles have bibliographies. Includes an index by country and area, and a supplementary index by organization names.

DC19 *The Encyclopedia of Missions: Descriptive, Historical, Biographical, Statistical*. Edwin M. Bliss, ed. 2 vols. New York: Funk and Wagnalls, 1891.
Covers mission organizations, the countries where missions were located, mission stations, missionaries, special topics, etc. A-Z dictionary format with numerous (and sometimes extensive) entries. Of importance in studying the history of missions. The appendices are an extensive bibliography; a list of Bible versions; a list of mission societies and addresses; a list of mission stations; an extensive set of statistical tables; and a general index.

DC20 *Mission Handbook: USA/Canadian Protestant Ministries Overseas*. W. Dayton Roberts and John A. Siewert, eds. 14th ed. Grand Rapids: MARC/Zondervan, 1989.
Editors and titles of earlier editions vary. Aims to provide "a convenient reference to descriptive and statistical data on all North American Protestant overseas ministries or related ministries with overseas operations, plus analytical and interpretative material." Includes brief essays on missions topics, information on the many agencies listed, a mass of statistical data, and various indexes to this material.

DC21 *World Christianity.* 5 vols. Monrovia, CA: MARC, 1979-1986.
    Contents: v. 1 -- Middle East; v. 2 -- Eastern Asia. v. 3 -- South Asia.
v. 4 -- Central American and the Caribbeean. v. 5 -- Oceania. A project of the
Strategy Working Group of the Lausanne Committee for World Evangelization.
Each regional list is arranged by country, with some larger countries (e.g., India)
subdivided. Gives a brief profile of Christianity among the peoples of each
country, including information on unreached peoples, national churches, foreign
missions, major Christian activities, and the nation and its people in general. Each
chapter also includes a selected bibliography.

DC22 *Directory: North American Protestant Schools and Professors of Mission.*
    Monrovia, CA: MARC, 1982.
Arranged in two main sections: part one is a directory of 217 colleges and
seminaries, listing mission-related degrees, course offerings, and faculty.
Appended is a geographic index to these schools. Part two is a list of 453 mission
professors, including their areas of specialization.

Note: see also the *World Christian Encyclopedia* (D1) for extensive information
for missions research.

** ENCYCLOPEDIAS AND DIRECTORIES -- U.S. AND CANADA

DC23 *The Native American Christian Community: a Directory of Indian, Aleut,
    and Eskimo Churches.* R. Pierce Beaver, ed. Monrovia, CA: MARC,
    1979.
Includes an introductory essay; directories of denominational agencies,
nondenominational agencies, and independent churches working with native
Americans; a list of native American churches in cities over 30,000; a directory
of councils, service agencies, and educational ministries; Christian population
reports; and statistical tables. A valuable source of information and statistics
difficult, if not impossible, to find elsewhere.

DC24 *Harvard Encyclopedia of American Ethnic Groups.* Stephan Thernstrom,
    ed. Cambridge: Harvard University Press, 1980.
Includes long articles on major ethnic groups and short sketches of many other
smaller and lesser known groups. Treats their cultural, social, economic, religious,
and political history. Also includes 29 essays on general themes such as
education, health, religion, etc. Lacks index and cross-references. An important,
scholarly, and authoritative work.

** OTHER TOOLS

DC25 *A History of the Expansion of Christianity.* Kenneth S. Latourette. 7
      vols. New York: Harper, 1937-1945.
An extensive authoritative work on the missionary work of the church from its
beginnings up to the present. Covers Catholic, Protestant, and Orthodox mission
work in a comprehensive scholarly survey. Each volume includes an index,
extensive bibliographies, and maps.

DC26 *The Twentieth Century Atlas of the Christian World: the Expansion of
      Christianity Through the Ages.* Anton Freitag, ed. New York: Hawthorne,
      1964.
Contains a series of 29 colored maps, along with illustrations and explanatory text,
showing the growth of the church through its mission work. Indexed by proper
name.

** ASIA

DC27 *Christianity in Southeast Asia: a Bibliographical Guide.* Gerald H.
      Anderson. New York: Missionary Research Library, 1966.
"An Annotated Bibliography of Selected References in Western Languages." A
selective classified list with brief annotations. Intended to be representative of the
scholarly literature on the topic. Lists books, articles, dissertations, and relevant
periodical titles.

DC28 "A Selected Bibliography in Western Languages." Gerald H. Anderson.
      In *Asian Voices in Christian Theology*, pp. 261-321. Edited by Gerald H.
      Anderson. Maryknoll, NY: Orbis, 1975.
Lists books and periodical articles on Asian Christian theology, giving brief
annotations. Arranged by country, subarranged by author.

DC29 "A Selected Bibliography in Western Languages, Classified and
      Annotated." Douglas J. Elwood. In *What Asian Christians are Thinking*,
      pp. 458-497. Edited by Douglas J. Elwood. Quezon City, Philippines:
      New Day Publishers, 1976.
Lists, for the most part, the same materials as Anderson's bibliography (DC28) but
arranges the materials by subject. Classified arrangement with specific subject
index. Note the list of other bibliographies on Asian Christianity at the beginning
of this bibliography.

DC30 *1983 Directory of Theological Schools in Asia.* Bong Rin Ro, ed. Taipei,
      Taiwan: Asia Theological Association, 1982.
Part I lists about 500 theological schools and Bible colleges in Asia and the South

Pacific. Entries are arranged by country, subarranged by name of the school. Part II gives brief statistics for about 180 schools in Asia.

DC31 *1979 Directory of Theologians in Asia.* Bond Rin Ro, ed. Taipei, Taiwan: Asia Theological Association, 1979.
Gives short biographical information on over 350 evangelical theological scholars in Asia. Entries are arranged by country, then by theological school to which the person is attached. Includes a picture of each person.

DC32 *Christianity in China: A Scholars' Guide to Resources in the Libraries and Archives of the United States.* Archie R. Crouch, [et al.]. Armonk: M.E. Sharpe, 1989.
A list of 554 repositories, arranged by state, city, and institution. Provides address of library and a description of the China material housed there. Includes three union lists: of 700 journals related to Chinese missions, of oral histories, and of dissertations. Bibliography, subject index, name index, and institution index. Invaluable tool for study of the history of Christianity in China.

** LATIN AMERICA

DC33 *Bibliografia teologica comentada del area Iberoamericana, 1973/74-* . Buenos Aires: Instituto Superior Evangelico de Estudios Teologicos, 1975- .
Covers all aspects of "Iberoamerican" theology, including articles from over 400 periodicals as well as books. The major bibliography for the student of Latin American theology. Classified arrangement with subject, author, and biblical reference indexes.

DC34 *Protestantism in Latin America: a Bibliographical Guide.* John H. Sinclair. Pasadena, CA: William Carey Library, 1976.
"An Annotated Bibliography of Selected References Mainly in English, Spanish, and Portuguese and Useful Bibliographical Aids to Assist the Student and Researcher in the General Field of Latin American Studies." Lists more than 3,000 works in two major sections: a reprint of the 1967 edition and a supplement of new material. Classified arrangement with an author index.

DC35 *Catalog of The C. Peter Wagner Collection of Materials on Latin American Theology of Liberation.* C. Peter Wagner, ed. Pasadena, CA: Fuller Theological Seminary, 1974.
A 70-page annotated bibliography of "(1) materials directly addressed to Latin American theology of liberation, (2) other writings of the principal figures in the Latin American theology of liberation . . . and (3) background materials published in Spanish and/or Portuguese. . . ." Arranged by author, with entries under each

person subarranged by date. Includes books, periodical articles, and circulated but unpublished materials.

DC36 *The Catholic Left in Latin America: A Comprehensive Bibliography.*
Therrin C. Dahlin, Gary P. Gillum, and Mark L. Grover, eds. Boston: G. K. Hall, 1981.

Intended to be comprehensive, covering 1960-1978, for material relating directly to the topic; but only includes "representative" literature on Christian democracy, education, and liberation theology. Entries are arranged geographically, subdivided by topic.

** AFRICA

DC37 *Christianity in Tropical Africa: a Selective Annotated Bibliography.*
Patrick E. Ofori. Nendeln: KTO Press, 1977.

Lists 2,859 books, articles, theses, etc., on the history of Christianity in Africa south of the Sahara. Materials are arranged topically by the regions and countries discussed, subarranged by author. Includes author index.

DC38 *African Theology: International Bibliography, 1968-1977, Indexed by Computer.* Raymond Facelina and Damien Rwegera. (RIC Supplement 30). Strasbourg: Cerdic, 1977.

Lists 393 books and articles on the modern "Africanisation" of Christianity and theology. Stresses material produced in Africa, primarily in French and English. Arranged by author, no subject index.

DC39 *Christian Communication Directory: Africa.* Franz-Josef Eilers et al., eds. Paderborn: F. Schoningh, 1980.

Published cooperatively by the Catholic Media Council, the World Association for Christian Communication, and the Lutheran World Federation. A directory, arranged by country, of the Christian "church communication centres," publishing houses, printing presses, periodicals, radio/TV production studios, and AV and film centers in Africa, with brief descriptive data. Incomplete but still of value.

DC40 *Directory of Theological Institutions in Eastern Africa.* Nairobi: Association of Theological Institutions in Eastern Africa, 1981.

Information on 40 theological schools from 6 countries. Some entries more complete than others. Data include degree programs, size of student body, library holdings, and faculty.

Note: See also the section on "Christian Church and Africa," as well as other relevant items, in E. L. Williams, *Howard University Bibliography of African and Afro-American Religious Studies* (H32).

** CULTURAL ANTHROPOLOGY AND AREA STUDIES

A working knowledge of the reference works covering cultural anthropology and area studies is usually necessary when doing research on modern missions. However, "few general reference books in anthropology are available, as most works in this field treat specific countries or areas (Sheehy, p. 734)." For a bibliography of reference works covering particular countries, see Sheehy (A1), using the index. A few highly useful works are listed below.

DC41 *Nature and Use of the HRAF files; a Research and Teaching Guide.*
    Robert A. Legace. New Haven: Human Relations Area Files, 1974.
A description and guide to the Human Relations Area Files, a collection of data on over 300 primitive, historical, and contemporary cultures which is available in microform or hard copy at many libraries. Each culture is assigned a "Culture File" that holds material (books, articles, manuscripts, special translations, etc.) on that culture. Also allows for the study of specific topics (e.g. religion) cross-culturally.

DC42 *Abstracts in Anthropology,* vol. 1- , 1970-   . Farmingdale, NY:
    Baywood. Quarterly.
Publisher varies. Arranged topically by the major subfields of anthropology, indexed by author and specific subject. Provides abstracts of books and periodical articles.

DC43 *Area Handbook of . . .*and *Country Study of . . . .* Washington, DC:
    Superintendent of Documents, [various editions and dates].
A series of over 100 volumes -- each original "Area Handbook" is being retitled "Country Study" as a new edition is published. "Each Study describes a single country with a view toward depicting cultural and historical origins and the role these play in the country's present institutional organization and functioning." Written by an interdisciplinary team for the nonspecialist.

DC44 *Encyclopedia of the Third World.* George T. Kurian. 3rd. ed. 3 vols.
    New York: Facts on File, 1987.
"Provides a compact, balanced and objective description of the dominant political, economic and social systems of 122 countries of the world." Arranged by country, with an extensive name and subject index. Each article includes a representative bibliography of materials published since 1970. A useful tool that gathers information from a variety of sources.

DC45 *Third World Resource Directory.* Thomas P. Fenton and Mary J. Heffron,
    eds. Maryknoll, NY: Orbis Books, 1984.
An annotated list of organizations, books, and other resources arranged in two

parts. Section 1 includes 5 geographical areas, section 2 contains 5 topics: food, human rights, militarism, trans-national corporations, and women. Extensive indexes are included. Defining the third world as all people under economic domination and impoverishment, this work has a strong bias against the American government and corporate relationships with the third world.

DC46 *Bibliography for Cross-Cultural Workers.* A. R. Tippett. Pasadena, CA:
       William Carey Library, 1971.
Includes all types of materials. Arranged by subject without annotations or indexes. Covers two major areas: "The Anthropological Dimensions" and "The Religious Dimensions" of cross-cultural work. The second section covers only Animism.

DC47 *Bibliography for Training Across Cultures.* Marvin K. Mayers. Dallas:
       Summer Institute of Linguistics, 1979.
A 250 entry bibliography for cross-cultural research. Part 1 classifies entries in 16 broad categories. Part 2 is an alphabetical list with annotations. Also included is the location of each title in six Texas libraries.

DC48 *Ethnologue: Languages of the World.* Barbara F. Grimes, ed. 10th ed.
       Dallas: Wycliffe Bible Translators, 1984.
"Ties together in one volume the best information available on the languages of the world" with "special attention to the Bible translation needs of each language." For each language, lists number of speakers, location, dialects, linguistic affiliation, and Bible translation needs. Arranged by country, subarranged by language.

CHAPTER 38
CHRISTIAN EDUCATION

** EDUCATION -- GENERAL

DD1 *A Bibliographic Guide to Educational Research.* Dorothea M. Berry. 2nd
ed. Metuchen, NJ: Scarecrow, 1980.
"A concise guide to assist students in education courses to make effective use of
the resources of the library of their college or university." Lists 772 items with
annotations. Arranged by type of material (journals, research studies, government
documents, reference tools, etc.), subarranged by subject. Author, title, and
subject indexes.

DD2 *Education Index.* New York: Wilson, 1929- . 10x a year.
"A cumulative author subject index to a selected list of educational
periodicals, proceedings, and yearbooks." Published monthly except for July and
August; annual cumulations. Provides author and subject entries for articles from
about 250 educational periodicals, arranged in a single A-Z sequence. From
mid-1961 to mid-1969 had only subject indexing. An established periodical index
in the field; its format is similar to *Reader's Guide.*

DD3 *CIJE: Current Index to Journals in Education.* New York: CCM
Information Sciences, 1969- . Monthly.
Semiannual and annual cumulations. Currently indexes over 700 publications.
Each issue has four parts: main section (with full bibliographic information and
an abstract) arranged by "document number;" subject index; author index; and
journals' contents index. Provides wide coverage with good indexing.

DD4 *Resources in Education.* Syracuse, NY: Educational Resources
Information Clearinghouse, 1966- . Monthly.
Formerly titled: *Research in Education.* Known as "ERIC." Published monthly
with semiannual and annual cumulative indexes. Gives bibliographical
information and descriptive abstracts of unpublished materials "of interest to the
education community" -- reports, papers, etc., that have been submitted for listing.
Entries are arranged by "document number." To locate relevant abstracts, there
are indexes by subject, author, and institutions. Contains a great variety of useful
material, of varying quality, most of which is available on paper or microfiche
from the ERIC reproduction service (see preface to any issue).

DD5 *Encyclopedia of Education.* Edited by Lee C. Deighton. 10 vols. New
York: Macmillan, 1971.
Treats all aspects of educational activity in over 1,000 articles by specialists, most

with bibliographies. Given the relatively few and long articles, be sure to use the index (vol. 10) to locate material on specific topics. For additional tips on use, see the "Guide to Articles" in vol. 9.

** CHRISTIAN EDUCATION -- BIBLIOGRAPHIES

DD6   "A Selected Bibliography." Marvin J. Taylor, ed. In *Religious Education: a Comprehensive Survey*, pp. 418-430. New York: Abingdon, 1960.

DD7   "A Selected Bibliography Since 1959." Marvin J. Taylor, ed. In *An Introduction to Christian Education*, pp. 383-98. New York: Abingdon, 1966.

DD8   "A Selected Bibliography Since 1966." Marvin J. Taylor, ed. In *Foundations of Christian Education in an Era of Change*, pp. 271-83. Nashville: Abingdon, 1976.

Combined together, these three bibliographies list about 1,000 post-1950 books important to this field. All three use nearly the same outline for arranging the entries, which are not annotated. Major areas covered are: The nature, principles, and history of religious education; religious growth and the learning-teaching process; the organization and administration of religious education; curriculum for religious education; methods in religious education; and prayer and worship.

DD9   *Bibliography in Christian Education for Seminary and College Libraries*. DeWitte Campbell Wyckoff. New York: Program Agency, Mission in Education Unit, United Presbyterian Church in the U.S.A., 1960-1987. Annual.

Publisher and title varied. Issued in loose mimeographed (and later printed) format. Intended to be a selective, annotated guide to the most important materials for training church workers in Christian education. Primarily of material on Christian education, but also lists representative and important secular works. Subjects covered include Christian education; education theory; the theology, philosophy, and history of education; the behavioral foundations of religion and education; administration; curriculum; religion and higher education; religion and the public school. Ceased publication in 1987.

DD10   *Researches in Personality, Character and Religious Education; a Bibliography of American Doctoral Dissertations, 1885 to 1959*. Lawrence C. Little. With an index by Helen-Jean Moore. Pittsburgh: University of Pittsburgh Press, 1962.

Preliminary ed. in 1960. Lists 6,304 dissertations "of possible value to students who do research in personality, character, religious education, and closely related fields." Arranged alphabetically by author with minimal bibliographic information. An extensive subject index provides detailed specific subject access to the material.

DD11 "Doctoral Dissertation Abstracts in Religious Education." In *Religious Education,* 1906- .
Title varies somewhat. Now appears in the journal annually, but it appeared less frequently in its early days. It contains "selected abstracts of doctoral dissertations of interest to religious educators" condensed from *Dissertation Abstracts* (P9), arranged by major subject areas. "Criteria for inclusion have been: inclusion of studies from the major religious groups in the country; representation from as large a group of schools as possible; relevance to the concerns and problems of religious education."

DD12 *Protestant Theological Education in America: a Bibliography.* Heather F. Day. Metuchen, NJ: Scarecrow Press, 1985.
A very extensive (5,249 item) list of materials related to American Protestant theological education (although some Catholic material is also included). Arranged by author, the list is not annotated. Four subject indexes, including institutions and "individuals significant in theological education," greatly enhance access to the bibliography.

** CHRISTIAN EDUCATION -- OTHER TOOLS

DD13 *Harper's Dictionary of Religious Education.* Iris V. Cully and Kendig Brubaker Cully, gen. eds. San Francisco: Harper & Row, 1990.
Over 600 signed articles from 270 contributors (Protestant, Catholic, and Jewish). Up-to-date and concise articles covering educational topics, biographies, organizations, teaching methods, and history are interspersed with longer essays on general themes on the theory and practice of religious education, psychology, faith development, etc. A valuable resource.

DD14 *A Dictionary of Religious Education.* Ed. by John M. Sutcliffe. London: SCM Press, 1984.
Over 200 contributors have produced about 340 signed articles, most of which are accompanied by bibliographies. Very few biographical entries, but there is an index of names. Intended to be international in scope and inclusive of all religious faiths, but the heavy emphasis is on British religious education.

DD15 *The Basic Encyclopedia for Youth Ministry.* Dennis C. Benson and Bill Wolfe. Loveland, CO: Group Books, 1981.
Intended as a "ministry-helping tool" for those working with youth, particularly those with little training. Contains about 300 short entries offering brief direction and advice in many areas of ministry to youth. Some items include brief bibliographies. Contains some useful material.

DD16 *Christian Education Catalog.* Ruth G. Cheney, ed. New York: Seabury,
      1981.

A guide to a wide variety of Christian education resources -- books, guides,
filmstrips, cassettes, student pamphlets, and other teaching materials. Includes "a
cross-section of the best materials available from the mainstream Christian
publishers and institutions." A helpful guide, particularly in its coverage of major
curriculum series and of audio-visual materials.

CHAPTER 39
WORSHIP AND LITURGY, CHURCH MUSIC, AND PREACHING

** WORSHIP AND LITURGY

DE1   *The New Westminster Dictionary of Liturgy and Worship.* J. G. Davies, ed.
       Philadelphia: Westminster, 1986.
Covers the liturgy and worship of the major and minor Christian groups with brief
accounts of other major religions. Articles give a definition of each item, its
historical background, its interpretation, and its current significance. Most of the
articles, written by a wide variety of scholars, have bibliographies. Articles on
topics of widely varying opinion have two or more sections by representatives of
various viewpoints. The 1986 edition takes into account recent trends in liturgy
and worship.

DE2   *A Bibliography of Christian Worship.* Bard Thompson. Metuchen, N.J.:
       Scarecrow Press, 1989.
A massive (nearly 800-page) unannotated list of books, journal articles, chapters
from books, and dissertations on worship. Claims to cover through 1982, although
contains some later. Mostly English, but some foreign language. Arranged in
three sections: ch. 1 covers general works; ch. 2 (the bulk of the book) is arranged
historically: early church, eastern churches, Latin churches, Reformation, etc.; ch.
3-6 cover worship topics, such as sacraments, liturgy, church year, hymnology,
worship and the arts, etc. Very detailed table of contents and two indexes:
author/editor and organization.

DE3   *The Oxford Book of Prayer.* George Appleton, gen. ed. London: Oxford
       University Press, 1985.
A collection of 1,120 selections, arranged in seven chapters. Intended to be useful
both for private meditation and public worship. Primarily Christian, but also
includes prayers from other religious traditions. Author/source index and subject
index.

** CHURCH MUSIC

DE4   *The New Grove Dictionary of Music and Musicians.* George Grove, ed.
       6th ed., edited by Stanley Sadie.   20 vols.   New York: Grove's
       Dictionaries of Music, Inc., 1979.
A major revision of an established authoritative encyclopedic work on music.
Includes 22,500 articles, long bibliographies, 7,500 cross-references, 3,000
illustrations, and 16,500 biographies on all aspects of music and musicians. Has
a great deal of material of use in the study of church music.

DE5   *A Dictionary of Hymnology Setting Forth the Origin and History of Christian Hymns of All Ages and Nations.* John Julian. Rev. 2nd ed., with new supplement. New York: Scribners, 1907.
Still the most comprehensive and authoritative work on the Christian hymns of all ages. Includes signed articles with bibliographies on hymnology, hymn writers, and individual hymns. Besides the main A-Z dictionary section, the work includes a cross-reference index to first lines in English, French, German, Latin, etc.; an index of authors and translators of hymns; and various supplements to the main work.

DE6   *Key Words in Church Music: Definition Essays on Concepts, Practices, and Movements of Thought in Church Music.* Ed. by Carl Schalk. St. Louis: Concordia, 1978.
"Intended to provide the practicing church musician with information, largely historical, that may be helpful in addressing matters of contemporary practice in church music." Has 76 articles, each about five pages long, which include selected bibliographies.

DE7   *Women Composers and Hymnists: a Concise Biographical Dictionary.* Charles Eugene Claghorn. Metuchen, NJ: Scarecrow, 1984.
Brief, one-paragraph biographical sketches of 155 women composers and 60 women hymnists. Lists representative hymns or music for each entry; does not supply a complete list of works. Also lists hymnals where some works may be found. While the biographies are brief and incomplete, they do provide hard-to-find information.

DE8   *A Selective Bibliography for the Study of Hymns, 1980.* Keith C. Clark. Springfield, OH: Hymn Society of America, 1980.
Revision of the 1964 ed. A well done 42-page classified bibliography of significant works for the study of hymnology. Includes books, periodical articles, and unpublished materials. No annotations or index. Titles particularly valuable in a basic collection are indicated.

DE9   *An English-Speaking Hymnal Guide.* Erik Routley. Collegeville, MN: Liturgical Press, 1979.
Intended to be a companion to a hymnal, this work lists 888 hymns that are found 4 or more times in 26 major 20th century hymnals. For each hymn, it gives (as applicable) the first line, length and meter, author's name, original sources, notes of interest, and the hymnals in which the hymn appears. Includes chronological and author indexes, as well as brief bibliographies.

DE10 *Hymn and Scripture Selection Guide.* Donald H. Spencer. Valley Forge,
     PA: Judson, 1977.
Section 1 lists 380 hymns arranged by title. Under each hymn, brief phrases
identify its subject and selected relevant Scripture passages are listed. Section 2
is a listing of Scripture passages in canonical order. Under each passage, the
number(s) of the more appropriate hymn(s) are listed. Useful for appropriate
selection of hymns to go with a sermon on a particular text.

DE11 *Hymns and Tunes: an Index.* Katharine Smith Diehl. New York:
     Scarecrow, 1966.
Indexes the hymns from 78 English-language hymnals by first lines, variant first
lines, and authors. Indexes hymn tunes by names and variants and by composer.
Also includes a systematic index to the melodies and other useful appendices.

DE12 *Judson Concordance to Hymns.* Thomas B. McDormand and Frederic S.
     Crossman. Valley Forge, PA: Judson, 1965.
Provides a subject approach to 2,342 hymns from 27 major denominational
hymnals in the U.S. and Canada. The hymns included are listed alphabetically in
the "table of first lines." In the "line index" section, lines from hymns are
arranged by key word and refer the user to the correct entry in the table of first
lines.

** STUDY OF PREACHING

DE13 *Recent Homiletical Thought: a Bibliography, 1935-1965.* William Toohey
     and William Thompson, eds. Nashville: Abingdon, 1967.
A listing of over 2,100 books, articles, theses, and dissertations on preaching and
on Protestant and Roman Catholic homiletics. Most entries have brief annotations.
Divided into four major sections by type of material (book, article, etc.), then
arranged topically under 15 subject headings. An appendix lists periodicals of
interest. Author index.

DE14 *Recent Homiletical Thought: an Annotated Bibliography; Volume 2,
     1966-1979.* A. Duane Litfin and Haddon W. Robinson, eds. Grand Rapids:
     Baker, 1983.
Updates Toohey and Thompson (DE13) with a similar structure and scope, but
covering 1966-1979. Includes nearly 1,900 entries, listing articles in over 100
periodicals, as well as books and dissertations. Offers better coverage to the
writings of evangelicals than the first volume.

DE15 *Rhetoric and Public Address: a Bibliography, 1947-1961.* James W.
     Cleary and Frederick S. Haberman. Madison, WI: University of Wisconsin
     Press, 1974.

"A comprehensive listing of important publications on the subject of rhetoric and public address which have appeared in the major languages of Western civilization." Includes 8,035 books, periodical articles, and dissertations. Arranged by author with an extensive subject index. See especially the heading "Preaching" where numerous works, subarranged by narrower topics, are listed.

DE16   "Bibliography of Rhetoric and Public Address for the Year: 1951-1968." In *Speech Monographs* v. 19-36, 1952-1969. Annual.
Lists books, journal articles, dissertations, and book reviews from the major fields of interest to scholars in rhetoric and public address. Classified subject arrangement, no indexes. Note the section on "Pulpit Address."

DE17   "Graduate Theses: an Index of Graduate Work in Speech." In *Speech Monographs* v.2-36, 1935-1969. Annual.
In total lists 20,002 theses. Each annual list is arranged by the school where the thesis was done, subarranged by type of degree. Lists all types of theses -- M.A., M.S., M.F.A., Th.M., Ph.D., etc. Each list also has a classified subject index, see especially the subdivision "Homiletics-Preaching" under the division "Public Address." In addition, most years of this journal also include an "Abstracts of Dissertations in the Field of Speech" section which has abstracts for a limited number of recent theses.

DE18   *Index to Journals in Communication Studies through 1985.* Ronald J. Matlon, ed.; Peter C. Facciola, associate ed. Annandale, VA: Speech Communication Association, 1987.
The main section lists, issue by issue, the primary articles (reviews and short remarks are excluded) in 15 major speech journals, covering from the beginning of the journal through 1985. Each article is assigned a code number which the indexes use to refer to it. Has an author index and an extensive classified subject index (a key-word subject index to the classified subject index is included). Contains a fair amount of material on homiletics but it is difficult to find with the indexing used.

DE19   *Bibliographic Annual in Speech Communication, 1970- .* Falls Church, VA: Speech Communications Association, 1971- . Annual.
Lists and abstracts masters theses and doctoral dissertations in speech communication. Also offers a number of specialized bibliographies on aspects of communication.

DE20   "Pulpit Eloquence: a List of Doctrinal and Historical Studies in English." Harry Caplan and Henry H. King. *Speech Monographs* 22, Special Issue (1955): 5-159.
Lists all types of materials on the history and doctrine of preaching -- excludes

sermon collections, homiletical aids, and material on hermeneutics. Divided into sections by century of publication, subarranged by author. Unfortunately, no subject index (or any other subject access) is provided. Seventh in a series of 8 bibliographies: the other 7 list material in Latin, Italian, French, Spanish, Scandinavian, Dutch, and German. For bibliographical citations for these works, see the footnote on p. 5 of this bibliography, or see Toohey (DE13), pp. 222-223.

DE21 "Bibliography of Communications Dissertations in American Schools of Theology." Franklin H. Knower. *Speech Monographs 30* (1963): 108-136. Lists 913 doctoral, masters, and baccalaureate theses done before 1960 at 45 schools belonging to the American Association of Theological Schools. Theses are listed by school, then subarranged by type of degree and author. A classified subject index is also provided.

DE22 *20 Centuries of Great Preaching: an Encyclopedia of Preaching*. Clyde E. Fant and William M. Pinson. 13 vols. Waco, TX: Word Books, 1971. Has chapters on over 90 Christian preachers from many denominations, countries, religious vocations, and theological positions. For each preacher, the chapter includes a portrait, a brief chronology, a concise biography, a sample of his sermons, and a selected bibliography of material by and about him. Individuals covered are arranged chronologically. Vol. 13 contains an alphabetical list of the preachers included and excellent indexes of subjects, Scripture references, persons, sermon names, homiletical style and usage, and illustrations used in the sermons.

DE23 *Christian Communication: A Bibliographical Survey*. Paul A. Soukup. Westport, Conn.: Greenwood Press, 1989. An annotated bibliography of 1,311 (mostly English language) books and articles covering all general categories of communications studies *except* homiletics. Following an introductory essay, items are listed in eight sections: resources; communication theory; historical studies; rhetoric; interpersonal communicatioin; mass communication; intercultural communication; and other media. Name, title, and subject indexes.

** HOMILETICAL AIDS

DE24 *Familiar Quotations: a Collection of Passages, Phrases and Proverbs Traced to Their Sources in Ancient and Modern Literature*. John Bartlett. 15th rev. and enl. ed. Emily M. Beck, ed. Boston: Little, Brown, & Co., 1980. A standard tool for finding apt quotations on a given topic or for tracing the origin of known sayings. Quotations are arranged chronologically by the author's dates. Access to these is provided by an extensive 100,000-entry key-word index.

DE25 *The World Treasury of Religious Quotations: Diverse Beliefs, Convictions, Comments, Dissents, and Opinions from Ancient and Modern Sources.* R. L. Wood, comp. New York: Hawthorn, 1966.
10,000 quotations arranged under 1,500 subject headings, subarranged by date. Provides wide coverage, but only 2 of the quotations are taken from the Bible. Author index. No key-word index.

DE26 *Encyclopedia of Religious Quotations.* Frank S. Mead, comp. Westwood, NJ: Revell, 1965.
A collection of around 10,000 religious quotations arranged under 170 subject headings. Contains Christian and non-Christian sources. Includes index of authors and topics.

DE27 *Granger's Index to Poetry.* Edith Granger. 8th ed., completely rev. and enl., indexing anthologies published through June 30, 1985. Ed. by William F. Bernhardt. New York: Columbia University Press, 1986.
An extensive index to poetry by title and first line. Also gives a location in an anthology where the entire poem may be found. Includes author index and subject index.

DE28 *Masterpieces of Christian Literature in Summary Form.* Ed. Frank N. Magill with Ian P. McGreal. New York: Harper & Row, 1963.
Includes 2,000-word essay-reviews of 300 books dealing with the Christian movement. Materials were selected and reviewed from a Protestant viewpoint (see also the companion volume, *Masterpieces of Catholic Literature in Summary Form* (New York: Harper & Row, 1965). Useful for a quick summary of what a work is about and some idea of its importance.

INDEX

To Authors, Editors, Titles, and Alternative Titles

Atiya, Aziz S., BC13
ATLA Religion Index Special Bibliographies, H41
Atlas of Israel, AF10
Atlas of Religious Change in America; 1952-1971, BF13
Atlas of the Early Christian World, BB23
Atlas van de oudchristelijke wereld, BB23
Atlas zur Kirchengeschichte, BA18
Augsburg Historical Atlas of Christianity in the Middle Ages and Reformation,
     BD10
*Author and Added Entry Catalog of the American Missionary Association
     Archives*, DC8
Author Index to "Psychological Index", DB11
Aversa, Elizabeth Smith, A4
Avi-Yonah, Michael, AF7
Ayres, Samuel G., CA21

Bachman, Ernest Theodore, DC14
Baer, Eleanora A., N18
Bahmn, Archie J., CC13
Bainton, Roland H., BD4
Baker, Derek, BD18
Baker Encyclopedia of Psychology, DB21
Baker Encyclopedia of the Bible, AD5
Baker's Dictionary of Christian Ethics, CB7
Baker's Dictionary of Practical Theology, DA5
Baker's Dictionary of Theology, CA5
Baldwin, James M., CC12
Baptist Atlas, C21
Baptist Bibliography, BE12
Baptist Theological Seminary, AC8, CA15
Barber, Cyril J., A13, H23-H24
Bardenhewer, Otto, BB3
Barrett, David B., D1
Barrow, John G., G6
Bartlett, John, DE24
Basic Bibliographic Guide for New Testament Exegesis, AC5
Basic Bibliography for the Study of the Semitic Languages, AB14
Basic Encyclopedia for Youth Ministry, DD15
Basic Handbook of Child Psychiatry, DB6
Basic Tools for Biblical Exegesis, AA2
Bass, Dorothy C., BF21
Batson, Beatrice, H19
Bauer, Johannes B., AE2

Church and State in America, DA12
Church Growth Analysis and Learning Center, DC12
"Church-Related and Accredited Colleges and Universities in the U.S., E4
Church-State Relations, DA13
Churches and Church Membership in the United States, D13
Claghorn, Charles Eugene Claghorn, DE7
Clark, Keith C., DE8
Classification of the Library of Union Theological Seminary, H6
Classified Bibliography of Literature on the Acts of the Apostles, AC22
Classified Bibliography of the Finds in the Desert ..., AA30
Classified Bibliography of the Septuagint, AB18
Classified Catalog of the Ecumenical Movement, BE8
Clavis patrum apostolicorum, BB21
Clavis patrum graecorum, BB16
Clavis patrum latinorum, BB15
Cleary, James W., DE15
Clifford E. Barbour Library, BD35
Coggins, R. J., AD24
"Collections toward a Bibliography of Congregationalism", BE14
Collison, Robert L., G1
Commenting and Commentaries, AA6
Commission internationale d'histoire ecclésiastique comparée, BD5, BD18
Companion to the Bible, AE1
Composite Bibliography of Church Growth, DC12
Comprehensive Dissertation Index, P5-P7
Concise Dictionary of Christian Ethics, CB6
Concise Dictionary of the Christian World Mission, DC17
Congregationalism of the Last 300 Years, BE14
Consider a Christian College, E5
Constable, Giles, BC12
Contemporaries of Erasmus, BD12
Contemporary Research on the Sixteenth Century Reformation, BD2
CORECAT, H11
Coreham, Gary A., DA23
Corley, Bruce, AF14
Cornish, Graham, N13
Corpus Dictionary of Western Churches, BA11
Corpus Reformatorum, BD28
Corsini, Raymond J., DB18
Cottrell, Jack, CA2, CB1
Council on Graduate Studies in Religion, P15-P16
Council on the Study of Religion Bulletin, U3

Dictionary of the Bible, AD9
Dictionary of the History of Ideas, CC11
Dictionary of the Middle Ages, BC10
Dictionary of the New Testament, AD23
Dictionary of Theology, CA9
Dictionary of Universal Biography of All Ages and of All People, F4
Dictionnaire d'archéologie chrétienne et de liturgie, C18, BB10
Dictionnaire d'histoire et de géographie ecclésiastiques, C18, BA13
Dictionnaire de droit canonique, C18
Dictionnaire de la Bible, C18, AD7-AD8
Dictionnaire de théologie catholique, C18
Dictionnaire du Nouveau Testament, AD23
Diehl, Katharine Smith, DE11
Directory of American Philosophers, CC13
Directory of American Scholars, F25
Directory of Archives and Manuscript Repositories, S2
Directory of Departments and Programs of Religious Studies in North America,
    E7
Directory of Ecumenical Institutes, Centers, & Organizations, BE10
Directory of Faculty in Departments and Programs of Religious Studies in North
    America, F27
Directory of Religious and Parareligious Bodies and Organizations in the United
    States, D6
Directory of Religious Broadcasters, D15
Directory of Religious Organizations in the United States, D9
Directory of Theologians in Asia, DC31
Directory of Theological Institutions in Eastern Africa, DC40
Directory of Theological Schools in Asia, DC30
Disciples of Christ and American Culture, BE15
Dissertation Abstracts International, P9, P14
Dissertation Abstracts Online, U6
Dissertation Title Index, P16
Dissertations in Philosophy Accepted at American Universities, CC6
Dittes, James E., DB27
Doctor William's Library, London, BD21
"Doctoral Dissertation Abstracts in Religious Education", DD11
Doctoral Dissertations in the Field of Religion, P15
"Doctoral Dissertations on Mission, 1945-1981", DC14
Dodson, Suzanne Cates Dodson, J16
Dolan, J., BA15
Dölger, Franz J., BB11
Doughty, Harold R., E3

Living Themes in the Thought of John Calvin, BD32
Livingstone, E. A., BA8
Livres de l'année--Biblio, K13
Livres disponibles, K14
Longman, Tremper, III, AB1
Longstaff, Thomas R. W., AC16
Lovejoy's College Guide, E2
Lueker, Erwin L., C25
Luey, Beth, T17
Lutheran Cyclopedia, C25
Lutheran World Federation, C24, DC39
"Lutherbibliographie", BD26
Lutherjahrbuch, BD26

McAlpin Collection of British History and Theology, BD19-BD20
McCabe, James Patrick, A7
M'Clintock, John, C9
McDormand, Thomas B., DE12
McGreal, Ian P., DE28
Macgregor, Malcolm B., BD22
McLean, George F., CC17
Macmillan Altas History of Christianity, BA19
Macmillan Bible Atlas, AF7
McNeil, Barbara, F1, F2, F3
McQuarrie, John, CB5
Magazine Index, U13
Magill, Frank N., DE28
Malatesta, Edward, AC20
Malcom, Howard, H30
Malony, H. Newton, DB30
Mann, Thomas, A14
Mansell, J1-J2
Manual for Writers of Term Papers, Theses, and Dissertations, T15
Manual of Style, T14
Marconi, Joseph V., L1
Marrou, Henri, BB10
Marrow, Stanley B., AA2
Martin, Dennis D., C28
Martin, Jochen, BA18
Martin, Ralph P., AC2
Master Search Bible, U21
Masterpieces of Christian Literature in Summary Form, DE28
Masters Abstracts, P10-P11